From Small Wins to Sweeping Change

AMERICAN ALLIANCE OF MUSEUMS

The American Alliance of Museums has been bringing museums together since 1906, helping to develop standards and best practices, gathering and sharing knowledge, and providing advocacy on issues of concern to the entire museum community. Representing more than 35,000 individual museum professionals and volunteers, institutions, and corporate partners serving the museum field, the Alliance stands for the broad scope of the museum community.

The American Alliance of Museums' mission is to champion museums and nurture excellence in partnership with its members and allies.

Books published by AAM further the Alliance's mission to make standards and best practices for the broad museum community widely available.

From Small Wins to Sweeping Change

Working Together to Foster Equity, Inclusion, and Antiracism in Museums

Edited by Priya Frank and Theresa Sotto

ROWMAN & LITTLEFIELD
Lanham • Boulder • New York • London

Published by Rowman & Littlefield
An imprint of The Rowman & Littlefield Publishing Group, Inc.
4501 Forbes Boulevard, Suite 200, Lanham, Maryland 20706
www.rowman.com

86-90 Paul Street, London EC2A 4NE

British Library Cataloguing in Publication Information Available

Library of Congress Cataloging-in-Publication Data Available

ISBN 978-1-5381-6358-0 (cloth : alk. paper)
ISBN 978-1-5381-6359-7 (pbk. : alk. paper)
ISBN 978-1-5381-6360-3 (electronic)

∞™ The paper used in this publication meets the minimum requirements of American National Standard for Information Sciences—Permanence of Paper for Printed Library Materials, ANSI/NISO Z39.48-1992.

Contents

PART V: ENGAGING GROUPS BEYOND STAFF

Acknowledgments

This book is a testament to the power of collaboration and collective action. We began this project knowing of one another's work to further equity, inclusion, and antiracism; however, we had never worked with one another and neither of us had experience editing a book. Yet we knew the opportunity to collect the insights and recommendations of colleagues dedicated to fostering change in museums would cause a ripple effect across the field. It was an opportunity we couldn't pass up.

First, we thank one another for approaching this project with care, compassion, and the willingness to dive into uncharted territory, catalyzed by the belief that if we work together, we can overcome incredible challenges and make a difference in museums. The collective values and trust we shared with each other made every challenge worth it.

We are grateful for our respective institutions—the leaders who support this book and our equity work in general and the colleagues who work alongside us. Theresa thanks Hammer Museum Director Ann Philbin; Cynthia Burlingham, Deputy Director of Curatorial Affairs; and all of her coconspirators in the Hammer's Diversity and Inclusion Group and the Academic Programs Department. She also thanks Andrea B. and John H. Laporte Director of the Walters Art Museum Julia Marciari-Alexander and Walters Deputy Director Kate Burgin. Priya thanks llsley Ball Nordstrom Director and CEO of Seattle Art Museum (SAM), Amada Cruz; Board Chair Carla Lewis; and board member Dr. Cherry Banks. Priya would also like to thank SAM's former

Ilsley Ball Nordstrom Director and CEO Kim Rorschach. These four women exemplify courageous leadership, and their support and mentorship have been invaluable to Priya's growth.

Thank you to Jason Porter for his invaluable advice and who, along with Mary Kay Cunningham, generously shared resources and templates that were integral to the project. We also thank Joni Boyd Acuff and Laura Evans for sharing coediting tips and Kayleigh Bryant Greenwell, whose conversations with Theresa in the early stages of book development were crucial in the initial proposals.

We are especially grateful to those who played key roles in editing this book: Jeffrey Cheatham, Olivia Fales, Hallie Scott, and Brandon Vaughan, without whom we would not have survived the weeks leading up to the manuscript deadline.

Theresa is particularly indebted to her husband Mike Eaton, who provided editing and emotional support and endured the impact of this project on our time together. She also thanks her son Calder, who cheered every time she finished editing a chapter; her cousin Jessica Jacobo for sharing words of encouragement when she needed it most; and her parents and brother for their support. She also thanks her museum confidantes Veronica Alvarez, Jeanne Hoel, Sarah Jesse, and Kelly Williams, who never fail to give sage advice.

Priya could not have gotten through this project without the following people: her mom, Betty; dad, Eddie; brother, Sanjay; and aunts Elsie and Ursula. She would also like to thank her meww Jaimée; Gabriel and Matt; and the incredible community who lifted her during a transformational year—you know who you are. Thank you for wiping the tears, cheering the wins, and providing laughter, courage, and joy. Her light shines bright because you all lit the way.

We also acknowledge the American Alliance of Museums and Rowman & Littlefield for the opportunity to bring this book to life.

Finally, to the authors who contributed to this book: you are all exceptional humans. Thank you for your dedication to diversity, equity, inclusion, accessibility, and antiracism. We know that this work is difficult and ongoing, exacerbated in recent years by a global pandemic, increased media coverage of anti-Black racism, and proliferation of anti-Asian hate. Yet you have taken time to share your knowledge with our field. We thank you, and colleagues around the world thank you. This book represents what we are able to achieve when we work together toward equity—in our respective institutions and collectively.

Dear reader, we also thank you for joining us.

Preface

Priya Frank and Theresa Sotto

How does a diverse community thrive in spaces that were designed to be exclusionary? Museums, with histories tied to colonial violence and racist practices and whose survival is largely reliant on the generosity of wealthy donors, were not built to be inclusive. Yet many museums' missions and the people who bring these missions to life have egalitarian aims. There have been many moments when we, the coeditors—two women of color who are daughters of immigrants—have not felt a sense of belonging in the field to which we have devoted our careers. This tension has been simmering in museums for decades. Convenings organized by Museums as Sites of Social (MASS) Action beginning in 2016 and the American Alliance of Museums (AAM) annual conference's 2017 diversity, equity, accessibility, and inclusion (DEAI) theme are just two examples in recent years that demonstrate the urgency of confronting histories of colonization and advancing equity and inclusion in museums. The Mellon Foundation's second Art Museum Staff Demographic Survey, released in 2019, confirmed that we still have a great deal of work to do to diversify staff, especially at senior leadership positions.[1] The museum remains perilously at odds with the diversity of the United States.

In 2020, after the murders of George Floyd, Breonna Taylor, Tony McDade, and countless others sparked protests worldwide, and while the COVID-19 pandemic exacerbated existing inequities, museums were increasingly and vociferously called on to establish antiracist practices, take action in support of the Black Lives Matter movement, and authentically engage audiences representative of their diverse communities. Grassroots efforts to call out racist behaviors and push for more equitable practices in museums increased exponentially and have taken the form of open letters demanding change,[2] social media campaigns such as the @ChangetheMuseum Instagram account, unionization efforts,[3] and convenings with like-minded museum staff, such as "[Collective Liberation]: Disrupt, Dismantle, Manifest," which was organized in 2021 by members of Museums and Race, MASS Action, Museum Workers Speak, The Incluseum, Museums Are Not Neutral, Empathetic Museum, and Visitors of Color.

These efforts have galvanized museum professionals to examine institutional culture and to begin or augment the challenging work of looking inward to foster DEAI and antiracism within their own institutions. Museums and Race contributors Janeen Bryant, Barbara Cohen-Stratyner, Stacey Mann, and Levon Williams state in a 2021 AAM article:

> museums operate within a white supremacy culture, which informs the norms and practices of the museum field at large. This culture comes from museums' historic ties to the Atlantic slave trade and has remained embedded in institutional and individual practices. However, there are field-wide efforts to dismantle white supremacy culture, and there are ways that individuals can begin to see and disrupt this culture in their respective organizations.[4]

Indeed, in recent years museums have begun to form cross-departmental working groups and committees to critique their internal practices, review hiring processes, and ultimately foster a more inclusive environment for both visitors and staff alike. According to the Cultural Competence Learning Institute (CCLI), 30 percent of 580 museums that responded to a CCLI survey have active DEAI committees.[5] Additionally, since summer 2020, a proliferation of DEAI-related positions have emerged in the museum field. In personal communications with Andrew Plumley, Senior Director of Equity and Culture at AAM, he approximated a 300 percent increase in calls from folks with DEAI in their title looking for support.[6]

Although establishing positions focused on DEAI efforts in museums is a positive indicator of organizational change, it is critical that this work does not fall on one person but is integrated into all facets of museum operations and processes. All stakeholders have a part to play in this work, and we are more effective if we work together. But how do cross-departmental initiatives get off the ground? How do individuals build support and successfully advocate for limited resources to be allocated to new positions, programs, and cross-departmental working groups? How can colleagues work together to decolonize their museum practices and make space for institutional critique? What lessons are being learned from these internal groups, and how can they inform practices that are sustainable and responsive to changing needs? The process of initiating and implementing DEAI initiatives can be complicated, challenging, and resource-intensive. Conversations about inequities, privilege, and power in the workplace are often tense if not fraught, and many museum professionals are seeking resources to navigate uncomfortable terrain.

In this book, we bring together a collection of tools, solutions, and models from DEAI practitioners who have actively worked toward institutional change. This is the first book to focus specifically on collaborative and inclusive practices in equity and antiracism work in different types of museums.[7] Through a range of case studies, we demonstrate the importance of relationship building, authentic connections, and developing foundations together over time, providing a much-needed resource for museum professionals at every level who are grappling with challenges that are pervasive in predominantly white institutions.

BOOK OVERVIEW: OUR JOURNEY TOGETHER

This book offers a range of learning about how different groups have approached their DEAI work in museums and how it's often the small steps that lead to significant change. Whether the work is achieved through cross-departmental teams like those at the Minneapolis Institute of Art or Hammer Museum; inclusive assessment approaches such as those at the Minnesota Historical Society and Pacific Science Center; or collaborations with volunteers at the Cincinnati Art Museum, with community advisory groups at the Burke Museum, or with the board at the Seattle Art Museum, the experiences are as diverse as the museums that they represent. We intentionally asked authors to describe the processes that led to their accomplishments to help readers enact similar initiatives at their institutions. For many museums, this work is still new and the challenges and failures are just as important as the wins—perhaps even more so. Our hope is that these learnings can spark questions, discussions, and ideas for how to implement equity and antiracism work in your own organizations, assess those practices, formulate and prepare groups to support the work internally, and authentically connect with constituencies outside of staff.

As coeditors of this book, we consider ourselves to be coconspirators, amplifiers, and collaborators in shaping material whose original form had already been produced through collective will. When we put out our initial call, we contacted groups such as MASS Action, Museum Hue, Incluseum, as well as our personal and professional networks. We received more than thirty proposals, each of which recounted stories of change made possible through collaboration. Even the structure of this book was borne out of the wisdom of a collective. While we reviewed the proposals, five threads emerged across a range of types of and sizes of museums, which ultimately became the main sections of this book: Goals and Vision Setting; Structure, Sustainability, and Impact; Assessment and Accountability; Staff Learning and Training; and Engaging Groups beyond Staff.

After we chose the chapter authors, we held a virtual meeting for everyone to connect, introduce their chapter topic, and learn more about the vision for the book. We were overjoyed to convene many people doing incredibly powerful equity work from all over the country. Our hearts felt full knowing that this project had potential to help shift our field. For many of the practitioners, writing about their work in a chapter format was a new experience, and we wanted to make sure they felt supported and understood that this process was new for us too. We expressed that we would be embarking on this book journey together.

The book authors represent a range of institutions—art and history museums, science centers, and children's museums—and a diversity of perspectives, approaches, positions, and experiences in the field. Of the forty authors in this book, 60 percent identify as Black, Indigenous, and people of color (BIPOC). In contrast, 28 percent of staff in art museums are people of color, according to the Mellon Foundation's Art Museum Staff Demographic Survey 2018,[8] and between 0 percent and 20 percent of executive staff and senior leadership at four major museum associations (American Alliance of Museums, Association of Science and Technology Centers, Association of Children's Museums, and American Association for State and Local History) are people of color.[9] When making decisions about authors for the book, we felt it was essential to center BIPOC voices in a field that is predominantly white. Moreover, as we read proposals from across the country, we saw that in many cases, BIPOC museum professionals were the ones who were catalyzing change.

As coeditors new to the publication process, the challenges to complete this book were numerous, and we received little direction or support from the institutions that called on practitioners to share their knowledge with the wider field. We knew that coediting a book would be a heavy lift, but the weight was even greater than we anticipated. We felt enormous pressure to produce a resource that does this work justice and ensures the authors get the recognition that they deserve. This was particularly crucial because we learned after our book proposal was accepted by the American Alliance of Museums, that chapter authors are not compensated for their labor, and editors receive a small percentage of the profits on book sales. This practice is in line with academic publications that work with authors who are ostensibly compensated by their employers to share their specialized expertise. Museum workers, however, are hamstrung by predominantly low wages, as demonstrated by The Art + Museum Salary Transparency Google spreadsheet, which includes more than twenty-five hundred salaries from museum workers at all levels. As an article in the *Chronicle of Philanthropy* pointed out, this spreadsheet "shows that pay and benefits differ radically across locations with one stark exception: Low wages are the norm for most of those who don't hold top director or chief curatorial posts."[10] Every field, including publishing, has a long way to go to become more equitable and offer fair compensation, especially to BIPOC museum workers who are disproportionately impacted by salary inequities.[11]

During the process of completing this project, our motivation for helping other BIPOC writers and editors navigate these inequitable structures has grown, and we have become advocates for greater transparency in fields, like the publishing industry, whose work coincides with ours. Our expertise is shifting these fields to better serve communities in line with the changing demographics of the country, and our work should be recognized, supported, and compensated accordingly. The authors have worked incredibly hard to shape complicated initiatives into cohesive stories with little or no compensation. Some, during the writing of this book, have decided to leave the museum field or are actively planning an exit strategy. We share these details with a desire for full transparency about the inequities that are pervasive in our field and the emotional labor that results. Even practitioners who see a vision for inclusive and equitable museums and have the passion and drive to realize that vision are burning out. Being BIPOC women leading this effort, the pressure to do it "right" feels insurmountable. Moreover, while reviewing authors' stories of frustrations and struggles resulting from institutional roadblocks, we would relive traumatic moments as well. As we approached each chapter with editorial care, we needed to extend the same care to ourselves, and fortunately, while reading about small wins from colleagues across the country, these accounts rekindled moments of joy we experienced in parallel situations. Ultimately, working on this project helped energize our DEAI and antiracism efforts, and we believe that reading about advocates and accomplices all over the country will energize and galvanize you, too.

MANY PATHS FORWARD

We hope that years from now we can look at this book as a collection of collaborative actions to forge new paths in DEAI and antiracism work. We also recognize that this work is constantly shifting, so this is by no means a map with only one path. We also hope that maps will no longer be necessary to arrive at places of inclusion and equity and that DEAI will be the foundation of every organization. This work must be considered fundamental to the excellence and success of a museum, and this includes dedicating time, people power, relationship building, and resources toward it. Our equity lenses must be affixed every day, across all departments, to be most effective.

This is a book for those who recognize that we are not going to undo structural and institutional inequities overnight, a resource for people who are willing to step out, have courage to take risks, and build pathways where there are none. This is a book for those invested in pushing for equity and inclusion long term, no matter what stage in their careers. It is for those struggling to make a difference in an institution whose white supremacist roots run deep. Of course this book is specifically about museums, but we also believe that the strategies and tools described can be applicable to a variety of industries, organizations, and communities looking to build more equitable processes and programs. This is a book for allies, for agitants/advocates (see chapter 4) as well as those who don't know where to start. This is for you, for our field, for the millions of people who visit museums online or on-site, and for those who won't visit until our spaces become more equitable and inclusive.

NOTES

1. Westermann, Schonfeld, and Sweeney, "Art Museum Staff Demographic Survey 2018."
2. See Randle, "'We Were Tired of Asking': Why Open Letters Have Become Many Activists' Tool of Choice for Exposing Racism at Museums."
3. See Greenberger and Solomon, "Guggenheim Museum Workers Push to Unionize Amid Wave of Organizing across U.S. Museums."
4. Bryant, Cohen-Stratyner, Mann, and Williams, "The White Supremacy Elephant in the Room."
5. Garibay and Olson, *CCLI National Landscape Study: DEAI Practices in the Museum Field.*
6. Andrew Plumley (personal communication, August 11, 2021) also stated that "most museums lack the ability/capacity to understand what the function of this role must be, and tend not to hire who they really need."
7. Collaborative efforts to further DEAI have been referenced in online resources and articles such as the Museums as Sites of Social (MASS) Action Toolkit or "Facing Change: Insights from the American Alliance of Museums' DEAI Working Group." There are some book publications on DEAI strategies in museums; however, those that exist focus on curatorial practices, such as *Decolonizing Museums: Representing Native America in National and Tribal Museums* (2012) by Amy Lonetree; center strategies for individual leaders and change agents, as in Cinnamon Catlin-Legutko

and Chris Taylor's *The Inclusive Museum Leader* (2021) and Mike Murawski's *Museums as Agents of Change* (2021); or offer foundational starting points, such as *Diversity, Equity, Accessibility, and Inclusion in Museums* (2019), edited by Johnnetta Betsch Cole and Laura L. Lott, and *Understanding and Implementing Inclusion in Museums* (2018), by Laura Edythe Coleman.

8. Westermann et al., "Art Museum Staff Demographic Survey 2018."

9. Garibay and Olson, *CCLI National Landscape Study*.

10. Dimento, "Crowdsourced List of Museum Salaries Goes Viral, Exposing Pay Inequities."

11. See Dafoe, "Arts Workers of Color in Los Angeles Earn 35 Percent Less in Wages than Their White Colleagues, a New Study Finds"; and Miranda, "Column: Are Art Museums Still Racist? The COVID Reset."

Part I

GOAL AND VISION SETTING

Chapter One

Carving a Path from Diversity to Justice

Anniessa Antar and Elisabeth Callihan
with contributions by Alice Anderson, Gretchen Halverson, Frances Lloyd-Baynes, Thomas Lyon, Tobie Miller, Krista Pearson, Frederica Simmons, Jamie Van Nostrand, Keisha Williams, and Jill Ahlberg Yohe

> I interrogate museums not because I abhor them or because I want to see them die; but because I want to witness and be a part of their necessary rebirth. I love museums, deeply. I just don't like where they appear to be headed.
>
> —Dr. Porchia Moore[1]

Our journey to this current moment in 2021 has not been a straight line; there have been periods of time when it feels as if we are moving backward—perhaps an inevitability given the complex and intertwined systems of oppression that institutional change work must engage.[2] As our understanding of these complex systems has deepened, the goals for the intended outcome of our individual and collective work have transformed as well.

Throughout the institution's history, the Minneapolis Institute of Art (Mia) has made various attempts to address the underrepresentation of racial and socioeconomic diversity in its audience, staff, and programming. Mia articulated an institution-wide commitment to this work in 2015, using the language of diversity and inclusion. Although the museum initially gained some small wins in this area, over time staff began to see that this approach was only making surface-level reforms to an otherwise unaffected system. A focus on equity led the next phase of our journey, as we developed an understanding that it would be necessary to examine and address the complex systems of power within which we operate. Most recently, staff engaged in this work have begun to accept that these systemic structures are deeply resistant to change as long as they continue to operate; therefore, we must act radically—working holistically from the root of the tree to its fruit—to overcome these systems of oppression and become a space of justice and collective liberation. While transformational work is challenging, focusing on these aspirational values is a reminder that this work can be joyful; it is generational and, in many ways, will always be necessary. It is essential that we look beyond this current moment and envision a radically transformed, liberatory museum of the future to build toward it effectively and sustainably.

The phases of our work over the years can best be defined by the language we applied at the time, which has changed accordingly and necessarily, to support our long-term vision and intended impacts. The language is less important than the values the work is rooted in, but the evolution is necessary to stay in motion, one step ahead of the whitewashing that threatens to co-opt and silence these efforts, one step ahead of the magnetic pull of the status quo that threatens to pull them back to the well-worn path.

TOWARD DIVERSITY AND INCLUSION

In order to create a roadmap to navigate toward where museums need to go, we must first understand their origin. As authors of the *MASS Action Toolkit* write, "Historical and social context informs the conditions under which museums [were] created and within which their roles and purposes are defined. These sites cannot separate themselves from the collective memories that link their development with white supremacy, . . . structural racism and other oppressions."[3] At Mia, we recognize that addressing our history enables us to learn about harms caused during the museum's formative years to move toward collective repair and healing. As Rose Paquet and Aletheia Wittman explain, "Legacies based on systems of power and oppression will not go away simply by ignoring them. Dealing with them allows us to get to the heart of who our museums are for . . . and, by extension, whose experiences are acknowledged by museums and whose are not."[4] It is within this contextual framework, therefore, that we share some of our institutional history here as grounding for our present work.

Through oral histories and informal sharing of narratives, we have been able to put together this account. We are not the first, or the only, to have attempted to repair historical harms. There are many stories missing from this collective sense-making, and we honor the unnamed who have been pushed out, left quietly, left loudly and are unable to share their own story today. Although we do not wish to perpetuate the worship of the written word, we do offer this chapter as a snapshot of institutional memory for those who follow after us in this work to know that you are not alone.

BOX 1.1. ACTIONABLE PRACTICE: INSTITUTIONAL LEGACY

We must connect our past with our present to effectively address the future.

We encourage a deep dive into the founding of your institution, which is a vital first step in transformational, generational work.*

Individually, or as a group, consider the following: Who founded your institution and why? Who or what was displaced for its creation? What else was happening in your city, region, or nationally when it was founded? Who has it traditionally served; Who has it excluded? What narrative about its creation do you tell publicly, and how does that differ from the history you just constructed via these prompts?

Creating a People's History: Who has been responsible for past inclusion and equity efforts? How are you documenting this work for future generations of staff?

* For more information on this inquiry process and a resource for approaching this work, see Wittman, "Creating a Framework for Institutional Genealogy."

Our Founding History

Mia is located on the traditional lands of Dakota people, who were coerced[5] into ceding them to the US government in 1805 through deceitful tactics so that a military base could be built at the confluence of the Minnesota and Mississippi rivers, or the *bdote*, a sacred site of creation for the Dakota. Seven miles away lies the parcel of land the museum resides on, bequeathed to the city in 1872 by its third mayor with the stipulation that the site become a public park and an art museum. The museum opened its doors in 1915 with support from the Park Museum Fund[6]—a property tax to support green and cultural spaces, which continues to this day to be levied and reapportioned.

The white founding members of the Society of Fine Arts hoped the museum would elevate the perception of the Midwest in the eyes of those on the East Coast. Yet, they were also committed to making the museum an accessible place "for the people, all of them, from wherever they may come."[7] Free admission was offered several days a week—a requirement per the museum's bylaws—and attendance the first year exceeded 148,000, nearly half of the city's entire population.

Understanding this foundational context—being shaped and guided by the wealthy elite, while receiving public funds and purportedly existing "for the people"—is informative because its legacy has continued in the intervening century and has resulted in various degrees of tension and existential questioning. Since its opening, Mia has been in an oscillating cycle between the mythical identity of a "universalist museum,"[8] an institution that purportedly serves all people, and the exclusive, "monocultural club"[9] it was formed to be. For every attempt the museum has made toward diversity or inclusion, there have been opposing efforts that reinforce a narrative centering whiteness. The work has remained on the surface without ever impacting the bedrock. Thus, we cannot make substantive change through a one-off initiative; rather, it necessitates a complete change in our culture, practices, and larger vision.

Shifting Culture

Around 2010, Mia began to experience a culture shift that would lay some foundation for our future equity-related work. Under the leadership of its then director, staff began a practice of experimentation, embracing risk and potential failure in pursuit of innovation. The addition of contemporary art to the collection created opportunities to interrupt canonical art historical approaches. Staff began to work more collaboratively across divisions and hierarchy. Efforts were made toward cocreative models that moved programs from the stage to the circle and offered space for both subject "experts" and traditional knowledge keepers. The words *relevance* and *engagement* began being embedded in our vocabulary because staff began to expand on the idea of what a museum—and who its audience—could and should be.

These efforts were supported by museum leadership to the degree that they would not require a larger systemic evaluation. However, this embrace of experimentation naturally led to an examination of our historical modus operandi, which began to surface questions about how and why we do things—and again, *for whom*. This would reach a pivotal point in 2015 as Mia, and the field more broadly, began reflecting on its responsibility as a civic institution in responding to social injustices, such as police brutality. This was spurred on by the joint statement issued by a collective of museum bloggers in December 2014, followed by the weekly #MuseumsRespondtoFerguson Twitter conversations started by Adrianne Russell and Aleia Brown, and amplified by the #MuseumWorkersSpeak insistence that the social justice lens must be applied inward, as much as outward toward the public.[10] Mia, like many other predominantly white organizations, felt an internal tension arise around whether making a statement about human rights was aligned with our mission as a museum; and if it was, how might we even begin to do so.

Recognizing this as an opportunity to catalyze a field-wide commitment to social justice, Mia's head of multigenerational learning presented the museum's director of learning innovation with an idea for a national, collaborative initiative that would work toward developing actionable equity practices. Mia's then director and president agreed that Mia could support and host the idea. In collaboration with colleagues engaged in social justice efforts from across the field, Museum As Site for Social (MASS) Action was born.

Concurrently with this field-focused work, Mia's associate curator of Native American art began developing a large-scale exhibition of Native women artists, which would put some of these equity commitments into practice. From its inception, this exhibition broke the established curatorial paradigm, eschewing the individualist model to convene a roundtable of Native advisors, artists, and scholars to cocreate and collaboratively shape the exhibition. This process aligned more closely with Indigenous practice than the neocolonial approach art museums typically take toward Native material. Together, these initiatives, MASS Action and the exhibition that came to be called *Hearts of Our People*, provided an opportunity for a radically different approach to museum practice.

This direction was further reinforced with the creation of a new strategic plan in 2016, which prioritized engaging communities, acknowledging the importance of working collaboratively with partners outside its walls, as well as focusing internally on diversity and inclusion training for staff. Mia began its first attempts at directly addressing the topic of race, exclusion, and the pervasiveness of whiteness in museums. To support these efforts, Mia's head of multigenerational learning convened the cross-departmental resource team (later renamed equity team) with ten BIPOC and white staff representing areas of learning innovation, membership, human resources, accounting, and curatorial. This space gave staff members the chance to gather formally to discuss the challenges and inequities of the current work environment, propose solutions, and build a supportive community of allies. This early group was small, had no formal reporting structure to leadership, and no budgetary support; therefore, initial efforts had a somewhat ad hoc feel. Yet, as staff continued to gather and collectively address these issues, hope began to grow that these grassroots efforts might lead to more transformational change.

Diversity without Inclusion

While these staff-led initiatives were underway, Mia leadership was also creating some institutional goals around its newly named commitment to diversity and inclusion. These metrics were primarily focused on quantifiable diversity: How many staff are people of color; how many community partners we had; how many exhibitions representing nondominant identities, and so forth. Although the word *inclusion* was also being used, the emphasis was on "including" racial diversity in the existing system, with much less attention given to involving these perspectives in a way that would meaningfully change those systems. Predominately white institutions (PWIs) like Mia often start with the diversity approach because it allows the institution to make some visible changes to achieve tangible results and create a few easy "wins."[11] Institutions often think focusing on a statistical representation of diversity will be a stepping-stone to transformative work—or perhaps some regard diversity as the terminal goal.

The diversity fellowship model is a popular example of this tactic.[12] This model aims to redress the absence of staff of color through explicit invitations. However, without also considering the changes to the dominant culture needed to support the fellow's experience, the program risks being tokenistic at best and harmful at worst—a gesture of reform and not transformation.[13] The challenge with this kind of gesture, adding diversity to existing structures as an afterthought, is that it has the paradoxical effect of reinforcing whiteness as the norm. No transformation of the larger system is necessary if diversity is just a statistics problem that can be logistically and tactically "fixed."

This diversity ideology also allows white members of staff to construct a positive identity of themselves and the organization "as open-minded and accepting of difference . . . while maintaining the social and legal benefits of systemic whiteness."[14] It excuses white people from the conversation about their own participation and complicity in the system that invisibly benefits them and the need to change their own individual behaviors or mindset.

To counteract this, white people need to actively practice antiracism in their own lives and deepen their tolerance with discomfort. Often white individuals do not understand the relationship between institutional systemic racism and personal racism.[15] They may take offense or shut down from taking personal responsibility for unlearning white supremacy culture. Pushing through that discomfort can serve as a step toward transformation, and the willingness to adapt the conditioned responses of our bodies and minds can open the space for healing. At Mia, members of the equity team address this by creating opportunities to engage in critically self-reflexive practice,[16] examining one's individual mindset, assumptions and actions, and their impact on the organization.

White Supremacy Culture at Work

As challenging as it is to be critically reflexive at the individual level, museums—built on a foundation of white supremacy and from a history of colonization over land, people, and cultural and spiritual material—are especially ill-equipped to examine themselves. An effective tool we have used to encourage institutional-level reflection at Mia is Kenneth Jones and Tema Okun's insightful examination of the fourteen characteristics of white supremacy culture.[17] Although many employees who encounter these characteristics will find them so familiar and banal as to be harmless, Jones and Okun state this is precisely what makes them dangerous. Organizational culture is profoundly influential on our behaviors because it is ever present and, yet, invisible and unspoken. These characteristics are the norms and standards without ever having been intentionally named or chosen by the organization.

This is not without purpose. The characteristics displayed in white supremacy culture work are mutually reinforcing and keep the system operating as it always has. So, despite organizational leaders outwardly saying they are looking for multicultural diversity, they also expect—sometimes explicitly, sometimes subconsciously—that subordinated identities entering the space will assimilate to the organization's current cultural norms. For the people in the organization who have benefited from this system, there is no reason to question this way of operating. For anyone else, it creates a precarious dynamic wherein proposing a variation from the status quo might result in being labeled disgruntled, a troublemaker, or "not the right fit." Every organization has their own coded language for labeling employees who advocate for substantive transformation. At Mia, we noticed the word *rogue* was often used by management to describe any attempt to deviate from cultural norms. Whenever this word is used, it sets off alarm bells that white supremacy culture is being challenged.

White supremacy culture is damaging to everyone in a global sense, but it is materially harmful to the people of color who are brought into the space, who attempt to advocate for change and are shut down, reprimanded, or retaliated against in subtle to tangible ways. This yields a painful experience of tone-policing, gaslighting, and undermining the lived experiences of harm and trauma of BIPOC staff, forcing them to compartmentalize or sublimate their feelings. As a result of this, museums will continue to see a harmful cycle of disengagement[18] or departure of BIPOC staff as long as white supremacy characteristics go unchecked.

While the cultural change at Mia over the past decade, which moved staff from a dysconscious racism[19] to an explicit focus on "diversity and inclusion," felt like a seismic shift to some; for others, it felt insufficient to radically transform our practice. For change to happen, change must happen at

BOX 1.2. ACTIONABLE PRACTICE: INTERSECTING CULTURES: WHITE SUPREMACY CULTURE AT WORK

Consider how your organizational culture might be centering white dominant culture. At Mia, we did this by presenting one of the fourteen Characteristics of White Supremacy Culture* at each of our monthly all-staff meetings for more than a year; then we held a series of one-hour deep-dive sessions to unpack each characteristic.

As individuals or in groups reflect on the following questions:

Can you identify ways characteristics of white supremacy manifest in your work culture?

What are some antidotes and strategies you could develop to interrupt and counteract them?

---

* Jones and Okun, "White Supremacy Culture."

all levels—from individual mindsets to institutional policies. This requires an examination of larger systemic issues and a commitment to learning and changing behaviors. Over time, we realized that the *product* of our labor cannot and will not change until we address our *processes* and, most importantly, the root cause of current injustices within our organization.

This realization played out saliently in the planning of a recent exhibition, where a group of community voices most impacted by the exhibition content were invited to provide input on interpretive and programmatic strategies. Members of this advisory group were identified through existing Mia partners and offered an honorarium to compensate their time and contributions. Community members shared three main concerns: the exhibition erased local Native presence; prioritized content for the museum's predominantly white audience over those whose identities were reflected within the exhibition; and highlighted artists who they felt were profiting off the pain of BIPOC subjects. Staff shared these concerns with museum leadership in several meetings and in a formal letter outlining the disconnect between the museum's purported desire to invite community voices and the refusal to hear them. The critiques from staff and community were minimized and dismissed. In perhaps the most painful instance, an interpretation panel—featuring a quote by a BIPOC community member expressing their disapproval of an artist's use of Black death spectacle[20]—was removed after the exhibition opened because it was deemed too subjective.

This experience reinforces the negative impact of the diversity ideology. As in the case with the diversity fellowship, by seeking to reform current structures just enough to allow space for diversity, the museum only succeeds in inviting people of color into the systems that were designed to exclude and oppress them.

TOWARD EQUITY

Recognizing the harm of "solving for" diversity without designing for real inclusion was the first step in the next significant shift at Mia. It helped us differentiate between reformist tendencies that maintain the status quo and deeper transformational strategies focused on equity, which will bring about new ways of operating. Mia's working definition of *equity*[21] had been a relatively passive concept rooted in the ethos of diversity until the museum hired its first manager of diversity and inclusion in 2018. This staff member led us to a more explicit definition of equity—one which necessitates a systemic power analysis, action, and accountability. Although Mia had historically avoided explicitly addressing race, this new approach would intentionally be race-specific, though not exclusive.[22] With expertise in organizational development and change management, the diversity and inclusion manager provided structure and strategies that would help staff collectivize, prioritize their efforts, and gain momentum.

To begin, we used the multicultural organizational development (MCOD)[23] framework to examine the current institutional environment. MCOD is a process of change that supports an organization moving from monocultural and exclusive to multicultural and inclusive and equitable. This became a key tool for staff to understand not only where Mia fit along the continuum but also the structural areas that needed to be addressed to effect real change. The other key element brought in to help organize our work was an annual compression planning session,[24] through which we were able to identify various pillars of organizational structure (e.g., personnel, policies and procedures, programs, and exhibitions), map out how they intersected with the MCOD chart, and prioritize the work needed to impact each area.

Applying these frameworks, staff from the larger equity team community began to organize strategically in a matrix of work groups aimed at making an impact in each of the identified pillars and the organization as a whole. Two employee resource groups would also emerge for BIPOC staff and those identifying as two-spirit, lesbian, gay, bisexual, transgender and queer, questioning, asexual, and intersex+ (2SLGBTQAI+) and allies. Later, a racial equity roadmap would be developed by staff, administered by an interdepartmental

BOX 1.3. ACTIONABLE PRACTICE: EQUITY FRAMEWORKS

Group Discussion Questions:

Does your institution have an equity statement? What are some words or phrases that feel most resonant or powerful? Where is there a disconnect?

What are the actionable commitments your organization has made to equity? What accountability measures are in place to ensure the sustainability of those commitments?

Using the continuum of multicultural organization development,* break into small groups and identify where your institution falls on the chart. Compare and discuss findings with one another. Where do you align, and where do you differ? What are the areas needed to impact change?

---

* Jackson, *The NTL Handbook of Organization Development and Change.*

BOX 1.4. MIA EQUITY TEAM COMMUNITY AND WORK GROUPS

Equity Team Community

Mia's equity team "community" is a monthly meeting for equity team members, and open to all staff, to discuss broad topics that relate to equity and museums (usually kicked off by a short article, podcast, or video clip). It is also a chance to hear updates on Mia equity initiatives, share upcoming opportunities, or calls for support.

The following work groups were designed to support movement along the MCOD, as well as the frameworks of change mapped out by Mia's inaugural diversity and inclusion manager. Groups are listed in order of workflow process.

Equity Strategic Work Group

This team connects other work groups to the broader equity strategic vision, prioritizes workflow, and provides mechanisms for ongoing assessment.

Cultural Fluency

Cultural fluency is the ongoing journey of learning the language of equity and embedding it into our critical consciousness. This work group supports staff learning by organizing cultural fluency "sparks"—workshops or talks led by guest speakers that address the internal transformations needed to create a more equitable workplace and world.

Unpacking Characteristics of White Supremacy Culture

These monthly staff-hosted sessions explore one of the fourteen characteristics of white supremacy culture, examining how they may appear in our daily work. Understanding how each of the characteristics operate is the first antidote in dismantling them.

Mia Mindset

This group focuses on shifting from theory to praxis, by developing tools for implementing what staff are learning from cultural fluency sparks, ensuring that the staff's job activities, as well as the institution's policies, procedures, and external messaging are aligned and integrated with an equity lens.

Racial Equity Roadmap Task Force

This task force was formed by Mia's current director to address the racial equity roadmap created by staff.

Ad Hoc Groups

Shorter-term task-oriented committees regularly emerge. For example, a group rewrote Mia's performance evaluation to include DEAI commitment; another group was created to help support Human Resources to develop actionable strategies to hire and keep employees of color.

Employee Resource Groups

Two-Spirit LGBTQIA+ and BIPOC groups were created to provide safer spaces to build solidarity and respite for impacted staff.

Accessibility Team

This cross-functional team works to support staff learning, research effective practices, advocate for improved accessible design throughout our building, and support accessibility in public programs and digital tools.

Artist Identity Group
Mia's Artist Identity project works to match our collection documentation standards to our DEAI efforts by examining the artists—named, unnamed, living, dead—represented at Mia and considering how their unique identities impact their art. How we document and share that information with our audience relies on: self-identification; avoiding "othering"; and acknowledging that this work should remain as fluid as identity and language itself.

task force. Other independent groups, including an accessibility team and the artist identity group, also created intersections with the equity team.

Participation in equity-related initiatives grew tenfold, and at one point, members represented almost half of Mia's entire staff. However, just as it seemed that equity was becoming a standard consideration, we began to feel the beginnings of some resistance emerging. In 2020, we experienced a deep disruption: Mia's manager of diversity and inclusion resigned, followed shortly after by the diversity and inclusion coordinator, after assessing resistance from leadership to applying the mindset and strategy of equity through organizational development.

Although the decentralized power structure they established before their departure could support the continuation of this work for a period of time following their absence, it is not indefinitely sustainable. Further, despite strong efforts to build shared understanding and commitment around equity broadly across staff, it has yet to be embedded as a central tenet of the museum. While equity team and its subgroups have organized—frequent learning opportunities, frameworks, and audits for structural analysis, recommendations on how to move forward with these values in mind—they have not "trickled up" to the structural leadership level. Primarily, the work is "allowed" to happen insofar as it does not fundamentally challenge the status quo or the existing power dynamics.[25]

To counteract these moments of institutional inertia, we continue to adapt and develop resilient structures to help with the consequent burnout, including decentralizing leadership of initiatives to allow staff to step in/out and organizing to offer paid time for BIPOC staff mental health check-ins. We are better at naming our realities in our staff conversations on white supremacy culture characteristics, and we intentionally carve out meeting time to address topics of discomfort or disagreement head-on, in community with one another. We understand that generative conflict is necessary to interrupt cycles of white supremacy. There is a push and pull to this work, always, and it is this kinetic friction that propels us ahead.

The Death of DEAI

The work that equity-engaged staff has supported has set up new paths toward a values-based museum practice of the future. But broader institutional transformation will require uprooting norms around power, authority, and decision-making. Although we initially decided to shift the language describing our efforts from *diversity* to *equity* to address power and disrupt the harmful cycle of white supremacy, we are now seeing that white supremacy culture is even co-opting *equity* as a means of self-preservation.

As witnessed in June 2020 in the wake of the murder of George Floyd, an unprecedented number of museums issued statements on social media.[26] The challenge is, as evidenced from the noncommittal, "bothsidesism" language, it wasn't entirely clear what the statements were meant to convey. These largely empty posts (some of them, quite literally, empty black boxes) were devoid of accountability, lacking acknowledgment of harm caused by complicity in white supremacy, and commitment to do something about it.[27] As Angelique Power explains, these performative equity statements—words without actions—actually harm the broader movement: "Equity as a statement, an accessory, rather than a word that actually should create fear, [is] being used right now as a badge. And that is the death of the term 'equity.'"[28]

For staff engaged in this work at Mia, the moment felt like a passage for us as well. The museum's diversity and inclusion department no longer existed, and the equity team was becoming something more than a work group. We realized that the language of diversity, equity, accessibility, and inclusion (DEAI) was not the end goal; it could only ever be a starting point. We not only needed new language but, also, an aspirational vision to set our sights generationally into the future. Not "fixing" or reforming oppressive systems to be slightly less oppressive, but building a new world of radical hope and possibility. The death of DEAI at Mia was the birth of our vision for justice and collective liberation.

TOWARD JUSTICE AND COLLECTIVE LIBERATION

In response to the June 2020 statements, museum workers across the country began sharing personal accounts of racism in their institutions, detailing how these externally facing messages did not match their internal experiences.[29] At Mia, staff from the museum's BIPOC group and allies from the equity team expressed their own concerns and experiences to members of senior leadership. These were met with responses ranging from a sympathetic but beleaguered, "I know, but what can we do?" to denial. Feeling a growing sense of frustration from the avoidance and inertia, a group of staff intervened and took direct action. The result was the racial equity roadmap, a strategic plan for moving the dial toward racial equity within all aspects of the museum's practice, shared with Mia's staff, leadership, and board of trustees for consideration.

The racial equity roadmap envisioned a reparative workplace culture that would move beyond the performative toward substantive transformation through a series of short- to long-term recommendations. In the immediate, the document suggested the creation of a respite policy to support the physical and emotional well-being of BIPOC staff; a community review board to create transparency and accountability around museum budget, accessions, exhibitions, and programs; and a more democratic exhibit planning process to involve stakeholders most impacted by the content.

In response, Mia's director formed a cross-hierarchical task force to review the recommendations. This group was subsequently put on hiatus to create a labor management committee to address some of the roadmap's issues related to human resources. Although there are legal parameters and liability issues that leadership has to consider, this "step back" approach, pausing one committee to form another, is a time-honored resistance strategy to slow work down[30] and, in this case, to prevent staff from challenging white supremacy culture. It also signals that leadership either misunderstands or is intentionally preventing the radicality required to create meaningful change. Those in structural power are likely not even conscious of their motives. The white person's default reaction to protect its dominant culture is deeply ingrained in our patterned behaviors. Therefore, just as we need language to describe the change movement we are trying to shape, we also need language to identify emerging strategies of change resistance—and to recognize when we ourselves are perpetuating them.

The Ongoing Path

The need to cultivate a culture of imagination, emergent practice, and radical hope for what is possible are central components to change. *We cannot create what we cannot imagine.* We also cannot build anew without tearing down what no longer serves us. If we are to make real commitments to justice, there must be acceptance that we cannot continue to attempt reform. Accountability must be part of any work moving toward justice and is necessary for our path to collective liberation.

BOX 1.5. ACTIONABLE PRACTICE: RECOGNIZING THE 3 *R'S*

When this work stalls, it's helpful to recognize and understand the 3 *R*'s of resistance, repressive tolerance, and retrenchment, to work collaboratively to address them.

For Reading and Group Discussion (see Bibliography):

- Resistance: Active & Passive
  Resource: "Managing Resistance to Change" by Ken Hultman
- Repressive Tolerance
  Resource: "Repressive Tolerance and the 'Management' of Diversity" by Stephen Brookfield
- Retrenchment
  Resource: "Race, Reform, and Retrenchment: Transformation and Legitimation in Antidiscrimination Law" by Kimberlé Williams Crenshaw

This journey is difficult, and it is unresolved. Staff engaged in this work will feel tired, exasperated, and devalued because that's what white supremacy normalizes, and it can feel Sisyphean, witnessing a wave of retrenchment following a progressive measure. We have reached a turning point because the terminology of equity has been co-opted by the dominating culture as a tactic of repressive tolerance to paradoxically preserve its dominance. In response, we need to move ahead, not only to new language but also toward the ethics of care, transformation, truth and reconciliation, justice, and reparations. We encourage you to look at DEAI, not as an end goal but as a starting point. Create actionable and accountable commitments in your internal and external work. Recognize the forms and patterns of resistance. Activate and release your imagination for a radically hopeful vision of what is possible. Envision a fully transformed antiracist institution working toward our shared liberation. *What does it look like? What did you do to help create it?*

Working collectively, museums can become that which we imagine and need them to be—centers of creativity, reciprocal relationship, mutual aid, organizing, solidarity, and collective liberation. Until objects and the institution itself are no longer prioritized over the well-being of humans, we will remain in a crumbling foundation rooted in colonial extraction. The path that lies ahead is clear. As we move forward, we carry the narratives of those who came before, those who fought for the future that expands endlessly into the horizon ahead. We honor their sacrifices and deliver justice through our pursuit of a world reconstructed. Stepping forward from the shadows of oppression that extend centuries wide, we move forward into a space previously only held for dreams, now made reality, constructed without compromise.

We insist on a future that is:

Indigenized
Queer
Anti-capitalist
Decentralized
Collective
Cooperative
Trauma-informed
Practicing consent
Relational
Interconnected
Our tenacity is a testament to the viability of such a future.

It is ours to shape and to claim.

NOTES

1. Moore, "Reflexive Cartography: Or, a Ritual for the Dying Museum Landscape—the Socio-political Impact of Change in Museums."

2. As this work is complex, it is vital that staff from across the museum be part of the conversation so that a wide array of perspectives and job functions are represented. Therefore, the contributors to this chapter (Alice Anderson, Gretchen Halverson, Frances Lloyd-Barnes, Thomas Lyon, Tobie Miller, Krista Pearson, Frederica Simmons, Jamie Van Nostrand, Keisha Williams, and Jill Ahlberg Yohe) are all current and former Mia staff and members of the equity community who represent each of Mia's divisions: advancement, audience (formerly audience engagement and learning innovation), curatorial, finance, and operations.

3. Patterson, Wittman, Phillips, Guillotte, Quinn, and Russell, "Getting Started: What We Need to Change and Why," in *MASS Action Toolkit.*

4. Paquet and Wittman, "Bringing Self-Examination to the Center of Social Justice Work in Museums," 41.

5. Generally, the America Indian leaders who signed treaties did not read English, relying on interpreters paid by the US government. It is uncertain whether they were aware of the exact terms of the treaties they signed. Of the seven Dakota leaders present at 1805 negotiations, only two signed. Although their land was valued at

$200,000, when the US Senate later approved the treaty, they only allocated $2,000. See Minnesota Historical Society, "Minnesota Treaties."

6. In 2021, Mia received $15 million from Hennepin County property taxes, meaning about 40 percent of Mia's total operating budget comes from public dollars. Minneapolis Park and Recreation Board. "Resolution 2020-350."

7. Although democratic words in theory, in practice Wallace Nye—the city's mayor at the time who spoke—would most likely have been thinking specifically of *white* people. Although the state had technically been desegregated since 1885 with the passage of the Equal Accommodations Act, racial discrimination was still rampant and, at times, violent. See Burnside, "African Americans in Minnesota."

8. Raicovich, *Culture Strike: Art and Museums in an Age of Protest*, 24.

9. "The Club" is the second stage on the *Continuum of Multicultural Organization Development*, wherein an organization seeks: "to maintain privileges for those who have traditionally held social power," allowing entry to a limited number from other social identity groups if they have the "right" perspective and credentials. "The club . . . engages with social justice issues only when they can be approached with comfort and on club members' terms." See Jackson, "Theory and Practice of Multicultural Organization Development," 181, https://naaee.org/sites/default/files/mcodmodel.pdf.

10. Antar, Callihan, and Russell, "A Watershed Moment: Lessons from #Museums RespondtoFerguson and MASS Action."

11. Brownlee, "The Dangers of Mistaking Diversity for Inclusion in the Workplace."

12. A quick Google search of this topic will yield 173 million results (when accessed on May 12, 2021).

13. For a critical theoretical framework for thinking about the dynamics of these initiatives, see James, "White Like Me: The Negative Impact of the Diversity Rationale on White Identity Formation."

14. Mayorga-Gallo, "The White-Centering Logic of Diversity Ideology."

15. Van Der Valk and Malley, "What's My Complicity? Talking White Fragility with Robin DiAngelo."

16. Greenberg, Antar, and Callihan, "Change-Making through Pedagogy," in *MASS Action Toolkit*, 156–59.

17. Jones and Okun, "White Supremacy Culture."

18. Page, "The 'Problem' Woman of Colour in the Workplace."

19. Anderson, Narum, and Wolf, "Expanding the Understanding of the Categories of Dysconscious Racism."

20. Greenberger, "'The Painting Must Go': Hannah Black Pens Open Letter to the Whitney about Controversial Biennial Work."

21. With phrases like "seek to understand" and "strive to overcome," Mia's initial definition of equity relied on conservative, noncommittal wording that did not explicitly name how it would be adopted or implemented by the museum. See Minneapolis Institute of Art, "Inclusion, Diversity, Equity and Accessibility policy."

22. Race Forward, "Principles For Racially Equitable Policy Platforms."

23. Jackson, "Theory and Practice of Multicultural Organization Development."

24. McNellis, *The Compression Planning Advantage: A Blueprint for Resolving Complex Issues*.

25. Brookfield, "Repressive Tolerance and the 'Management' of Diversity."

26. Greenberger and Solomon. "Read Statements from Major U.S. Museums about the George Floyd Protests."

27. Callihan, "From Statements of Solidarity to Transformative Action and Accountability."

28. Power, "On the Death of Equity."

29. Durón and Greenberger, "In Open Letters, Art Workers Demand that Institutions Do More to Fight Racism."

30. Glaveski, "Stop Sabotaging Your Workforce."

Chapter Two

DEAI Committees as Drivers of Organizational Change

Jenni Martin, Marilee Jennings, and Cecilia Garibay

Many museums launch their equity efforts focused on audience, recognizing that they may not be reaching, serving, or representing a particular segment of their community. Museums undertake community engagement efforts, establish outreach programs, assess visitor demographics, convene advisory groups, and often, through these processes, make headway. However, this kind of external focus is often housed in one department of the museum, siloed from the organization as a whole, and sometimes considered more of a "side dish" than core to museum operations and overall success. If organizations examine assumptions about their ways of working, identify possible changes, and enact those changes, they can be empowered to take risks, opening up possibilities for fostering long-term, sustainable inclusion. Being proactive in changing internal practices throughout the organization can allow for a true shift in practice toward equity and inclusion.

In 2013, recognizing a growing need in the museum field for organizational change toward more inclusive practice, four organizations—a museum, two national museum membership organizations, and a research/evaluation firm—embarked on a new collaborative initiative. The four founding partners (Children's Discovery Museum of San Jose, Association of Science and Technology Centers, Association of Children's Museum, and Garibay Group) leveraged on-the-ground museum experience, national awareness, content expertise, and an organizational change research base to launch the Cultural Competence Learning Institute (CCLI). CCLI's mission is to help museum leaders at all levels to catalyze diversity and inclusion efforts in their institutions. CCLI's core program is a professional development institute for museum teams, which acknowledges that success for museums in the twenty-first century will depend on their ability to embrace organizational change so that they can meaningfully connect with new and diverse audiences. The yearlong CCLI cohort program consists of an in-person workshop and monthly virtual meetings, coaching, a comprehensive staff survey, peer networking, and specialized support for CEOs. Museums throughout the United States apply for the program as an organization, identify a cross-departmental team of at least three employees, including a senior leader, and select a strategic initiative to focus on over the course of their program year. Since its inception, CCLI has implemented seven yearlong cohorts, supporting thirty-five institutions and more than 125 museum staff members.[1] CCLI serves science centers and children's museums, aquariums, zoos, and natural history museums of various sizes and from rural and urban regions throughout the United States.

BOX 2.1. DEFINITIONS*

Inclusion denotes an environment in which each individual member of a diverse group feels valued, is able to fully develop their potential, and contributes to the organization's success.

Equity acknowledges differences in privilege, access, and need, and supports space for appropriate adaptation and accommodation.

Cultural Competence is a process of lifelong learning. It results in knowledge, skills, behaviors, and attitudes that allow people to work effectively with others from different cultural backgrounds, increases the ability of organizations to maximize the benefits of diversity within their workforces, and improves the services offered to various stakeholders.

* From Cultural Competence Learning Institute Curriculum, https://community.astc.org/ccli/philosophy-approach/history-and-definitions.

Over the past decade, in implementing its signature cohort model, CCLI has continued to learn from and lead museums as they seek to develop their organizational cultural competence and become more inclusive. Many of the museums who participate in CCLI establish, strengthen, or adapt internal diversity, equity, accessibility, and inclusion (DEAI) teams as part of their yearlong change efforts. Such committees can be instrumental in helping to advance equity efforts. Whether responding to current events or moving toward inclusive practice long term, DEAI committees can provide opportunities for reflection, professional development, and learning; a foundation from which to speak and act; or a platform for understanding and shifting organizational policies and procedures. DEAI committees can also be effective platforms for supporting equity efforts as *organizational change* efforts—a critical approach to embrace in order to create sustainable change.

In fall 2020, CCLI released a new study, the *CCLI National Landscape Study: DEAI Practices in the Museum Field.* With data gathered from across the United States from museums of all sizes and disciplines, the study showed that, among other things, only about 30 percent of responding museums have active DEAI committees. Additionally, the study found that there is no common position or method for driving accountability for DEAI efforts in museums. Less than a quarter (21 percent) of organizations surveyed indicated their CEO or another senior-level leader (16 percent) assumes accountability for DEAI-focused efforts within the institution.

Based on the experiences of CCLI cohort museums, we have found that committees are most effective when they (1) are cross-departmental and draw from across the institution; (2) have the power to make and implement decisions; and (3) have actionable and flexible plans. The stories of CCLI participating museums and their DEAI committees are included here. Embedded in the stories are details about how teams defined their purpose, adapted over time, coordinated structure and leadership, communicated, took risks, and took care of each other. CCLI believes that leadership capacity can and does emerge at all levels within the museum. In this chapter we aim to help all leaders, from wherever they are in the institution, to think about the *change* they want to make, the *leadership* that will be required, the *learning* they will engage in along the way, and the *reflection* that will be critical to success.

CHANGE

> Managing change is not about managing schedules, project scope or simply avoiding resistance to change. Change is about the impact on people, culture, systems, and structures. Change is bringing about a new state that better positions the organization for success in the future.
>
> —Garfein, Horney, and Nelson[2]

Organizational change is a process—an *opportunity* and a set of steps—that can help institutions identify where they are, how they might need to shift, and where they want to head. Engaging in an organizational change approach can help museums think more broadly about how to become more inclusive and have organization-wide impact. According to Garibay and Huerta-Migus, "Intentional organizational change requires assessing what needs to change, developing goals and a plan to move to the desired state, and implementing the change."[3]

Recognizing the need for change is often the impetus for establishing or reinvigorating a DEAI committee; the initiative may come from an employee hoping to gather with other BIPOC staff to talk about their experiences in the institution, from a senior leader noting the need for better cross-departmental communication or from a board member asking why museum visitor demographics don't match community demographics. As the committee convenes, the following planning steps may be helpful: surfacing ways of work that may contribute to existing tensions, brainstorming more inclusive communication processes, and identifying data that could contribute to greater understanding. One of the most important initial steps is to effectively articulate the purpose for the committee and the desired organizational changes.

Change Begins with Defining Purpose and Engaging across the Institution

Children's Discovery Museum (CDM) of San Jose, as one of the founding partners of CCLI, was both developer and participant in CCLI cohort 1. After pulling together a cross-departmental team that was diverse across many dimensions (including length of time and role at the institution, race, ethnicity, religious background, gender identity, sexual preference, parenting status, and age, among others), the museum convened their inaugural cultural competence team. The goal for the team was to create a written diversity statement for the institution. Implementation steps included: (1) team members gathered and read statements from other organizations and interviewed staff members from other departments about their responses to those statements; (2) the group worked together to identify important elements not to include, honing the purpose for the statement along the way; (3) one team member created an initial draft of the statement, and the whole group critiqued, debated, and came to consensus, acknowledging that the statement itself must be an evolutionary document—something that could change and shift; and (4) once the team felt good about the draft, they gathered stakeholder feedback. Individual staff interviews, full staff meetings, and one-on-one meetings with external stakeholders provided important suggestions and confirmed that the team was headed in the right direction.

By the end of that initial year, the statement, dubbed by the team as a "Welcoming Statement," was posted on CDM's website,[4] featured as a five- by five-foot sign at the museum's entrance, incorporated into staff onboarding processes, and revisited annually at all-staff meetings. The yearlong project initiated a change process for the museum, not only in the development of the words themselves but also in the steps engaged that considered multiple perspectives, gathered feedback, and communicated effectively across all roles within the institution. As a result of the extensive feedback process, the statement was well received by all of the staff.

At the start of the second year of the cultural competence committee, the team had some decisions to make. *How long would the term of service be for individual members of the committee? What should the team focus on now that the diversity statement was developed? How would the team prioritize next steps?* Recognizing that continuity was important, the group decided that some members would continue into the following year (including the CEO and a senior-level director), while others would cycle off, paving the way for new participation. The group also acknowledged that the purpose of the group in the second year was to put the diversity statement into action. One initiative that emerged was a reconfiguration of the bathrooms on the first floor of the museum. The cultural competence committee advanced this initiative based on visitor concerns brought by floor staff members, opportunities for funding leveraged by senior staff, and the establishment of new laws around gender-neutral bathrooms. As a member of that committee, the executive director prioritized reconfiguring the bathrooms into two spaces: (1) a single bathroom, which would work well for families with young children, elderly family members who need assistance, and gender fluid or transgender persons, and (2) a quiet room that could be used for nursing mothers, families who pray regularly throughout the day, and children with sensory challenges.

Six years later, the committee continues; it has established an annual goal-setting session designed to assess current needs for the community and an annual renewal process to incorporate new members. Not only does CDM continue to support DEAI initiatives internally, but the museum also supports other museums in this journey in its role as one of the founding members and lead faculty of CCLI.

LEAD

> The main focus of the committee is to keep the work moving forward, in a conscious and thoughtful way, making sure that we're looking across the organization. We acknowledge where we've made the mistakes and keep the work moving forward.
>
> —Sesheta Tanya Holder, Associate Director of Administration, on the work of the diversity team at Long Island Children's Museum (CCLI cohort 1)

The success of DEAI committees will depend on leadership—the engagement of the institution's senior leadership, the nurturing of new leaders within the committee, and the leadership from the committee for the institution as it reflects and adapts to recommended changes. Careful thought about committee composition, purpose, structure, and facilitation can contribute to the committee's ability to reach its goals and achieve the museum's desired DEAI changes.

BOX 2.2. LAUNCHING A DEAI COMMITTEE: REFLECTION QUESTIONS

Who will participate on the committee?
What is the purpose of the committee?
When will the committee meet? What will be the duration of service for each participant?
Who will facilitate or lead the committee? How will you ensure that all voices are heard?

WHO: When establishing DEAI committees and task forces, the first aspect to consider is team composition: *Who will participate? Will participants volunteer, be invited, or be required? How will you ensure broad representation, not only of different departments and roles within the museum but also by voices not often heard in your organization?* You might choose to ask for volunteer committee members but also put out special invitations to ensure broader representation. CCLI participating organizations have learned that engaging in dialogue about the dimensions of diversity represented on the committee can send a clear message about valuing multiple perspectives. Beyond organizational roles and departments, teams can look at some of the more commonly referred to dimensions of diversity (such as race, ethnicity, gender, age, or religion) and also consider factors that may help team members relate more closely with visitors, such as where they grew up or live currently, modes of transportation, and languages spoken at home.

WHY: Understanding why a DEAI committee is being established (focusing on reflection and learning or policy change) and clarity about decision-making and feedback are critical to the ultimate success of DEAI committees. Clarifying purpose can help tremendously in avoiding frustration and challenges. Without clarity, participating staff members may feel frustrated by the inability to initiate change, human resources personnel may be concerned about potential legal challenges, or senior leaders may feel blindsided by suggestions for policy changes. If the committee's purpose is to make changes to policies and procedures, senior leadership team involvement is critical. Teams that do not have a connection to senior leadership may have difficulty implementing lasting change. However, if the committee's purpose is focused on learning and reflection or on gathering a specific group to address a specific issue, the group might be most effectively led by someone with experience, expertise, and passion for that particular issue.

WHEN: Although the determination about when a DEAI committee will meet might seem a secondary decision, it is, in fact, an important one in ensuring equity. If a meeting is regularly scheduled at a time when part-time staff are unlikely to attend, the opportunity for broad representation is compromised. If the meeting is scheduled at a time that is convenient for senior staff but is in conflict with other existing meetings, this can send the message that senior staff are more important than other staff. If meetings are scheduled in the evenings, this can be challenging for parents, college students, or floor staff who work morning shifts. Consider assumptions about why meetings should be held at certain times and strive to make shifts to include a broad range of perspectives. Asking supervisors to fill in for visitor-facing staff to attend DEAI committee meetings is an effective strategy for broadening diverse representation on the committee and getting buy-in across the organization.

HOW: Consider who will play the lead role in convening, facilitating, and making decisions for committee meetings. Some CCLI organizations have found that changing or sharing leadership can be an effective and equitable strategy to help shift organizational power dynamics, increasing opportunities for newer staff to obtain leadership roles and for experienced staff to mentor newer staff. Additionally, as a range of perspectives are shared and in new ways, some staff may feel more comfortable contributing their ideas with someone new at the helm. However, this must be attempted with careful thought and support. Because DEAI work necessitates vulnerability and can be emotionally charged and potentially cause harm, facilitation of the group requires skill and empathy. The leader will play the important role of establishing a space that encourages sharing and hearing different perspectives, gathering an array of ideas, prioritizing as a group, and determining the decision-making process that is action-oriented and equitable. Organizations will also want to think about how leadership of the committee aligns with and replaces other responsibilities for the facilitator so that it is well integrated and not overwhelming within already existing commitments.

Some organizations have found that shifting the leadership dynamic for senior leaders accustomed to running meetings and for other staff in the habit of being guided by senior leaders can be an adjustment for all involved. Senior leaders will need to exercise restraint, compassion, humility, and vulnerability. Staff who are less familiar and comfortable with interacting with senior leaders may need practice speaking up in this setting and encouragement in understanding organizational roles and priorities different from their own.

LEARN

> Learning is a critical component of organizational change efforts—especially DEAI efforts, which require us to reconsider long-held values, beliefs, and ways of working. . . . A learning organization is one that is continually expanding its capacity to reflect in order to intentionally create its future—a future in which new ideas and expansive ways of thinking are nurtured and harnessed.
>
> —Garibay and Huerta-Migus[5]

Critical to the success of DEAI committees and organizations is the capacity to embrace an attitude of learning, including ongoing experimentation, questioning assumptions, and reflecting on practice. As organizations examine their assumptions, they can identify potential shifts and adapt their practice toward more equitable approaches.

Learning Includes Shifting Purpose and Adapting over Time

Generated initially by a project focused on cultivating relationships with their local Latinx community, Denver Museum of Nature and Science (CCLI cohort 4) launched a brown bag lunch series called "Conversations about Community" with the aim of providing individual staff members a place to learn, reflect, and share. The series included activities, small group dialogues, guest presenters, and the development of a resource library, with the primary purpose of fostering individual learning among participants. Following their work with CCLI, the group continued to meet and realized that their conversations were catalyzing many ideas about changes for the museum. However, this committee was not originally convened for the purpose of policy change but, rather, for individual learning; attendance at the monthly meetings was optional and leadership participation in the group was at the midlevel of the organization. The group realized that a new committee was actually needed, one that would include senior leaders and could be charged with making recommendations for changes in policy and practice. A new committee was formed, known as the Living Our Values (LOV) committee, which focused its efforts on institutional change. Both committees continued to operate simultaneously, meeting every two weeks because there was still a need for both functions.

In May 2020, the murder of George Floyd ignited new action by the staff and, ultimately, launched the creation of a third committee also focused on DEAI. After Floyd's murder, the museum's senior leadership released a public statement that, although well intended, was actually upsetting to many staff members. After this feedback was conveyed, leaders recognized the need for a space for processing and healing and agreed to provide this support through pop-up conversations. According to Andrea Giron Mathern, director of community research and engagement strategies for the museum: "We made a major misstep as an organization. . . . Had we not made such a big public mistake, we would not have opened the door to have some of these conversations."[6] As a result of these well-attended sessions, a separate group of BIPOC staff caucused and gathered, collectively crafted a call to commitments for the museum to engage in antiracist work, and presented it to the senior leadership team. Although this was a challenging and difficult time for BIPOC staff, senior leadership, and the museum staff as a whole, the organization now has an action plan in place and an affinity group model to become an antiracist organization. As Treloar Tredennick Bower, manager of program development, notes, "These committees now function well together to address the How, What, and Why of our DEAI work at the individual, interpersonal, and institutional levels."

As noted in CCLI's grounding organizational change framework:

> Organizations do not organically "become" learning organizations; it must be an intentional process. One of the most important outcomes of becoming a learning organization is the growth of internal responsibility across the organization for supporting change. The full involvement of all individuals across the organization in a collaborative process and collective accountability is critical. (Garibay and Huerta-Migus)[7]

Learning organizations are flexible, adaptable, open to new ideas, and supportive. They value risk-taking, asking questions, opposing perspectives, and time for reflection. At their core, learning organizations invest deeply in collaboration and trust-building.

REFLECT AND EVOLVE

> As we reflected on what this team was about, we realized that we needed to coordinate with other existing teams. We also realized that we needed to unite the teams and get better at communicating across teams and across roles. . . . We knew that there were structures we needed to change to have a broader diversity of voices.
>
> —Alexandra Pafilis, Director of Early Learning Initiatives, Chicago Children's Museum (CCLI Cohort 3)

For DEAI committees to continue to be relevant and responsive to the museum's internal DEAI efforts and external needs that arise, teams should incorporate both short- and long-term milestones with regular reflection on progress, structure, facilitation, and committee purpose.

Reflection Leads to Strengthened Structures and Leadership

Chicago Children's Museum (CCLI Cohort 3) has a rich history of investment in organizational change focused on advancing equity. Toward that goal, the museum has created a variety of committees that have been responsive to different needs and community efforts, including an access and inclusion team, a race and ethnicity team, a lesbian, gay, bisexual, transgender, and queer/questioning (LGBTQ) team, a translation team, and an advocacy team. As their organization reflected and evolved following their CCLI cohort year, they realized that the committee structures needed to change, and communication needed to be strengthened. The museum created the DEAI alliance, comprising leaders of each of the groups, to ensure that cross-organizational connection and historical memory are also part of the museum's equity work. Each individual committee continues to provide space for personal reflection and opportunities to surface potential policy changes, and the alliance helps to coordinate those changes across the institution. According to Jennifer Farrington, president and CEO of Chicago Children's Museum, "A goal of the committee structure was one of collective responsibility and accountability. The DEAI Alliance was able to create a structure that wasn't management-led or supervisory in nature, but which did help us to think about how we could insure a platform for review and accountability—and how we are all responsible to each other, in addition to our mission, visitors, and community."[8]

Effective Communication Evolves through Reflection

The Science Museum of Virginia (CCLI cohort 7) launched their inclusion, diversity, equity, and access (IDEA) team in 2020 during the pandemic with a goal of examining and improving internal practices; they determined that an internal webpage would be really helpful for communication. Spearheaded by one committee member, and using Google Docs for accessibility for all staff, the newly launched web page includes their diversity statement, descriptions of ongoing diversity-focused programs, and new, institution-wide efforts. The new tool is helpful for orienting new staff members and soliciting feedback about ongoing inclusion efforts.

SUMMARY

Museums are about capturing moments—moments in history, creativity, imagination, connection, play, and engagement. As museum professionals, our roles in capturing moments invite us to take the long view—to understand how these creative, historic, connected, and challenging moments are woven together to chronicle, to narrate, to engage, to embrace, and to make change.

We take this change journey as individuals, understanding how our identities, our experiences, our privileges or lack thereof, and the era in which we live shape our perspectives. We also participate in and impact our organization's journey. As organizations evolve and change, we, as individuals and as leaders, help our museums evolve toward more inclusive practices by centering equity.

Gathering together, choosing to focus on equity, and identifying a path to change can leave a lasting legacy. In CCLI, we have witnessed the importance of investing in organizational change by creating DEAI committees; however, to be successful, committees should have a clear purpose, broad representation, and the tenacity to reflect, recognize, and correct course. As we fortify our internal processes and build our capacity for change, our organizations will become more relevant in our communities: reaching, representing, and responding meaningfully to those we have not connected with in the past.

NOTES

1. CCLI wishes to express deep gratitude to the five museums, all CCLI alumni organizations, who have willingly shared their stories here so that other museum professionals could learn from them. These museums and the individuals represented have a deep commitment to equity and learning that has contributed greatly to their ability to shift toward more inclusive practice. They recognize, as do the authors, that the effort to change is an ongoing journey, one which is never completed and is worth the effort.
2. Garfein, Horney, and Nelson, "Managing Change in Organizations."

3. Garibay and Huerta-Migas, *Organizational Change Brief*, 1.

4. Children's Discovery Museum of San Jose, "Welcome Statement." https://www.cdm.org/wp-content/uploads/2016/08/Welcome_Statement.pdf.

5. Garibay and Huerta-Migus, *Becoming a Learning Organization Brief.*

6. Andrea Giron Mathern, in conversation with author, March 16, 2021.

7. Garibay and Huerta-Migus, *Becoming a Learning Organization Brief.*

8. Jennifer Farrington, in conversation with author, March 17, 2021.

Chapter Three

Using an Inspirational Read to Build an Institutional DEAI Action Plan

Brindha Muniappan and Neil Gordon

Institutional change does not need to start with a big idea or large amount of resources. It can begin with a few compelling words, even by someone completely unaffiliated with the institution, as it did for the Discovery Museum's diversity, equity, accessibility, and inclusion (DEAI) journey.

The Discovery Museum is a children's science center in a suburb of Massachusetts just outside the urban reach of Boston. Founded in 1982, the organization's mission is to inspire enduring curiosity and a love of learning. In its first year, the museum served forty thousand people with an all-volunteer staff and has since grown to include an audience of 240,000 visitors supported by twelve full-time and sixty-three part-time staff. The organization is committed to making our programs and spaces accessible to all visitors irrespective of age, ability, background, or economic circumstance. Although our mission and approach have not changed for thirty-nine years, our audience has expanded and diversified.

In 2007, the Discovery Museum formally made diversity a priority when we adopted a vision statement articulating respect for "differences of abilities, perspectives, background, and opinion," and in 2010 we set a strategic goal of "appealing to a larger and more diverse audience that reflects the communities we serve." During this time we established Open Door Connections, an initiative that eliminates barriers to access for our audiences through free or low-cost services to families with financial limitations and children with developmental or physical disabilities. In 2013 we initiated an $8.4 million capital campaign to fund a complete renovation and expansion of our museum building and our outdoor areas to better accommodate our visitors' diverse backgrounds and abilities. We opened the first phase of this project in 2016 with an accessible Discovery Woods playscape that is anchored by a 550-square-foot wheelchair-accessible treehouse. The expanded museum building opened in March 2018 and allowed for even more of the 4.5-acre campus, indoors and out, to be enjoyed by all.

In keeping with our strategic goal of appealing to a larger and more diverse audience, we offer free museum memberships to under-resourced families and subsidize outreach programs for underfunded school districts. We serve more than a quarter of our audience for free or at a deeply reduced cost through programs targeting underserved audiences, and recently set a five-year goal to grow this audience by 50 percent.

In 2019 we established Belonging as a key pillar in the museum's strategic plan in an effort to ensure that everyone in our community feels that they are a valued part of the Discovery Museum. This goal, as well as the additional pillars of People (emphasizing, for example, professional development, equitable pay, and improved recruitment practices) and Advocacy (determining when and how to take a public stance on issues that impact children and their families), helped lay out a five-year strategy for our continued work to improve DEAI in our community.

A recent survey of museums found that only 16 percent have a public DEAI statement despite 90 percent stating that it is a priority for their organizations.[1] Like many museums nationwide in 2020, we were in the early stages of formally articulating our values with respect to race. We recognized that creating meaningful, engaging experiences in our museum would require a whole-organization examination and understanding of the benefits and disadvantages we accept in how we work. Being able to recognize biases would enable us to embark on real institutional change while gaining experience with ways of helping children and families make sense of race-related experiences in a society encumbered by systemic racism.

Although our museum has a lengthy and successful track record with accessibility and diversity initiatives, we acknowledged that we had not prioritized inclusion and equity efforts. A local foundation's offer of a one-time, mini-grant to support organizations interested in antiracism learning provided an opportunity for the Discovery Museum's senior management team to expand our antiracist awareness and social justice knowledge base. Brindha, coauthor and senior director of the museum experience, proposed the idea after reading Beverly Daniel Tatum's book, *Why Are All the Black Kids Sitting Together in the Cafeteria? And Other Conversations about*

Race, and recognizing that there was tremendous relevance to our professional work with children and families. Not only does Tatum lay out the importance of supporting young children in specific ways as they form their racial-ethnic-cultural identities,[2] but she also encourages frank talk about racial identity as a means for fostering communication across racial and ethnic divides and gently encourages readers to take purposeful antiracist action despite fear of failure. Neil, coauthor and CEO, agreed that the opportunity for senior leadership to read the book, discuss the concepts and ideas, and begin formulating a potential DEAI plan of action would be a good way to acquire external perspective without committing too early to trainings or workshops with a consultant.

We wanted to investigate systemic racism that might exist within the organizational perspectives of educational experiences, development, marketing, finance, and operations so we felt confident that our senior leaders were the right group to begin this effort. We typically begin endeavors with clarity from this leadership group about the issues to be tackled and then form cross-functional task groups to think through questions, needs, strategies, and implementable actions. Our core group of staff are now familiar with this approach to cross-team organizational work and can jump right into new institutional topics without requiring much start-up energy.

We used our mini-grant to purchase copies of Tatum's book for the leadership group and allocated eight to ten hours of time for each person to read and then participate in weekly group discussions. Taking the approach of independently reading this important and meaningful book to advance antiracist learning allowed each group member a bit of time and privacy to think about their personal prejudices or privileges prior to the group discussions. The group's goal was to raise each person's level of understanding about systemic racism and focus on identifying inequities in organizational policies and practices rather than becoming entangled with personal biases. We kept the conversations focused on how to examine systemic racism within the institution's mission and operations, with the aim of ultimately creating goal statements and action plans for each senior leader's focus area.

The antiracist study group met weekly, online, for six discussions between September and October 2020. Brindha created a time frame for the group's progress, set meeting times, lightly facilitated the conversations, captured discussion notes, and provided supplemental readings for most sessions. Facilitation of each week's discussion was greatly helped by prompts from Tatum's book group discussion guide.[3] The group's conversations ranged from exploration of personal biases to analysis of the museum's present and past positions on DEAI, as well as tangible actions the organization could take to be more racially equitable in our work.

Tatum notes that "Talking about racism is an essential part of facing racism and changing it."[4] The antiracist study group meetings did increase the senior leadership team's awareness and comfort with language about racism and social justice, emphasizing to all participants that defining terms is critical for our internal conversations. Our discussions about Tatum's book reminded us about the nation's history of racism and inequity and how little has changed over time. The book also underscored how being passive is tantamount to supporting racism. The senior leaders recognized that to change a racist system, our organization needed to become proactively antiracist to best serve our community of children and families.

The antiracist study group, comprising White[5] staff except for one member, understood that much of the work to advance the organization's antiracist and social justice endeavors would require our personal introspection and acknowledgment that we are part of a racist system. The Discovery Museum is located in an affluent suburb in northeastern United States and our organization has benefited from economic, political, and social systems that traditionally support wealthy White Americans. Over the years the Discovery Museum has maintained a solid focus on playful learning for children, knowing that joy is a path to continued exploration. However, we had perhaps not fully recognized the importance of providing opportunities for children to notice and appreciate physical differences and ask race-related questions as part of the process of developing their own identities, something that is underscored in Tatum's book.[6] Our group became energized in brainstorming ways of creating a culture of inclusion and equity to encourage critical thinking beyond science principles: How might we help children better understand stereotypes and inequities? The ideas raised through our group's conversations suggested a different approach to the way we had been successfully operating for decades. Although exciting, they also created wariness about making mistakes, inadvertently tokenizing individuals, and acting insufficiently. However Tatum's encouragement to move to action—"a sincere, if imperfect, attempt to interrupt the oppression of others is usually better than no attempt at all"[7]—was reassuring and motivating.

During the final two meetings of the antiracist study group, a strategy was developed to widen the discussions and planning process to include more members of the museum's community. We created four antiracist working groups to focus on governance, communications, audience, and institutional activities as a way to examine the institution's full suite of operations. The plan for the working groups was discussed with the museum's board president and an initiative to involve the full board of directors in creating a board diversity statement was established. The board and staff leaders had conversations about the importance and value to the organization of taking

DEAI action and being antiracist, and the board discussed DEAI language and grappled with how to think about our relatively progressive children's museum's place in the context of systemic racism. The conversations were important and ultimately led to agreement and support for the staff's DEAI work. Strong consensus emerged about how diverse perspectives among staff and board would lead to better decisions and a stronger organization which, in turn, would lead to a more diverse visitor population and greater community support. Museum leadership intentionally framed the process of developing DEAI goals as an opportunity for organizational improvement and strength rather than for personal change.

We acknowledge that the decision to examine our operations and dismantle systemic racism in the organization was initiated by senior leadership. Again, this is a course we have followed in the past when embarking on critical organizational changes. Our process relies on the belief that effective solutions can emerge from focused conversations among dedicated teams of staff. We know that these solutions can be implemented effectively when the staff who develop the plans are also responsible for execution of the solutions. Throughout the process, however, we are careful to emphasize that we are producing a framework for action and that framework needs to stay flexible, especially with regard to time frame because other competing priorities that are not part of this process are likely to emerge over time.

To develop our institutional DEAI strategy, each senior leader in the Antiracist Study Group recommended additional members for four antiracist working groups based on their team members' primary duties and professional strengths. By January 2021 an additional ten managers had joined the working groups and the groups were asked to review their functional tasks with a DEAI lens and identify places for improvement or revision. The governance group was to create an action plan for diversifying the board of directors; the institutional activities group would consider administrative, purchasing, hiring, and compensation procedures; the audience group would examine the museum's programs, exhibits, outreach endeavors, and visitor welcoming efforts; and the communications group would review the content and methods of communicating with the museum's current communities, identify ways to improve those connections, and create a strategy for connecting and engaging with new audiences.

The antiracist working groups were to each meet monthly to focus on their specific area (although overlaps with other groups were bound to arise) and share discussions and progress at monthly all-group convenings chaired by the CEO. Everyone was encouraged to be actively involved, incorporating the opportunities for group discussions into ongoing organizational work. The process was defined by time—roughly six months—and each group was charged with creating their own strategic objectives and actions. Ultimately the objectives would be consolidated into a unified institutional statement and a strategy for addressing DEAI inequities in the organization.

Our institutional antiracist work had begun with reading Tatum's book. Motivated by her words, we wanted to share them beyond our internal working groups so we invited Tatum to be part of the museum's annual public speaker series. We knew our community would want to have a discussion with her about antiracist language, when and how to talk with children about race and racism, and the development of racial-ethnic-cultural identity. Because of the COVID-19 pandemic, Tatum's talk was held online in January 2021.[8] A record-breaking thirty-five hundred people from forty-eight states and three countries registered for the event and another eight hundred requested access to the postevent recording when the video conference capacity was filled. (We typically have 250–300 attendees at our speaker series events.) It was clear to our team—and perhaps all staff, volunteers, and board members who attended the talk—that Tatum's perspectives not only aligned with the Discovery Museum's mission and ethos but are also desired by so many members of our growing community.

The antiracist working groups immediately began working on creating goal statements and action plans. All participants were encouraged to access the museum's copies of Tatum's book and to look for examples of DEAI statements and work by other museums and related organizations. The governance group revisited the museum's approved statement of inclusion and accessibility with the board of directors, which was reaffirmed, and facilitated the creation of a statement on board diversity. These statements by the board were important for the ensuing work by the other task groups and provided staff with reassurance that the directors were in agreement about the need for a widespread, institutional antiracist strategy.

It was gratifying to see each group take ownership of their task, with some establishing their own particular ways of working, as the audience group did. As the largest team with members from every museum department, the audience group adopted a "book club" approach and identified a different leader, secretary, and spokesperson to report out to the full antiracist team at each monthly meeting. While reflecting on Tatum's message about the importance of supporting children's development of their racial-cultural-ethnic identities, at least one of the groups discussed how our DEAI aspirations require a shift in the organization's long-held view of not calling out or highlighting any specific visitor identity. Without meaning to be colorblind we wondered if we had been invalidating some visitors' identities. And, by not intentionally supporting nonwhite, noncisgender visitors through representation—for example, in programs, exhibits, and marketing materials—we may have been inadvertently reinforcing dominant viewpoints. The cross-department working groups additionally served as opportunities for staff to share how they had already been thinking and advancing DEAI goals that are specific to their departments, such as providing programs about women and people of color year-round and intentionally reaching out to local organizations to learn about each other's missions and work to build meaningful new relationships.

Three months into the strategic planning process we asked all members of the antiracist working groups to participate in an anonymous survey about the overall effort and effectiveness of our way of working toward an institutional DEAI strategy. Survey respondents (79 percent of the total group) answered positively about the work process, especially about the opportunities to have discussions with colleagues they hadn't been seeing regularly as a result of the COVID-19 pandemic. The responses indicate familiarity with the cross-team work and agreement that this planning process is the right one for the Discovery Museum's DEAI work. All respondents felt their voices were being heard and one person reminded us of the importance of hearing from our primary floor staff as we think about the needs of our audience. When asked for ways to improve our DEAI strategic process, about 30 percent suggested that an external consultant would be helpful to weigh in on our planning work or help the team members better understand DEAI issues and develop shared perspectives and perhaps even enable us to move forward more quickly and confidently. (In full disclosure we are not opposed to working with external advisors but prefer to create a strategic framework and then assess what additional training or assistance may be needed to accomplish the organization's goals.) All respondents said they know that DEAI work is important to the museum although one person wrote "I thought we had more important things to do. After learning more about it . . . it became apparent how important it really is."

A total of 100 percent of respondents believe the museum's leadership is committed to DEAI work, with the caveat that because we are still developing the strategic institutional DEAI plan they reserve full evaluation until we implement the action steps. This survey provided leadership with a check-in for our DEAI planning process and the suggestions that were made will be presented to the antiracist working groups for discussion prior to our next steps.

Tatum's guidance, via her inspirational and motivational book, energized us to get started on a path to be proactively antiracist. Our staff have recognized that we must be explicit about providing visible opportunities for children and their families to see themselves reflected when they visit the Discovery Museum, participate in outreach programs or online events, and see or hear from us in publicity materials. We will be proactive about creating a culture of inclusion and equity for children and their families and encourage critical thinking about racial-ethnic-cultural identity. We acknowledge that our organization has benefitted, and continues to benefit, from privilege created through systemic racism and know that we can do much more to support children and their families, including continued DEAI self-education.

In less than one year we have moved from reflection to the creation of an organizational DEAI statement, unified from goal statements developed by the four antiracist working groups. Our next steps may include external consultation about our work to date, refining action steps to achieve the strategies underlying the organizational DEAI statement, and implementing the effort with full staff involvement. In January 2021 we added questions to our annual staff engagement and satisfaction survey to assess interest and valuation of potential DEAI endeavors and, therefore, now have a tool to gauge how the institutional work affects staff beliefs going forward. We will present our plan to outside reviewers for input and to our board of directors prior to adoption. Just as we have done with our sustainability plan we will post our DEAI action plan publicly on our website and create an annual work strategy and appropriate budget to achieve our goals.

Our approach to learning about systemic racism and creating our organizational DEAI process may not be a model that will work for all organizations. However, we are enthusiastic about the internal wellspring that drives much of our creative success and feel comfortable supporting and encouraging our staff to step forward. We applied a familiar organizational process to a challenging and, potentially, uncomfortable topic. Although some might argue that our process should be more "disruptive," we have stayed true to our way of working. Our institution's DEAI work is ongoing—as are our personal DEAI journeys—and we are eager for our staff and community to continue journeying together with purpose.

NOTES

1. Garibay and Olson, *CCLI National Landscape Study: The State of DEAI Practices in Museums.*

2. We have followed Tatum's written use of the term *racial-ethnic-cultural identity* to encompass the related constructs that an individual uses in developing their sense of self.

3. See book discussion guide in Tatum, *Why Are All the Black Kids Sitting Together in the Cafeteria? And Other Conversations about Race?* https://www.beverlydanieltatum.com/wp-content/uploads/2020/01/Beverly-Daniel-Tatum-Book-Group-Discussion-Guide.pdf.

4. Tatum, *Why Are All the Black Kids Sitting Together in the Cafeteria?*, 8.

5. We use the term *White* (or *Black* or *Brown*) to reference a specific group of people, as Tatum does in her book. This approach is used by many writers, including the National Association of Black Journalists, who advocate for consistency when referring to people and not color.

6. Tatum, *Why Are All the Black Kids Sitting Together in the Cafeteria?*, 111–29.

7. Ibid., 236–37.

8. Discovery Museum Speaker Series, *Talking to Kids about Race and Racism: A Conversation with Dr. Beverly Daniel Tatum moderated by WBUR's Tiziana Dearing.*

Chapter Four

The Individual as Agitant

Catalyzing Transformational Change

Christian Blake

I've titled this chapter using the word *agitant*; it seemed fitting for the way advocacy often unfolds in museums. It has *troublemaker* connotations (in the John Lewis sense), which I like, but also centers the individual agitant as critical to change. Having worked in a museum with a large natural history collection,[1] the word *agitant* naturally also makes me think of mollusks (clams, oysters, mussels) because of how they respond to agitants—specifically, the ways in which they are transformed by them.

When an agitant works its way into a particular species of clam, oyster, or mussel, it begins a strange and wonderful process. Firstly, the mollusk's defense mechanisms kick in—the agitant is new, worrisome—klaxons blare and alarms are raised (one imagines). The mollusk coats the agitant in a secretion as a way of identifying it as something that is different. Yet still, the agitant remains recognized as something else by the mollusk and so another coat is added, and another, all signaling this difference, all transforming what lies inside the shell.

After years, the individual agitant is no longer identifiable, its influence having grown to encompass layers on layers of new forms. The product of all these layers: a pearl. A beautiful culmination of an agitant-induced transformation.

Within capital *I* institutions, the ones with long (and often problematic) legacies,[2] the individual is the agitant. Particularly, those individuals who advocate for a departure from how things have been, with an aspiration to what could be. Throughout this chapter, you'll find I use the words *agitant* and *advocate* often, interchangeably, and intentionally to refer to those who spark and shape organizational transformation through their presence and their labor. In recognizing the work of agitants/advocates it is also critical to examine the structures into and under which they operate to effect change.

As mentioned, the Institution of the museum is rooted in several problematic legacies. Collections were built through oppression, erasure, theft, and worse, only to then be offered back to the masses for the collective good of public enlightenment—and of course, the price of admission. This is likely familiar to many who work in the museum world; organizers created space at conferences dedicated to grappling with museums' legacies, others have imagined what a decolonized museum could be, and many have protested to crystallize for the public the problems present in museums.[3] So if the very premise of what museums are, and the structures in which they find their origins are so deeply flawed then why, or how, do they persist?

Museums persist as they are because, like the structures that underpin them, they have an uncanny ability to maintain what has been. This is why true deep change within institutions will always require the individual—the agitant or advocate—who is unwilling to be complicit in sustaining the problematic aspects of legacy and who will rehabilitate the museum through uncomfortable, necessary transformation.

CONCERNING FRACTALS: CHANGE FROM ANY SEAT

The work of advocacy within museums is one of individual labor and collective solidarity against the intentional or unintentional perpetuation of the status quo. How then, does one find opportunities for movement? They begin in ways that are small.

In *Emergent Strategy*, adrienne maree brown[4] cites Octavia Butler's Earthseed philosophy—"all that you touch, you change. All that you change, changes you. The only lasting truth is change"—as the grounding for how people create change.[5] If change is a constant, then it is also a balm to the individual who feels as though the work of shaping institutions is futile or unlikely. But if change is happening, then where? This is a good question, and one that requires microscopic looking.

During my early museum years working with youth programming, I learned about the concepts of fractals, the never-ending, infinitely complex patterns that emerge from the repetition of a single unit over and over again.[6] The concept was perhaps a bit heady for my elementary-aged group, but they took to it with accessible examples like broccoli, fern leaves, and snowflakes—all things that display their simple, repeating pattern in ways that move from microscopic to massive. Our discussion turned into an enjoyable art project and also gave me a theory for growth that I find myself remembering in moments where I wonder about the impact of a single individual.

The change that we aspire to create on the level of institutions begins at the level of the individual. Within simple interactions—in those spaces that we have the ability to influence and control—we reclaim justice and equity. This is how change can be catalyzed from any seat. For example, those of us who work directly with the public may embody deep listening and the affordance of grace in our interactions. These simple acts create small moments of care and justice in our workdays. For those who manage or support teams, we can decentralize power and decision-making authority in ways that support deeper, more thoughtful, and more imaginative explorations of our work. For leaders (regardless of title), we can interrogate the qualities of our leadership against a future vision that requires a grand departure from "the way things have always been done." Leaders who do this exemplify the humility required to lead through transformational change.

In the work of shaping change, we can then aspire to be like fractals—that is to say, embodying the vision we have for the whole on the level of the individual with the hope that one day, the two will be identical. And this does happen.

BOX 4.1. ALL ACCESS: A CASE STUDY IN FRACTALS

To further understand how fractals expand within an Institution, I'd like to share the experience of Melissa Smith, a friend and a fellow museum agitant/advocate. At her organization,* she has agitated/advocated for deeper access within all facets of the institution's work, while also building it into her practice in roles growing from coordinator of volunteers, adult education and access to assistant curator of access and learning.

Melissa has worked with design students and individuals with lived experience to reimagine how collections can be presented to better engage people who are blind or partially sighted. She's also advanced the ways in which her organization uses art as a tool to support mental health and well-being. And she's created free opportunities for deep (often facilitated) engagement for individuals who would benefit from participating in the museum but experience barriers to do so.

As others in her organization noticed Melissa's work, fractals began to appear (undoubtedly in spaces close to her orbit first). Exhibition design and interpretation teams found methods for consulting with individuals with disabilities to ensure that the display and communication of the exhibition's materials are accessible. The volunteer docent group received additional training on ways to facilitate discussions around art and the collection that are inclusive of experiences and narratives that have historically been excluded. Fractals continued to build, and in 2019, the organization made *access* a core pillar of its strategic plan and rolled out a brand new admission model that significantly reduced the financial barrier to access for many.† The whole now mirrors the values of the individual.

* The Art Gallery of Ontario.
† Wong, "AGO to Keep Free Entry for 25 and Under, $35 Annual Pass."

But the fractalization of our change work in museums does not occur by one individual simply existing; rather, it is similar to the movement of a flock of birds, a process which involves closeness, observation, and trust.

FLOCKING TOGETHER: BUILDING CHANGE THROUGH TRUST

In another museum memory, a kind ornithologist colleague of mine explained to me the process of flocking,[7] the way in which birds can twist, dive, and turn in perfect unison. In my understanding, each bird pays close attention to the birds directly near it,[8] keeping watch and adjusting for changes in speed, heading, and elevation. The magic of the flock though is not in the watching but in the trust built among individuals. In flocks, when a bird begins to turn, so too do the birds paying close attention to it and those paying attention to those birds and on and on, until the collective is producing wonderful twists and turns.

My digression into flock dynamics is particularly important after thinking about fractals and the individual. If the work of the individual agitant/advocate is to shape change in small ways then flocking is how change is further built through shared purpose and trust. For the agitant/advocate shaping change within institutions, what we can learn from the dynamics of flocking birds is to start close among those you trust and who trust you. These trusting

BOX 4.2. TRUSTING TURNS: A CASE STUDY IN FLOCKING

For me, the work of turning an organization toward a more equitable tomorrow began among the BIPOC affinity group at my institution. This group came together organically over lunches and coffees, as a collective capable of agitating/advocating for change within the institution while also creating space where we could offer solidarity and care for one another in the face of resistance.

A fundamental trust existed within our group such that when a few of us began to advocate for more substantial work to foster right relations with Indigenous peoples, so too did the rest of us. Or when a group of us called on our organization for deeper, more transparent accountability practices, so too did the voices of the rest.

These individual movements of solidarity and shared direction took the form of conversations within our spheres of influence, contributions during meetings, inclusions in email communications, and a general commitment to creating visibility in our orbits. We were flocking, turning with the trust of those around us and, in doing so, turning the organization toward a more equitable future beyond the ability of any one individual.

collectives may be colleagues or organized collectives like affinity groups or unions. They may be within or outside of the institution.

Despite the power of flocking, individuals, even collectives, face resistance. As a sector, our affinity for the way things have always been is strong. So, in the face of a lackluster institutional imagination and the profound ability for organizations to downplay, diffuse, and outright suppress internal advocacy, a tool of the agitant/advocate is an ability to harness the currents of our broader environment, the momentum of moments (events that spark public consciousness, drive people to the polls, or into the streets) beyond the walls of our organizations, to advance work within them.

MOMENT-MOMENTUM: LEVERAGING THE POWER OF PUBLICS

The events of summer 2020 seemed to spark a collective awakening to the insidious, lingering, and traumatic nature of anti-Black racism and other systems of oppression across institutions. The murder of George Floyd, followed closely by a litany of violence perpetrated against other BIPOC at the hands of the police, drove people to organize, to march, and to call for the defunding, dismantling, and abolition of systems which did not serve the public good. Museums were not spared from these calls.

From my observation of the sector, many museums lacked the capacity to navigate these new waters in which they found themselves. Perhaps unsurprisingly this lack of capacity was often most prominent in spaces with a distinct and noticeable absence of leadership of color.[9] In many spaces it seemed that the duty to chart a course fell to the agitants/advocates. For those of us who had been working within institutions to shape a deeper reckoning of our organizational baggage, it was complex to experience these topics now suddenly on the tongues of leadership, discussed in-depth across panels and conferences, and integrated into every institutional talking point. I have found there are two truths of moment-momentum and harnessing it within institutions: it can drive work in important ways, and it can also feel kind of gross.

It feels gross to recognize that it took visible incidences of Black trauma played out across our televisions and phones to incite institutional discussions of change. And gross to realize that the desire to change in most institutions is rooted in a desire to survive, to remain relevant, to persist rather than a desire for true justice. Yet, like flocks, turning and twisting, I believe that many agitants/advocates recognized the opportunity to begin to turn our organizations toward deeper, more equitable futures and to do so in alignment with those around them who were paying close attention to their movements.

For me, much of the work that I'm most proud to have been a part of in museums happened during the complex days of summer 2020. During this time, agitants/advocates helped shape new policy, governance structures, methods of evaluation, and more. Many of these moves were sparked from external critique which catalyzed internal discussions.[10] It was within these days that many agitants/advocates laid the foundations for the sustainable futures we aspire to see.

BEYOND NONPERFORMATIVES: GROUNDING ACCOUNTABILITY AND SUSTAINABILITY

Despite the momentum harnessed within moments, many agitants/advocates, myself included, were uncertain of how organizations would continue to hold themselves accountable when people were no longer marching in the streets and #justice was no longer trending on Twitter. Many of us felt that the momentum would not be sustained, that the turns toward justice and equity were just too sharp for institutions to bear, and that, despite their commitments, they would snap back to their previous shape. Because institutions have an affinity for making commitments (which should make us skeptical of their authenticity).

Institutional commitments are often in response to some type of internal or external calls for change, a "moment," and are typically along the lines of:

> At [organization] we are committed to the important ongoing work of [whatever the rallying call of the moment is around] and aim to support a more [socially conscious adjective], [another socially conscious adjective], and [one more socially conscious adjective] society, organization and workplace through our actions. We stand in solidarity with [community who the moment is centered around and who may have called us out] in their calls for deeper [copy-paste movement action points] and acknowledge that we continue to grow by listening and learning.

These commitments can be public or just shared internally, but a commitment is not action and it does not mean that commitment will be acted upon. In her book, *On Being Included*, Sara Ahmed tactfully lays out the habits of institutions when it comes to commitments, particularly that these commitments are generally nonperformative, meaning they do not produce (perform) the function that they name and, therefore, do not tangibly commit organizations to anything.[11] Instead, institutional commitments can provide cover from critique. Ahmed's conceptualization of performative and nonperformative is different from how I had previously used, or seen used, the term *performative*. To keep things clear as we dive further, a performative commitment produces tangible action and a nonperfomative commitment does nothing.

So, in a world of nonperformative commitments, a seemingly simple way to create accountability is to support the creation of performative commitments. Agitants/advocates are often the ones looked to in the moments when the institution needs to "say something." These are opportunities for us to ensure institutional commitments are performative and, importantly, public. In supporting the development of such public performative commitments, it's important to include specific actions, metrics, and criteria for success and how the ongoing growth of this work will be shared publicly.

When given the opportunity to write publicly on behalf of the institution, write in the language of justice and liberation that you aspire to see. Make it bold; make it revolutionary; because before it goes out, it will be edited. I have generally experienced the process of putting out an organizational commitment to be an exercise in watering down and have yet to see a statement that has not had at least two people review it for "tone, messaging and/or brand alignment." But in knowing that and writing boldly toward the future you aspire to see for the organization, you can better ensure that even when watered down that the ethos and performative nature of the commitment remains.

Once a performative commitment is made public, the work of ensuring accountability and sustainability becomes an exercise of pointing. Pointing to that performative commitment and stating, "This is what we said we would do. We've told the public that we will update them on progress. So how should we go about moving toward it?" This type of statement places institutions in a position of continual expectation wherein both the public and those within the organization expect transparency on progress. An institution without consistent expectations can easily snap back into previous habits, whereas one under the scrutiny of the public will have a much more difficult time doing so. Such is the power of transparent accountability.

FULL TRANSPARENCY: ADVOCATING FROM WITHOUT

Full transparency, I no longer work in a museum. I took my exit from the sector in the early part of 2021. I'm of the belief that you should leave a job while it still feels bittersweet to do so, and I could tell that window was closing for me. I held deep respect for many of my colleagues, enjoyed the wonder of the collections, and the behind-the-scenes world that helped to tell its stories, but the progress of equity work all seemed too slow, the actions not radical enough, and the impact too surface-level. I experienced the draining interplay of feeling as though the moment of transformation was right on the horizon, only to continually be confronted with institutional inability to move forward in substantial, meaningful ways. So, when an opportunity for deeper growth came along, it seemed like the right time to let the winds of change carry me to more fertile soil. In departing, I have found that many organizations are keen to shape change and that there are spaces in which the skills of an agitant/advocate can grow, thrive, and fractal into growing and thriving organizations and communities. These are perhaps not revelations, but they were certainly welcome rediscoveries for me.

In rediscovering, I've also experienced an interesting redefinition of my professional life outside museums. I still work in the not-for-profit space, but find myself sporadically missing the strange wonders of the museum; a coprolite on a desk here, a full albatross for preparing there, that foam cat which inexplicably appeared everywhere.[12] Yet, only a few months into a new role, I find myself more grounded where I am. I am in community with the families, members, and partners our organization serves. As a team, we are flocking, twisting, and turning at a pace that is refreshing, timely, and impactful and making those moves in ways that truly support a more equitable, inclusive, and just practice.

I still find myself wondering how much the agitant/advocate can impact institutions from outside of its walls, only to remember the good work being done by individuals and collectives not directly linked to any single organization: folks like Change the Museum, Museums Are Not Neutral, Death to Museums, MASS Action, and more. With these examples I've recognized that the external agitant/advocate can still foster internal discussion, drive deeper institutional reflection, and shape public perception in ways that flow into organizations. In my analogy of mollusks, I've come to think of the external agitant/advocate as a barnacle, sitting within the currents and, in large enough numbers, directing the flow of those currents.

NACRE: LAYERING IT ON

Nacre, or as it's more commonly known, mother of pearl, is the name of the secreted layers that encircle an agitant inside a mollusk, eventually turning it into a pearl. This is a slow process, certainly jarring for the mollusk (the production of a pearl is an immune response after all) and likely disorienting for the agitant that sits at the center as all these new things form around it.

Yet within this jarring and disorienting process the formation of all these layers leads to transformation, to creation, to something entirely new. Rooted at the center of organizational transformation is the individual, the agitant/advocate, whose presence and embodied commitment to change catalyzes change around them. Others see the ways in which agitants/advocates work, and they start to work similarly, beginning the process of fractalization—the expansion out of values, principles, behavior, and so on from the level of the individual to beyond and beyond again, again and again.

These opportunities for expansion, for fractalization, are often begun among flocks—networks who trust each other and share an aspiration of what change could be. In these flocks, change is layered on through the actions of each individual working in alignment with the movements of others. Yet even with the collective purpose of a flock, the ability to elicit change can be challenging, but opportunities can arise in which the momentum of moments can be harnessed to drive organizational change.

Often, in these moments, large numbers of barnacles redirect the currents outside an organization. In doing so, they provide flocks of agitants/advocates with the conditions in which change can take place. It is within these moments that task forces are formed, commitments made, accountability created, and actions advanced. It is in these moments that agitants/advocates can work toward the futures we aspire to see. This is the time in which soil can be tilled and made fertile for change to take root.

Will I return to museums some day? Maybe. I still believe in their potential to become spaces that create connection and deepen understanding in ways that promote and imagine more equitable futures. But there is substantial work to be done to achieve that potential. The museum sector needs deeper introspection at the most fundamental levels of what a museum is, who it serves, and how it serves (in ways that would make ICOM blush).[13] A reimagining of who holds power, how institutions are structured, funded, and guided will also be crucial. It will require agitants/advocates.

For now, my role is as a barnacle. Operating without and redirecting supportive currents to those within. To those agitants/advocates transforming change within institutions through fractals and flocks, moments and commitments, I am grateful to you for the work you continue to do. My belief in museums is a belief in you, you who lay the foundation of the pearl to-be-produced, who prepare the soil for change to take root, and who shape the change we aspire to see.

NOTES

1. The Royal Ontario Museum, if you're curious.
2. Primarily defined by, but not limited to, significant ties to colonialism, white supremacy, imperialism, capitalism, etc.
3. For an example of a conference presentation, see Stevenson, "The Truth Starts Here: Museums' Role in Truth, Reconciliation, and Healing"; for an example of a call for a decolonized museum, see Shoenberger, "What Does It Mean to Decolonize a Museum?"; and for an example of museum protests see Bishara and Novick, "Decolonize This Place Launches 'Nine Weeks of Art and Action' with Protest at Whitney Museum."
4. I owe much of the clarity in the way I imagine shaping change to adrienne marie brown. For all the agitants/advocates this is certainly a book worth reading. See brown, *Emergent Strategy: Shaping Change, Changing Worlds.*
5. Butler, *Parable of the Sower*.
6. I was delighted to find this again in *Emergent Strategy* by brown. Again, you should read it.
7. Yet another concept rediscovered within the pages of *Emergent Strategy* by brown. Seriously, you should read it.
8. Somewhere between five to seven birds.
9. See Grady, "If Museums Want to Diversify, They'll Have to Change. A Lot," and O'Neil, "A Crisis of Whiteness in Canada's Art Museums."

10. For organizations, this external pressure can be anything from a comment on social media to a *hyperallergic* exposé; all are valid and all should inform change.

11. Ahmed, *On Being Included: Racism and Diversity in Institutional Life.*

12. Including, remarkably, in one of our exhibitions.

13. The International Council of Museums proposed a new definition of museums in September 2019 that included language around social justice, equality, and planetary well-being which was met with significant pushback for being "too radical" and "too political." A reimagined definition of a museum could certainly go further.

Part II

STRUCTURE, SUSTAINABILITY, AND IMPACT

Chapter Five

The Hammer Museum's Diversity and Inclusion Group

Evolution and Impact

Alexander Barrera, Tara Burns, Theresa Sotto, and Nick Stephens

The Hammer Museum's diversity and inclusion group (DIG) began in 2016 without a clear purpose nor defined leadership, without a clear pathway for proposing and implementing initiatives and with no budget to realize a single goal. We weren't sure if we truly had agency to foster change in our organization or whether our meetings were spaces for frank and vulnerable discussions. However, we knew that a core group of our members had, and continue to have, a lot of passion for strengthening equity and inclusion at the Hammer, buoyed by a firm belief in our organization's mission: "We believe in the promise of art and ideas to illuminate our lives and build a more just world." In those early DIG meetings, Hammer employees would gather to share a mixture of disappointments and hopes for how we could do better to live up to our mission by more proactively fostering inclusion internally and externally. Five years later, after a significant amount of difficult conversations and new understandings, our work has become more embedded in policies, procedures, and work culture. Initially, between twenty and thirty people (out of more than one hundred full-time staff) attended in-person DIG meetings. In 2020, our attendance doubled in virtual meetings as several working groups continued to push forward initiatives while working from home.

In this chapter, we describe DIG's structure, how and why it evolved from a series of informal convenings to a formalized set of working groups, and examples of successes and challenges as a result of this shift. As we continue to learn from one another, we anticipate further shifts in our structure and processes, additional strides in our equity and antiracism work, and undoubtedly more difficult conversations. We know that working through the difficulties is at the heart of this work, and we are committed to this practice so long as we are able to lift up and lean on one another.

THE DIG STRUCTURE

DIG members work together to foster diversity, equity, accessibility, and inclusion (DEAI) initiatives at the museum with the support of museum leadership. The goals of DIG are to propose and initiate internal and external strategies that embed inclusive practices in museum work and to ensure that the diversity of Los Angeles is reflected in all Hammer activities. DIG members are considered to be anyone interested in DEAI-related topics and active in DIG meetings from all levels of the institution. DIG general meetings, which take place quarterly, are open to all staff and provide vehicles for individuals to voice their opinions about any DEAI-related topic or provide feedback on an existing initiative. If an individual is interested in becoming more involved, they can propose a new initiative or join a subgroup that focuses on more specific projects. DIG currently includes the following subgroups:

- Accessibility: Improves accessibility across Hammer initiatives, digital platforms, and spaces
- Black Lives Matter Taskforce: Works on divestment initiatives at the museum and facilitates antiracist group discussions
- Employee Orientation: Develops resources for new employees to promote a culture of inclusion and belonging from the start of employment
- Inclusive Language: Establishes inclusive language practices in both written and verbal forms
- Spanish Language: Explores opportunities for incorporating resources and programs for Spanish speakers at the museum

These groups have evolved over time, each for different reasons. Some emerged from an idea initiated by a couple of staff members and required additional staff to develop the initiative; others addressed an immediate need that DIG members felt were within their power and capacity to address.

In addition to the subgroups, a DIG steering committee supports short- and long-term DEAI goals, advocates for and communicates DEAI initiatives across the institution, creates the agendas for DIG meetings that are open to all staff, and provides guidance to DIG members and subgroups as needed. The group also advocated for and now manages a modest budget intended for staff training sessions and honoraria for speakers. The cross-departmental steering committee comprises staff at different levels in the institution and includes at least one representative from each of the DIG subgroups. Three steering committee leads liaise between the committee and the museum's executive team (museum director and three deputy directors) to discuss DEAI initiatives led by any of the working groups and to share working agendas for DIG general meetings.

Participation in any DIG general meeting or DIG-initiated projects is completely voluntary unless an initiative becomes a departmental or institutional procedure, process, or program. Knowing that voluntary commitments are not sustainable, our executive team created a full-time, senior leadership position focused on DEAI work, which has been essential to the sustainability of this work over time. Created in 2020, the position of chief of human resources, equity and engagement (CHREE) was formed to prioritize DEAI initiatives for the museum. The CHREE is a senior member of the museum's management team who is responsible for organizational and performance management and the direction and oversight of human resources strategy, budgets, staff operations, and a team of human resources, visitor experience, and gallery operations employees. The CHREE incorporates inclusion initiatives and racial equity best practices by collaborating with staff across the museum to proactively champion the continued evolution of an inclusive culture in which everyone can thrive.

It took several years for employees to shape DIG into its current structure, which would not have been possible without the support of museum leadership in providing space and leeway for employees to advocate for change. We outline DIG's evolution in the hopes that lessons learned and missteps can provide insight to colleagues at other organizations who are interested in embarking on or fortifying their own DEAI or antiracism actions.

THE EVOLUTION OF DIG: FIVE LESSONS LEARNED

Lesson 1: Normalize Ongoing Learning and Care while Having Challenging Conversations

At the suggestion of the Hammer's artist council, which is an advisory group of Los Angeles–based artists, museum leadership invited a company to lead a cultural competency workshop for key staff members, select board members, and several members of the artist council in December 2015. The goals were to discuss the relationship between dominant culture and racism and explore the ways in which the Hammer might uphold institutional racism despite both personal and professional commitments to equity and inclusion. The tension of the latter goal proved to be a sticking point for many participants. In what ways could the museum simultaneously resist and benefit from the structures of white supremacy? Following this generative space of reflection, an assembly of engaged staff members began meeting, and DIG was born.

Those initial DIG meetings were focused on defining diversity and inclusion, brainstorming objectives, and sharing what we believed were our expected outcomes. We claimed DIG as a critical and progressive space and encouraged honest and courageous communication. These meetings provided the only space where staff who would not normally interact with one another, let alone discuss personal and often vulnerable subject matter, could gather to reflect on the institution as a whole. Because the Hammer's exhibitions and public and academic programs aim to provoke dialogue, the museum tends to draw employees who believe in the importance of critical discourse. Very early on, most DIG members were willing to engage in dialogue across departments and hierarchies and were eager to try a different mode of engagement not bound by traditional patterns of communication at the museum. The conversations were sometimes messy, and often emotional, but ultimately they established DIG meetings as spaces where criticisms about work culture and processes could be shared in a semiformal manner and validated by colleagues who felt similarly.

The desire of many members of DIG was to create a "safe space," but this concept is often a complicated one to realize in the workplace. For some people, this meant believing that our sensitive conversations wouldn't be shared with outside parties. For others, this meant a freedom to publicly call out other's behavior and being shielded from consequences. And still for others, the concept of a safe space seemed incompatible with any professional environment. We eventually mitigated the problem by prefacing sensitive statements as being "off the record" to request confidentiality. We also developed community agreements, stating aloud a range of guidelines that demonstrated how we want the group to interact with one another, writing them down, and collectively agreeing to them. Over time, we normalized challenging conversations about diversity and equity, which became one of DIG's most valuable features.

Lesson 2: Provide Clearly Defined Opportunities for Staff to Lead (Not Just from Leadership Positions)

DIG conversations functioned best when diverse voices were in the room, representing a range of races, ethnicities, genders, ages, and staff positions. Our proactive inclusion of positions across the staff hierarchy proved to be essential: The younger and more junior staff members were often the individuals with the initiative, spirit, and willingness to propose ideas and push them forward. However, support from senior staff members was vital in guiding that energy through our museum's bureaucracy. Although many senior staffers were uncomfortable with discussing institutional shortcomings, others would operate as supportive guides. For example, our chief curator understood that her role in DIG was not as an authority figure, and she often offered strategies for moving an initiative forward. To see any project to completion, we needed to balance both the foot on the pedal and the hand on the wheel. There were many moments when there was too much of one and not the other, either too much enthusiasm or too much managing. When we were increasingly able to strike a balance between the two energies, we enjoyed a sense of harmony and momentum.

Structurally, our original intention was to have a flat hierarchy with no singular leadership and to allow all voices to have equal weight. Nevertheless, leaders emerged organically from among different departments and across levels of hierarchy. We established a steering committee, which initially generated agenda items for the full group meetings and kept the executive staff updated with our activities. We also created three subcommittees: staff training and development, access and outreach, and best practices. After some time, it became clear that some of the subgroups grew into hubs of activity while other subcommittees were feeling underused. One reason for this discrepancy was due to the presence of strong leaders in active groups, who were proactive in initiating projects and seeing them through to completion. The DIG steering committee decided to rethink each subgroup's focus—from broad thematic categories to specific projects that were initiated by DIG members and, therefore, less likely to be neglected when those members began working toward subgroup goals. From these conversations, we arrived at the current DIG structure described in the prior section.

Lesson 3: Seek Broad Representation and Openly Discuss Motivations for Participation

A formalized structure for DIG has been beneficial for a variety of reasons: DIG leadership roles were more clearly defined, DIG subgroup members had a clear focus, and the Hammer community as a whole understood the communication channels among subgroups, the steering committee, and the executive team. However, we share these benefits with a word of caution. The increased formalization and defined structure also came with disadvantages for those who wanted the institution to be more nimble. The structure established processes that enabled change to be enacted on an institution-wide level; however, proposals took longer to be reviewed and we could no longer act quickly to pursue an initiative.

To manage the size of our leadership team we restructured the DIG steering committee to twelve people. Although our intent was to keep the team from being unwieldy, our new membership consisted of fewer people with the bandwidth to take on tasks or with the passion and drive to initiate them. This was particularly challenging because steering committee members had different motivations for being involved. Some joined because their jobs entailed providing oversight of museum operations, such as legal or human resources staff members, rather than a passion to foster equity and inclusion. Meetings did not feel like safe spaces to discuss sensitive topics, there were inconsistent levels of trust among members, and roadblocks were raised before ideas could become developed proposals. To mitigate these challenges, we restructured the steering committee to include more representation across departments and the organizational hierarchy in an effort to provide a greater balance of perspectives. Eventually most of these challenges were resolved through staffing changes but, more importantly, by proactively embracing compassion and being patient with one another, including ourselves. Once the motivations of all steering committee members were more closely aligned, DIG was able to function productively as a group of colleagues collectively mobilizing for change.

Lesson 4: Clearly Define and Communicate Expectations about Processes

Following the murder of George Floyd and the increased calls for museums to dismantle systems of oppression, our executive team committed to two hires: a new senior leadership role at the Hammer Museum—the aforementioned CHREE—and an outside DEAI consultant. The DIG steering committee recognized that DIG was not initially involved in the hiring processes of each of these positions. We asserted the importance of our participation in the searches, which led to the appointment of three committee members, fondly referred to as the DIG 3, assigned as liaisons to the executive team.

With the support of the executive team, the DIG 3 played an active role in the hiring process for the new CHREE, including editing the job description, reviewing curriculum vitae of final candidates and interviewing candidates separately from the executive team. Although the executive team reiterated more than once that the ultimate decision was theirs to make, luckily everyone came to a unanimous decision. For the first time in the history of the institution, a Black person was hired to join the senior leadership team. The hiring process for this position took approximately three months from beginning to end due, in part, to the services of a Black-owned hiring firm.

For the DEAI consultant position, the DIG 3 led the search, incorporating consultant research and interviews into their main job responsibilities. This process did not go as quickly or smoothly. Although DIG had researched and proposed consultants the year prior, the executive team established criteria (e.g., consultant must be based locally in Los Angeles) that required the DIG 3 to expand their research. After ten months of diligent work, the DIG 3 identified two consultant firms that fit the criteria the executive team had requested. While presenting their research, the museum director informed the liaisons that one of the identified firms provided an estimate for services that was too excessive. Instead, the executive team suggested a solo consultant that DIG had previously proposed early in the search but had been rejected because he was moving out of state. Ultimately, the executive team made the decision to shift priorities and hire the solo consultant in the end. The decision-making process was not ideal nor as inclusive as we had hoped, and the DIG 3 openly shared their disappointment and frustration.

As a result of the unsatisfactory process, the DIG 3 and executive team learned an important lesson: It is essential to clearly identify the process and limitations for an assigned task, incorporate these details in a written document that can be shared with all parties, and continually provide updates to make sure everyone is headed in the right direction. Furthermore, we share this example to reflect the mutability of equity work; there is always a possibility that the priorities of museum leadership will shift based on new information. It can be helpful to continually seek and share information that will provide rationale for a formerly rejected proposal in the hopes that perspectives will shift in the future. The goal may be reached eventually—just not via the path you envisioned.

Lesson 5: External Consultants Need to Work in Concert with Staff Doing the Work

In late 2019, the Hammer Museum hired an organization to facilitate an antiracism workshop, which focused on broadening understanding of systemic racism. Unlike the training in 2015, senior leadership made this daylong session mandatory for all staff. Employees across hierarchies, departments, and backgrounds sat around a circle and discussed race, prodded into participation by assertive facilitators despite discomfort with positionality and power dynamics. Although many individuals stepped up and bravely shared how racism had played a role in their work, others shared a desire for a different avenue to express their perspectives.

The academic programs team of educators organized a follow-up discussion that was open to all staff. They wove together opportunities for anonymous written feedback with facilitated discussions in an effort to create an open and brave space for colleagues to speak out on the ways that racism had affected our work. Many staff spoke about what we understood "progressive" to mean as a descriptor for our work in a contemporary art museum. We then examined the ways we believe the museum upholds its progressive beliefs (e.g., free admission, social awareness programming for kids and adults, the existence of DIG) and, via anonymously shared sticky notes, described areas where we stood to improve (e.g., silos among departments, less racial diversity in higher positions). By the end of the debrief we arrived at thematic pain points in the organization: the need for greater transparency and cross-departmental communication; structural inequities in staff hierarchies; the need to examine all aspects of museum programs and operations from an equity lens; wage disparity; and a lack of resources and allyship for DIG work. The topics that arose out of the debrief needed more time and attention from staff to unpack, analyze, and, if possible, resolve.

CONTINUING EQUITY WORK DURING A PANDEMIC

The critiques raised during the debrief meeting were still top of mind during what would be our last in-person all-staff meeting early in March 2020. During this meeting many topics resurfaced from the antiracism workshop: how we practice care in the museum, how we respectfully share and hear each other's stories, and how complicated it can be to challenge seniority. Within two weeks of that meeting we began working from home because of the COVID-19 pandemic. Staff settled into remote work and established new working norms and then our lives were shaken once again by the brutal murder of George Floyd. We, along with the audiences and artists we serve, were overcome by our shared grief. This full emotional context is necessary to underscore the depth of the various DEAI needs that the museum was experiencing at one time.

As all of these issues mounted early in summer 2020, the limitations of the DIG structure became clear. A small group of DIG members convened to check in on one another and brainstorm about how the museum might better address the immediate needs of its community both internally and externally. This group of twenty or so members (what would become the DIG BLM taskforce) was not prompted by the steering committee or any subcommittee to begin doing this work. The BLM taskforce worked collaboratively to craft a robust statement of support for the movement for Black lives and the protestors of Los Angeles, while simultaneously working to hold the museum accountable for specific immediate steps it could take toward antiracism. The group also began to investigate opportunities for divestment by researching the scope of the institution's relationships with various police forces and then drafted recommendations for divestment for senior leadership's review, which remains an ongoing conversation as of the writing of this chapter. The steering committee, recognizing a flurry of activity happening outside the formal structure of DIG, had to reckon with itself. DIG was no longer the most vocal body at the museum pushing for structural change. The steering committee had to adjust its approach to organizing the larger DIG group to better meet the ever-evolving needs of Hammer staff.

The first virtual DIG general meeting occurred a few weeks after Floyd's death. We knew that his murder and its emotional aftermath would be central to this meeting, and we also knew that we had many topics to cover that predated the pandemic. With the aim of being more inclusive than before, we engaged and invited part-time staff to attend this meeting. In structuring the virtual meeting, we used breakout rooms to provide staff with an opportunity to speak and be heard in ways that are sometimes lost in a larger setting. We fostered open dialogue by carefully orchestrating each breakout room in advance, pairing members of leadership with individuals whom we felt would be able to navigate power dynamics in productive ways and would make space for colleagues who may be shy to share in this context.

Nearly seventy people attended this meeting, including full-time, part-time, and student staff members. In breakout rooms, we posed thought-provoking questions that were still lingering from the antiracism workshop debrief:

- How can staff initiate better communication and transparency?
- How can we ensure that our exhibitions and programming reflect the various publics we serve?
- How can we foster more inclusive decision-making and creative input across departments and hierarchies?
- How do we examine the construct of whiteness in museum spaces?
- How do we cultivate a more caring and equitable culture?

The discussion that ensued was a return to the early days of DIG; we were primarily holding space for one another to share our feelings on DEAI topics like racism, privilege, and access. This time, because we were separated and experiencing layers of trauma simultaneously, instead of feeling chaotic it felt more cathartic.

CONCLUSION: COLLECTIVE CARE AND COLLECTIVE ACTION GO HAND IN HAND

Museum leadership has made it clear that DEAI work is an institutional priority. Although participation in DIG is currently voluntary, the authors believe that all staff should assess their work through a DEAI lens, regardless of whether they are members of DIG. In fact, the CHREE has affirmed that annual performance evaluations should reflect when employees demonstrate effectiveness in DEAI work, and he has added a requirement to all new job descriptions that states that successful candidates will demonstrate a commitment to DEAI initiatives. Our hope is that DEAI work will be embedded in the processes, protocols, and structures of the Hammer and will therefore no longer require the advocacy and oversight of a core group of individuals.

As DIG continues to evolve over time, there is one aspect of our work that we believe will remain a constant: the ongoing challenge of participating in or bearing witness to difficult conversations with colleagues whose perspectives vary. The frequency of these conversations has increased across the institution, resulting in a climate where conversations about race, power, and inequities are expected and encouraged. In general, these conversations have become more courageous but no less difficult, and we know that working through difficulty is a big part of DEAI work. Combating white supremacy within institutions that have benefited from it is mentally laborious and emotionally strenuous on staff members. For this reason, we encourage all members of DIG to practice self-compassion and vocalize crucial moments when they need support. Sometimes we do not have the mental or emotional capacity to be active in DIG work. We encourage each other to practice self-care and support DIG members who want to step down from a subcommittee or DIG projects for a period or indefinitely. We rely on like-minded colleagues in DIG to support each other through this work, and as a result, many friendships have grown between colleagues who otherwise may not have had the opportunity to work with one another and form bonds.

One pivotal DIG meeting in 2020 was not focused on inequities and its impacts; instead, the DIG steering committee designed an intentional space for collective healing. Staff were exhausted—from the constant onslaught of news about anti-Black racism and anti-Asian hate as well as from the challenges of difficult conversations about systemic inequities in our own institution, all while pivoting to working from home against the ongoing trauma of the COVID-19 pandemic. We needed to lift one another up. In our DIG general meeting in December 2020, we spent one hour focused on gratitude, highlighting aspects of our colleagues' work that we found particularly helpful or meaningful. It was a time where we were given institution-wide permission to take a step away from our responsibilities and to individually and collectively honor our work. Many staff members were in tears. We end with this anecdote to emphasize the necessity of praise to unify institutions. Although we all acknowledge there is still a lot of work we need to do to foster antiracism and equity at the Hammer, we know that we cannot engage in this difficult work if we don't have a foundation of collective care and mutual respect.

NOTE

The views and opinions expressed within this chapter are those of the authors and do not reflect the views, opinions, and beliefs of all members of DIG, the Hammer Museum, or the University of California, Los Angeles.

Chapter Six

The Accessibility Task Force at The Museum of Modern Art

Francesca Rosenberg and Lara Schweller

Imagine that you have entered a meeting room at The Museum of Modern Art (MoMA) to join one of our disability equality trainings. Typically, we begin each session by asking a series of questions. We would ask you to raise your hand or in some way acknowledge if you or someone you know has a physical disability and uses an assistive device, such as a wheelchair, walker, or cane. We would continue by asking about other disabilities. Do you or someone you know have hearing loss? Vision loss? An intellectual or developmental disability? Dementia? A chronic illness? Depression or another mental illness? Each time the answer is yes, we would ask you and the individuals in the group to acknowledge this as we ask about a vast range of disabilities. By the end, most people have signaled with whatever mode they are able, most often with a hand in the air, likely two, and maybe even a foot because they have run out of hands. We all experience or know other people living with disabilities and it's meaningful for everyone in the room to acknowledge this together. According to the Centers for Disease Control and Prevention (CDC), as of 2018, 26 percent of adults in the United States reported having a disability.[1] Although one in four adults in this country have a disability, even more adults know someone with a disability—a family member or a friend. Staff, artists, and visitors at the museum may have a disability themselves or may be visiting with someone who has a disability. The number of visitors seeking an accessible museum experience is high.

The accessibility task force (ATF) at MoMA, formed in 2011, is a cross-museum collective of staff dedicated to advancing accessibility across all aspects of the museum's physical spaces, exhibition content, programming, and staff professional development. This working group has been steadily advocating to not only increase accessibility across the museum's physical and intellectual spheres but also to shift the attitudes of staff toward a more inclusive understanding of people with disabilities as part of the general public. MoMA's approach to accessibility emphasizes a shift away from thinking of the disabled body as an outlier to the norm. Planning spaces, content, and experiences for a wide diversity of bodies and minds is much more "normal" than planning for a limited set of bodies, which research shows "most-often include audiences [that] are disproportionately white, older, more affluent, and more highly educated."[2] Or, as social practice artist Carmen Papalia writes:

> As a museum visitor I seldom feel like the museum cares about whether they can make a returning customer of me. Of course they have a visitor experience that they can offer me as a non-visual learner, but, as is the case with so many public institutions, the experience that I am allowed as a disabled person is a bad one. Sure I can go on an "accessible" tour once every week or so, or put on a pair of headphones while I walk through an exhibition, but, still, my experience of the museum is a derivative of the experience that the museum offers other visitors.[3]

To become accessible, museums need to actively work toward expanding inclusive design and broadening the audience that they consider.[4] And as Papalia notes, accessibility shouldn't be a "derivative" experience, simply an accommodation that translates the experience for people who access the work in an alternative way. Making a museum accessible to a diverse audience is a creative opportunity. In this chapter, we share insights from MoMA's ATF, including successes and strategies for advocating for accessibility—creatively and with empathy. Our goal is to demonstrate what can be accomplished through a task force like this as well as the work that still needs to be done.

Before moving on to these more in-depth examples, we need to account for our own position in this work. Francesca and Lara are cis, white women without disabilities. Although we are both committed to the field of accessibility in museum education, we recognize our own privilege in securing positions in this field at MoMA. We feel that it's most important to share the platform we hold to provide access to people with disabilities and to always continue to learn with and from others. MoMA is actively working to diversify its staff, including bringing on staff with disabilities. In this chapter we aim to bring in the voices of people with disabilities with whom we work—staff, artists, and self-advocates.[5] In our resources for this chapter we incorporate papers by individuals with disabilities to redirect readers to these writers. When referring to people who have disabilities, we often use person-first language. For example, we might say "a person with a disability" rather than a "disabled person." Although identity-first language emphasizes disability as the primary marker of someone's identity, person-first language emphasizes that disability is just one part of a person's identity, naming the person as the primary rather than their disability. However, some individuals with disabilities prefer to use identity-first language and it's most important to defer to the language a person uses to describe themselves.[6]

We begin this chapter with brief informational groundwork in this introduction and have organized the rest of this chapter into three sections: The first section will cover the history of MoMA's ATF in the hopes that telling this story will empower other museums to continue this work. The second and third sections dive deeper into the dual focus of the ATF work: staff training and professional development as well as physical and programmatic accessibility.

THE SOCIAL MODEL OF DISABILITY

The history of disability advocacy is aligned with the civil rights movement in the United States in its practice of political action. In 2020, MoMA presented the New York premiere of Nicole Newnham and Jim LeBrecht's documentary film *Crip Camp*, which narrates this history through the lens of collective action forged through friendships at a summer camp for teenagers with disabilities. Though disability advocacy is a part of the US civil rights movement, specific considerations for accessibility—and accommodations to the built environment of a cultural space—are often elided in conversations around diversity, equity, and inclusion. In 2021, many museums are actively pursuing much-needed and long overdue diversity, equity, accessibility, and inclusion (DEAI) work. As DEAI initiatives come to the forefront of cultural institutions' work in response to our country's reckoning with ongoing, systemic racism, it is more essential than ever to identify that ableism has always been an intricate part of systems of oppression and that disability rights are civil rights.[7]

The World Health Organization (WHO) defines disability as the, "results from the interaction between individuals with a health condition such as cerebral palsy, down syndrome [*sic*] and depression as well as personal and environmental factors including negative attitudes, inaccessible transportation and public buildings, and limited social support."[8] Disability is what happens in the interaction between a person's body or mind and their environment. If a person has a visual disability but wears corrective lenses that augment their vision so that it's what one "typically" experiences, then they may be able to seamlessly navigate a museum. However, if a person has a visual disability but doesn't have access to corrective lenses—whether that's because the technology isn't adequate, there is a lack of access to health resources or financial reasons—then that person's experience of the same environment becomes a disabling experience. Disability lies in that interaction and in the inability of a culture, laws, technology, or the built environment to provide equitable opportunities for a diverse population. Simi Linton writes that:

> Briefly, the medicalization of disability casts human variation as deviance from the norm, as pathological condition, as deficit, and, significantly, as an individual burden and personal tragedy. Society, in agreeing to assign medical meaning to *disability*, colludes to keep the issue within the purview of the medical establishment, to keep it a personal matter and "treat" the condition and the person with the condition rather than "treating" the social processes and policies that constrict disabled people's lives.[9]

The social model of disability works to identify cultural, ideological, attitudinal, political, and architectural barriers to experience that cause the disabling experience.

Access to arts and culture is a civil right, and yet people with disabilities still face a range of barriers in accessing museums. We recently interviewed a self-advocate, Julian Reiss, who identifies as autistic and, for years, has attended MoMA's Create Ability program, an art-looking and art-making workshop. We asked Julian to tell us about his interest in art. He wrote:

> I remember going with my parents to study about artists before I could talk. I was able to be expressive with art projects without using my voice. I am not a good artist but I am enthusiastic about expressing myself. It does not matter how art is made. It is an expression of my soul. I really like to learn about the different artists and different artistic mediums.[10]

For Julian, who worked to develop and hone his verbal expression as a teen, access to the arts was access to self-expression.

ACCESSIBILITY IN THE MUSEUM

For the last twenty-seven years, Francesca has foregrounded the voices of and advocated for the rights of museum visitors with disabilities by increasing museum-wide accessibility and creating a range of programs for visitors with disabilities through collaborations with individuals and community advisory groups. Prior to the museum's closure in 2020, due to the COVID-19 pandemic, the museum's community and access programs typically served upward of twenty thousand individuals each year.

Although MoMA's access programming is currently robust and staff from across the institution are firmly committed to making the museum accessible to all, for years Francesca worked on her own, siloed in the education department.[11] MoMA's ATF was started to begin building accessibility into the workflow of departments across the museum. Our colleague Annie Leist, associate educator in community and access programs shared:

> When institutions strive to make accessibility a part of everyone's job, it shows. I know personally that I can sense that more holistic welcome as a disabled museumgoer. When I joined MoMA's staff in 2020, I was thrilled to learn about the Accessibility Task Force, and the commitment to barrier removal made by colleagues all across the museum. To me, it means that accessibility at MoMA is not just an add-on; it's a fundamental part of our museum's culture. Weaving accessibility more fully into the fabric of the institution allows us to more meaningfully consider disability as an aspect of identity, and to begin to address issues of diversity, equity, and inclusion for disabled audiences, artists, and staff.[12]

MoMA's ATF is always working to embed accessibility across a museum and to build capacity for this work through staff collaboration.

In the hopes that this chapter will be less of a reflection on MoMA's own experience and much more so a tool for other institutions to implement new and different modes of working on accessibility, we'll summarize these key strengths that we'll continue to return to in a few different case studies:

- The ATF prioritizes a collective of voices over one individual perspective. When it comes to thinking big and broadly about accessibility across the museum, it's best to have as many perspectives represented as possible.
- Accessibility isn't the purview of one department and needs to be a cross-museum initiative. Different roles at the museum have different and varied expertise. A staff member trained in museum education will think about exhibition accessibility much differently than a curator or an exhibition designer. Making a museum accessible is a creative opportunity for each department to think about what this means in their work.
- Accessibility is always changing as technology advances and culture shifts. Working toward accessibility is not a project that has a beginning and an end, and a working task force ensures that the work is not project-based.
- The goal of the ATF has always been twofold: striving to ensure the museum's physical and programmatic accessibility as well as to break down attitudinal barriers toward disability equality through staff training.

While we can share the path we've taken at MoMA, it is particular to our institution's history and culture. We hope these highlights will serve as a roadmap for other institutions creating working groups to enhance accessibility.

THE DETAILS AND LOGISTICS OF THE ACCESSIBILITY TASK FORCE

James Gara, MoMA's chief operating officer, launched the ATF in 2011. He had previously collaborated with Francesca on specific accessibility projects and was dedicated to supporting accessibility at the museum and her work in the education department. While attending a MoMA film screening he watched as a visitor requested an assistive listening device and the frustration they then experienced when the accommodation didn't work and no one knew how to fix it. While staff in MoMA's audiovisual (AV) department or access programs team would have been able to assist, there was no one on hand at this particular screening, and there was a lack of awareness that extended across departments and frontline staff.

James launched the ATF to consider accessibility holistically across MoMA. If the working group could embed a commitment to accessibility across the museum then all staff would feel empowered to not only confidently troubleshoot accommodations but would welcome visitors with disabilities as part of the museum's general public. The task force has since overseen large-scale projects to implement T-coil loop systems and a variety of assistive devices in the theaters and has also developed and implemented years of disability equality and accessibility training for MoMA staff. James appointed Francesca and Tunji Adeniji, director of building and safety at MoMA, as the two co-chairs of the task force to complement the group's focus on accessibility in the building and exhibition design as well as programmatic accessibility and staff training. Alexis Sandler, associate general counsel, was integral to this working group to ensure the museum's compliance with Americans with Disabilities Act (ADA) guidelines, though it was the museum's mission to go above and beyond compliance. The group meets twice a year to review successes, identify areas in need of improvement, and report on anything related to accessibility in MoMA's physical building, exhibitions, programs, staffing, and the visitor experience. We meet with this cadence to keep long-term projects on track and to stay accountable to goals. Throughout the year, smaller teams from this larger group meet to work on exhibition-specific content or more large-scale projects.

The ATF is made up of senior level staff from almost every department at the museum because accessibility work touches all aspects of the museum's operations. The group, which includes self-advocates, typically includes staff from the following departments at MoMA and MoMA PS1: AV, building facilities and safety, communication, curatorial, education, exhibition design and production, exhibition planning and administration, general counsel's office, graphic design, group services, information technology, membership, special events and visitor engagement.[13] Having staff at the director level who are able to make decisions quickly in the group ensures that projects can be conceived and implemented efficiently, rather than getting caught in a tangle of approvals. Decisions are made by consensus in conversations during meetings, and Francesca circulates action items for specific group members.

There are many other institutions that have formed working groups for accessibility on a voluntary basis by recruiting people who are personally interested in advancing accessibility and growing the group organically irrespective of each person's department or position. At MoMA, one person from each department, typically in a leadership role, is asked to serve on the task force or to identify someone from their department to join. In a volunteer-based model, people who self-select to join a group like this are typically already passionate about advancing accessibility and bring that energy to the group.

The ATF has its own operating budget of capital funds approved by MoMA's finance department. These funds have been allocated to diverse cross-museum initiatives, from purchasing stools that visitors can access in the lobby, to creating staff training videos on disability equality, to funding exhibition-specific accommodations like captions for audio or video artworks. Although each exhibition budget has a line for accessibility, it has been essential to have funds allocated for use in advancing accessibility and working with living artists who want to make their work available to the widest audience possible.

This working group has always focused on how to advance accessibility not only through changes to the building or accommodations in the artwork but also in shifting perspectives around disability equality. Ellen Rubin, a longtime collaborator, consultant, and participant in our programs, told Francesca years ago that the biggest barrier she faced as a woman who was blind was other people's attitudes about what she could and couldn't do. Through staff training and professional development, we all work to collectively chip away at the inherent biases many of us hold about what it means to be disabled and occupy space in a museum. Because accessibility is always changing, and MoMA building upgrades, retrofits, and redesigns take the form of multiyear projects, it's almost impossible to be 100 percent accessible to 100 percent of people all the time. We're always working on it. When someone encounters a barrier in the museum it can ruin their visit. Continually working toward a more and more accessible space means that the work of how we welcome people and who we welcome is always top of mind. We also focus on staff training because staff are often stepping in to make the museum a welcoming place despite inefficiencies in the built environment. LaPlaca Cohen, a strategy and marketing consultancy firm, reports, "People with disabilities are 59% more likely than those without to say they do not attend cultural activities because they 'had a negative experience last time.'"[14] We all have work to do to empower our staff to feel comfortable and confident welcoming everyone into cultural spaces, including people with disabilities.

DISABILITY EQUALITY TRAINING AT MOMA

From its beginning, the task force focused on disability equality training workshops for frontline staff who interface directly with visitors. Yearly sessions with staff from visitor engagement, security and facilities, operations, membership, and retail provided an opportunity to focus on this important topic, but the sessions had limitations. The impact of these sessions was limited due to the brief time allotted for each meeting (frontline staff need to be on the floor); the auditorium-style seating in a large, dark room needed to accommodate larger groups; and the information-heavy content (rather than interactive discussions revolving around real-world situations). Refresher sessions were needed throughout the year as well as opportunities to incorporate this information when onboarding new staff, but neither were logistically possible. We found that MoMA staff felt so uncomfortable talking about disability that it got in the way of realizing that people with disabilities are more like us than not.[15] We all are or know people with disabilities, but we live in a culture where having a disability is stigmatized. We knew that we needed to redesign these trainings so that our staff could learn about disability equality directly from the disability community. Additionally, we wanted staff to meet in smaller groups for longer periods of time, with opportunities to process information together and break through some of the discomfort that was preventing meaningful shifts in attitude.

At the time, Francesca, Lara, and Carrie McGee (former assistant director of MoMA's community and access programs), were facilitating these trainings on behalf of MoMA's access programs team in the education department. We wanted these sessions to be a platform for the voices of our visitors with disabilities. However, given MoMA's large staff size (at that time this included more than nine hundred employees) and the volume of training we were conducting, we knew that the logistics of bringing multiple speakers to each training would be an unrealizable effort. Our colleague Jackie Armstrong (associate educator in visitor research and experience), designed an all-staff survey to better understand what our colleagues felt they knew and what questions they had, both about accessibility at the museum but also about disability experience more generally.

Roughly 35 percent of MoMA staff responded. We learned that although staff felt like they provided good customer service to people with disabilities, the language staff used in survey responses confirmed that they were still thinking of visitors with disabilities as a separate group from our typical visitors. They used words like *special*, *other*, and *different* when describing visitors with disabilities. Additionally, staff wanted to learn more about disability experience and that that process could be the key to building empathy and shifting attitudinal barriers. As a direct result, we reached out to seven self-advocates to assist us in making a training video that we used in interactive staff trainings to open up a conversation around disability experience.

In the summer of 2018, while MoMA closed to finish a renovation project, frontline staff were available to participate in a variety of professional development opportunities, including disability equality training. More than seven hundred MoMA frontline staff and volunteers participated in a three-hour disability equality workshop. Maureen Gilbert, a disability, intercultural, diversity and equality consultant, worked with MoMA to develop our approach to the trainings; we also collaborated with nine disability self-advocates to create content for the trainings, which took the form of interview videos.[16] We asked these consultants about their most frustrating and disabling experiences at museums and then created scenario videos in which they, along with MoMA frontline staff, acted out their disabling experiences. We also filmed a version of how these scenarios could unfold in a more accessible MoMA.

As part of the trainings, staff collectively designed and set an internal guide for how to be welcoming to visitors with disabilities. When asked what they enjoyed most about the training, the majority of staff cited the importance of getting to know colleagues through the conversations we facilitated around what it means to feel welcome at a museum and how we, as MoMA staff, can create that environment. This cross-departmental collaboration has been key to advancing accessibility across MoMA and is one of the task force's most impactful outcomes.

EXHIBITION ACCESSIBILITY AT MOMA

The ATF brings together staff situated in curatorial, design, and visitor engagement to think of the creative opportunities for accessible design. One exciting focus of the task force is collaborating with living artists to ensure that their work will be accessible to the widest possible audience. Curators and exhibition designers involved in this work—either through participation in the task force or through related disability equality training—often raise opportunities for accessible design with artists. They may consult with the access programs team on realizing initiatives because our team has collaborated with curators across the museum. Recently, a number of artists have specifically sought out ways to make their exhibitions more accessible. Park McArthur, whose *Projects 195* exhibition was exhibited at MoMA in 2018, said:

> Creating access is often understood as a translation of loss from the "original" work of art, rather than a constitutive part of every visual, aural, or performance work. The team I worked with at MoMA understood that encountering works of art within built environments only occurs through accessible presentation; accessibility itself has aesthetic qualities that artists and curators can engage both within and alongside the content of their work. At a time when contemporary artists are questioning the roles and limits of institutional life and procedure, access is a lodestar. Accessibility is infrastructural and organizational and it serves as a useful term for transformation more broadly.[17]

Park distills how the accessibility of artworks and spaces can be a marker for an institution's transformation and, perhaps, its attitude toward welcoming its visitors to experience art. Kevin Gotkin, NYU Steinhardt Professor, whose work combines research, artistry, and activism, shared with us that, "accessibility is about choice, options, about giving folks more than one pathway." And that rather than simply meeting compliance, it can "allow people to engage in really creative and curious ways."[18] Both artists point to the opportunity for accessibility to be a catalyst for more creative design.

MoMA's access programs team and AV department often consider opportunities for building T-coil loop systems into artworks, which requires built flooring into which the loop can be installed as well as a single-channel sound installation that won't have competing sound from nearby artworks. From December 2012 to January 2013, MoMA exhibited Christian Marclay's film *The Clock*. The design for this film involved building a theater specifically for this work, which presented an ideal opportunity for incorporating a T-coil loop. This was the first time the twenty-four-hour film had ever been shown with a T-coil loop, enabling it to be accessible to the many people who are deaf or hard of hearing who use a hearing aid or a cochlear implant. Through collaborations with the ATF, MoMA staff designed an installation that would support the accommodation. Marclay was delighted that his film would be available to a wider audience, who was now able to experience the work with the sound amplification of a loop system.[19]

These working relationships gain traction over time and instill a culture of teamwork across departments. This type of teamwork isn't just about playing together nicely; it means that staff with different professional and personal backgrounds come together to provide ideas about how to design creatively for a diverse audience. Sometimes this takes the form of staff providing feedback, and sometimes it involves providing support in thinking about how to activate artworks and exhibitions in new ways. Aaron Louis, director of AV at MoMA, has implemented technology-based accessibility solutions ranging from hearing loops to personal closed captioning systems to infrared assistive listening systems, and a new technology that streams audio content from an artwork via Wi-Fi live and in-sync with a visitor's personal handheld device or hearing aid. Aaron says, "Access at MoMA is implemented through multiple technologies at once, which together work to create a seamless, intentional, and positive experience throughout the Museum. I approach this part of our work as both a priority and opportunity to experiment with new technologies as these innovative systems so often are adapted for wider use and provide value to all patrons and staff."[20] Technologies that are first developed to serve individuals with disabilities often benefit the entire public and are adapted more widely. For example, the assistive listening devices used on group tours to amplify sound for visitors who are hard of hearing were so useful in the often cacophonous museum that they were incorporated into all public tours.

In 2015 the museum exhibited *Yoko Ono: One Woman Show, 1960–1971*. Ono's artwork *To See the Sky* (2015) includes a black spiral staircase that leads to a skylight in the roof of the museum where you could watch the sky. Curatorial, exhibition design and production, and AV staff worked with Ono to make this work accessible by adding a camera pointed at the skylight that transmitted to a monitor across the room. Visitors with physical disabilities, young children and their parents, and anyone who could not climb the stairs for any reason could experience the work through this alternative. We share this as an example for what museums can do to provide accessible experiences. Building relationships and rapport between departments takes time as well as a willingness to share resources and ideas and the work of thinking outside of the typical or expected experience of an artwork or a space.

Curators of *Judson Dance Theater: The Work Is Never Done* (September 2018–February 2019), collaborated with exhibition design and production, AV and the access programs team to imagine how they could share a series of oral histories about Judson Dance Theater within a single gallery. To make these histories accessible, a monitor with scrolling captions was added to provide a textual and visual experience of these stories. The histories were accessible to a wider audience and also provided a multimodal experience overall, which served visitors in addition to those who were deaf or hard of hearing. This exhibition stands out as an example of what an accessible exhibition could be—planning for accessibility in advance, thinking through multimodal experiences of content, and working across teams. We are working toward more of this in the future.

CONCLUSION

Over the last decade, the ATF has instilled a culture of sharing expertise and labor through collaboration among its participants. It has strengthened relationships among departments, led to exciting professional friendships and collaborations, and has honed every participants' critical assessment of what it means to be accessible and welcoming in all aspects of MoMA's work. Lana Hum, director of exhibition design and production at MoMA and a critical ATF member, shared, "The only way to become an accessible institution is to approach it pan-institutionally, from multiple perspectives, and with DEAI as core to our being. Task forces are great at capturing multiple perspectives and keeping important work alive. The effort does not end at a set of rules or policies but requires ongoing thought."[21] Accessibility shifts and staff need to be attuned to these changes and open to creativity, change, and redesign.

BOX 6.1. ACCESSIBILITY TASK FORCE RECOMMENDATIONS

- Form a task force that has the ability to enact museum-wide policy and change. Consider what type of institutional support is needed for this.
- Advocate for each department to include accessibility considerations in their budget as well as a separate budget for a task force that can be applied to cross-museum initiatives or accommodation support.
- Schedule your group meetings across the year with enough time to hold everyone accountable for completing projects as well as enough time for progress between each meeting. Every institution has a different rhythm.
- Involve as many departments as possible in the task force, with a mix of frontline and back-of-house staff.
- The disability civil rights movement's slogan is "Nothing about us without us." Design programs and resources with disability consultants for these projects.
- Create an inclusive culture. Incorporate recruiting and hiring people with disabilities when job openings become available. Review hu-

man resources policies for applications, interviews, and accommodation requests for accessibility.

- Representation in an art museum includes representation in the museum's collection. Engage with disability aesthetics and disability artistry.

The ATF is currently working on developing a training for curatorial teams co-led by exhibition design and production and access programs staff to inspire teams to think creatively about accessible exhibition design. Lana says, "One-size-fits-all solutions do not work. The ATF made us better designers. Considering the diversity of our audiences has made us better designers/listeners and more creative thinkers." When we design for people with disabilities in mind, we design for everyone. When we add ramps within buildings, we serve individuals who use wheelchairs, caregivers using strollers, and anyone who prefers to walk up a ramp rather than climb stairs. When we feature wall text in an exhibition with a larger font size, it not only makes information accessible to visitors with low vision, but it also enables more people to read the information from further away. This is essential to avoid crowding and eliminates visitors having to get dangerously close to the artwork. Adding captioning to digital content on moma.org not only makes the video accessible to people who are deaf or hard of hearing, but they also become more accessible for people whose first language isn't English, or for anyone who prefers to watch the video without sound.[22] We all benefit from disability advocacy and disability design. We look forward to continuing to work toward a more and more accessible MoMA.

NOTES

1. Centers for Disease Control and Prevention, "Disability Impacts All of Us."
2. LaPlaca Cohen and Slover Linett, "Culture + Community in a Time of Crisis."
3. Papalia, "A New Model for Access in the Museum."
4. Guffey, "Beyond Compliance."
5. Self-advocates are individuals with disabilities who are also invested in disability advocacy work.
6. For more information on distinctions between identity-first and person-first language, please see this roundtable discussion hosted by the Museum, Arts and Culture Access Consortium; Gotkin, Lurio, Matos, and Zalopany, "Mindful Communication: Language and Disability Discussion and Best Practices."

7. For more reporting on this, see the recent report from the National Disability Institute, "Race, Ethnicity and Disability: The Financial Impact of Systemic Inequality and Intersectionality." For more coverage of current health disparities, see reporting by Aaron, "Doctors and Racial Bias: Still a Long Way to Go." Also see Geiger, "Racial and Ethnic Disparities in Diagnosis and Treatment: A Review of the Evidence and a Consideration of Causes." For reporting on the increased likelihood of BIPOC with disabilities entering the incarceration system, see Cohen "Young People with Disabilities More Likely to Be Arrested."

8. World Health Organization, "Disability."

9. Linton, *Claiming Disability: Knowledge and Identity*, 11.

10. We encourage you to watch the entire interview with Julian as well as interviews with other self-advocates on MoMA's website at https://www.moma.org/visit/accessibility/resources#disability-equality-training-resources.

11. There were a handful of museum workers in the 1990s who found themselves in a similar situation and reinstated the Museum Access Consortium, now known as the Museum, Arts and Culture Access Consortium (MAC). The original MAC was launched in the 1980s and the MAC group in the 1990s was formed to create a mutual network of support, which is key, because it supports an ethos of sharing knowledge, resources, and power that has been essential to the success of accessibility work.

12. Annie Leist, e-mail message to author, August 2021.

13. MoMA PS1 is a contemporary outpost of The Museum of Modern Art located nearby in Long Island City, Queens.

14. LaPlaca Cohen, "Culture Track 2017."

15. "More like us than not," is a phrase that we often invoke in our disability equality trainings. It is Larry Bissonnette's phrase from the film *Wretches and Jabberers*. Bissonnette, an adult with autism, is asked what he would want others to know about him. He responds, "more like you than not."

16. Interview videos are available on moma.org/access as well as on YouTube at the following link: https://www.youtube.com/watch?v=0-kZXqSfNlY&t=34s.

17. McArthur, "Correspondence with Park McArthur," 2019.

18. Kevin Gotkin. "Interview with Kevin Gotkin," May 21, 2019, courtesy of MoMA.

19. T-coil loop systems require a high degree of expertise to install and can be costly, but other accommodations can support sound accessibility: describing the sound in the wall label for the artwork, making a transcript of dialogue available, captioning the work if it's video or film-based as well as installing a loop system. Different options suit different audiences and are more or less feasible depending on an institution's access to that technology and budget. Layering accommodations is always most useful.

20. Aaron Louis, e-mail message to author, June 2021.

21. Lana Hum, e-mail message to author, June 2021.

22. When the word *deaf* is spelled with a lowercase *d* it refers to the disability experienced by someone with hearing loss. When the word *Deaf* is spelled with a capital *D* it refers to someone who also identifies with Deaf culture and belonging to Deaf community.

Chapter Seven

Be Bold

Small Actions Lead to Big Change

Julia Latané and Stacey Gevero Swanby
with contributions by George Luna-Peña

> The museum field, the profession I love, has to make the commitment to change. It is not a choice, it is an obligation. . . .We should live up to our stated ideals. If we truly believe that we are a better profession when we embrace diversity, then let that diversity permeate and shape the staff throughout our museums. . . . It is in our power to change this profession, if we have the courage, the creativity, and the will.[1]
>
> —Lonnie G. Bunch III

Although many museums have been developing more formal structures for diversity, equity, accessibility, and inclusion (DEAI) working groups or hiring full-time positions to focus on this work, two midlevel hiring managers at The Broad museum in Los Angeles sought to impact hiring across their own institution.

We, Julia Latané and Stacey Gevero Swanby, represent different generations, races, and disciplines; and we are both passionate about social justice. After working toward equity on our own separate teams at The Broad, we joined forces in 2016 and proposed changes resulting in institution-wide shifts in hiring practices. As a result, The Broad's staff came to better reflect the diversity of Los Angeles.

OUR BACKGROUNDS

Stacey Gevero Swanby

I started at The Broad in summer 2015 before the museum opened to the public. I had the exciting opportunity to be a part of opening a new museum and building all aspects of the visitor experience. As a mixed-race Filipina American, it was intimidating to navigate the white dominant work culture of the contemporary art world. I had previously worked at the Wing Luke Museum of the Asian Pacific American Experience, an immensely supportive environment. The Wing instilled in me the urgent necessity of pushing for social justice. My time there working with the Chinatown-International District community will forever shape the way I approach my work. I gathered strength from my BIPOC peers at other institutions and was committed to building strong and productive relationships with coworkers. My experiences led me to commit to creating the most equitable hiring and promotion decisions possible wherever I worked.

Julia Latané

As a white, cisgendered, middle-aged, able-bodied woman, I strive to live by my ideals, use my position and my privilege to remove barriers to entry to museum careers, create welcoming and inclusive workspaces, and to empower staff to grow and achieve their goals. Some of my ancestors were Jews who came to the United States fleeing persecution, and some of my ancestors held enslaved people and profited from their labor. Partly because of this shameful connection to slavery, I feel a personal responsibility to break down the white supremacist structures that my people built and that I continue to benefit from. My work in social justice continues to evolve as I learn from scholars and colleagues from different communities. I have worked in the mostly male fields of construction, fabrication, and art handling for more than thirty years. I have spent the last fourteen years working as head preparator, first at the Autry Museum of the American West, then at The Broad from 2014 to 2018, and now at the Los Angeles County Museum of Art (LACMA).

RECOGNIZING THE NEED FOR CHANGE

In 2015, the Andrew Mellon Foundation's Art Museum Staff Demographic Survey[2] quantified for the first time how white museum staffs are. It showed that 72 percent of museum staff are white non-Hispanic and 28 percent are people of color. The survey also confirmed that most of the museum professionals of color are concentrated in facilities, security, and finance/human resources (HR). Within museum leadership positions fewer than 10 percent are people of color. Museums have struggled with diversifying their staff for decades; we should not wait any longer to set out concrete actions that can move us toward more diverse, inclusive, and equitable work environments. To best serve our communities we need to represent our communities, which means the demographics of the community should be reflected in the demographics of our staff. Optimally, this means that all perspectives, viewpoints, and voices are present and respected.

The Broad is a contemporary art museum located in Downtown Los Angeles. Since opening in September 2015, more than 3.5 million people have visited (as of September 2021). The average visitor age in 2019 was thirty-five, which is more than ten years younger than the average art museum visitor across the country.[3] The *Los Angeles Times* dubbed The Broad as the millennial museum.[4] More than 60 percent of the museum's visitors self-identify as people of color compared with the national art museum average of just 29 percent. We set an intention to make changes in our hiring practices so that staff is representative of the communities that we serve.

Julia's Work with Preparators

In 2015, The Broad advertised an open call for eighteen preparators (preps) to install its inaugural exhibition. Most of the candidates we interviewed were white and male, an applicant pool I was committed to transforming. I did research and spoke with colleagues about equitable hiring practices and creating inclusive work environments. At the time, a lot of the language around the issue was new to me, as I had last deeply studied these issues in the early 1990s. Galvanized, I revamped the job description and hiring process for preparators at The Broad, which had been based on typical job descriptions for the field.

In 2016, we began a new round of hiring for on-call preparators. We still found that most candidates we interviewed were white men. Then, a young woman of color came in for an interview. She did not have enough experience to be an on-call prep, but she was so passionate about the position I could not forget her. A week later, I asked then Deputy Director Rich Cherry if I could hire her as a preparator apprentice for our next exhibition change out. He said "Absolutely! And, let's write a grant to start a program!" Just as the first preparator apprentice was hired, I wrote a grant to the Institute of Museum and Library Services to start the Diversity Apprenticeship Program (DAP). To test out the program, we created mini-apprenticeships for visitor services associates (VSAs), many of whom were just starting out in the museum field and eager for opportunities for growth. Three VSAs were hired through a process that piloted many of the components we would use for the DAP. They were each assigned to work on separate exhibition change outs and were relieved of their VSA duties for that period of time. This allowed them to work full-time with the prep team for the duration of the projects, which ranged from five to seven weeks long.

Stacey's Work with Visitor Services

Although the visitor services team was flat in organizational structure for the first two years, it became clear we needed to expand the leadership of the team to better support our operations. This provided an opportunity to promote from within the museum. At the time, The Broad did not have a formal decision-making process in place for internal promotions. The visitor services team was often staffed with 150 people, and understandably, there were a lot of interpersonal dynamics at play. I sought to eliminate processes that allowed unconscious and perceived bias to impact decision-making. Independently and then with the consultation of the HR manager, I created scoring rubrics based on the core competencies needed for each of the positions. I also developed a decision-making process that used a hiring committee to allow for varying perspectives and to ensure that one person did not have too much control or power over the process.

Working with HR

We started this work independently and then brought it to the HR manager for refinement. At the time, the HR team consisted of one staff member, the manager, who received backend support from a separate office. Because the museum had newly opened, we were not working against entrenched systems; staff and leadership were open to ideas. The Broad also has an entrepreneurial spirit, always looking for new approaches. By committing to building our relationships with the HR manager, we were able to learn from her expertise while also sharing the latest resources on hiring practices, including the ones listed in the bibliography. We advocated for the adoption of equitable hiring practices across the museum, and we scheduled regular meetings with the HR manager and deputy director to discuss DEAI issues, creating a de facto DEAI task force.

In an effort to get HR excited about the changes both of us had made to the hiring process, Stacey presented it to the department as an opportunity to set best practices within the museum field. We were fortunate that the museum's leadership understood the need for this work and sought and supported opportunities for innovation.

BUILDING A CULTURE OF INCLUSIVITY

Although demographic data is tracked (staff self-identify during the onboarding process), equity and inclusion work is not solely about the numbers but also about building a culture of inclusivity—communicating to colleagues that they belong. We began by learning from inspiring colleagues who came before us and by having open dialogues with each other. We created equitable processes to give staff opportunities for growth and to build more diverse candidate pools. We then shared these processes and conversations about DEAI with more staff. There is a need for patience, empathy, and honesty during this process. Although the journey toward more equitable practices can be uncomfortable and often messy, we reminded staff that this discomfort should not hinder moving forward and making impactful progress.

To share a specific example, Julia learned a lot from a team member who was in the process of transitioning to the gender with which they identified. This person changed their name and pronouns several times and was instrumental in helping Julia and the team learn how to create an inclusive work environment for them. At one point, Julia started a meeting by asking everyone to introduce themselves with their pronouns—only to learn that this in itself was harmful to those who may not be comfortable with sharing their pronouns. Julia has since adopted the strategy of introducing herself with her pronouns, leaving space for others to choose whether to do so. Admitting when we make mistakes and continuing to learn and grow are essential to building the trust required for open dialogue to continue. It is only through open dialogue that we can create truly inclusive workspaces.

EQUITABLE HIRING PRACTICES

In this section we will outline six specific steps we took to make our hiring practices more equitable. All of these steps are intentional actions to reduce bias in hiring. We all carry biases,[5] and unconscious or implicit bias is often a major barrier to an equitable hiring process.[6]

1. *First and foremost, begin with yourself; examine your own biases.*[7] All hiring managers should do this. Ideally, everyone should do this. You can use Harvard's Project Implicit[8] website or follow MTV's Look Different Campaign[9] to learn about the ways bias impacts real people. Examining your biases takes courage, self-awareness, and honesty. It can be difficult to face but it is critical to creating a more equitable process.

2. *Audit and improve your current practice.* Before posting a position, take the time to fully review your last hiring process. Compare each of the steps along the way with current research before proceeding. If budget allows, you can hire an outside consultant to audit your institution's practices and suggest improvements.
3. *Evaluate job descriptions and postings.* Remove unnecessary criteria such as education requirements, transportation requirements, and previous museum experience. Consider the way you describe physical abilities and skills with the intention of being as inclusive as possible. Use an app such as Textio (https://textio.com/) or Hemingway (https://hemingwayapp.com/) to check for gendered language, jargon, reading level, and accessibility.
4. *Make your recruiting strategy inclusive.*[10]
   - Is the position only posted on the organization's website? Get creative with how the job posting is circulated and share with contacts outside of the museum field.
   - Are there local job fairs you could attend to meet possible candidates in person? Our staff have met some of the most dedicated employees at local job fairs.
   - Reach out to recruit from more communities. Build relationships with community centers, workforce development organizations, churches, synagogues, temples, and so forth.
   - To broaden the candidate pool, leave jobs posted longer or on an ongoing basis, especially if you hire for multiple openings for the same position regularly.
   - Ensure candidate pools are diverse. If you continue to see a lack of representation on your staff, then broaden your outreach and extend application deadlines. Consider using a search firm that specializes in assembling diverse candidate pools even for midlevel positions.
   - Read every single resume before moving people to the next stage to increase the likelihood of a bigger and more diverse candidate pool.
   - Don't give preference to referrals. If your team is already homogenous and you favor referrals you perpetuate the problem.[11]
5. *Use objective decision-making methods.*
   - Consider anonymous resume screening[12] to reduce bias. This could be the HR team removing identifying information such as names, addresses, and schools from resumes and cover letters before forwarding to the hiring manager.
   - Allow space to evaluate experience creatively; for example, a candidate who has years of experience as a restaurant server may have skills applicable to art-handing.

- Write interview questions that relate specifically to the required core competencies from the job description and ask all candidates the same questions in the same order,[13] which formalizes, standardizes, and simplifies the process.
- Use a scoring rubric to rate candidates' responses to interview questions.[14]
- Use skills tests or ask for work samples or assessments to demonstrate a candidate's actual skills rather than solely relying on their resumes and what they say they can do. At The Broad, we implemented the following skills tests for preparators: a written spatial reasoning test;[15] carrying precariously balanced items through an obstacle course; and installing prop two-dimensional artworks. It is important to respect candidates' time by limiting the length of skills tests.

6. *Use interview panels and ensure that different perspectives are represented on the panel.*[16] Interview panels should be small enough to avoid intimidation but should include enough people to counteract and check each others' biases. Panelists should evaluate each candidate and write down their thoughts before discussing them to avoid influencing one another.[17] It is also important to inform the candidate of the panel ahead of time: let them know who will be in the room, what their roles are, and why they are there. For example, the prep team would often ask for a member of the visitor services team to be a part of an interview panel to provide a varying perspective (front of house versus back of house). Consider how the candidates may feel when they enter the interview location. Are you creating a comfortable environment where they feel welcome? Are staff of different backgrounds reflecting different communities?

TRAINING FOR HIRING MANAGERS

We wanted to share resources across the museum to help make change on a broader level, so we asked for and were granted the opportunity to present our process to all hiring managers. Prior to the training, we sent out a list of readings to provide them with some foundational knowledge to better prepare the group for discussion. We curated the list so that the minimum reading requirements could be done in an hour and added more resources for those who wanted more information. We also instructed them to come to the training with job descriptions for their open positions and specific questions in mind. We began the training with a presentation on the changes we made in our recruitment and hiring for our teams, much of the same information contained in this chapter.

Following the presentation, hiring managers set up individual meetings with one of us to discuss the details of their recruitment and hiring. During these meetings we discussed how they had conducted their processes in the past and the changes they were planning to make with the information they learned. We acknowledged that while each hiring situation is unique, using consistent equitable hiring practices in all scenarios leads to less bias, more diverse candidate pools, and ultimately a more diverse staff. Ideally, hiring managers would be required to follow equitable hiring practices and HR would provide support and hold them accountable.

IMPACT ON STAFF DIVERSITY

Between 2015 and 2017, we saw progress toward our goal of representing the city of Los Angeles in our demographics, as demonstrated by figure 7.1. The graph shows the demographics of the city of Los Angeles, and The Broad preps in 2015, 2017, and 2019.

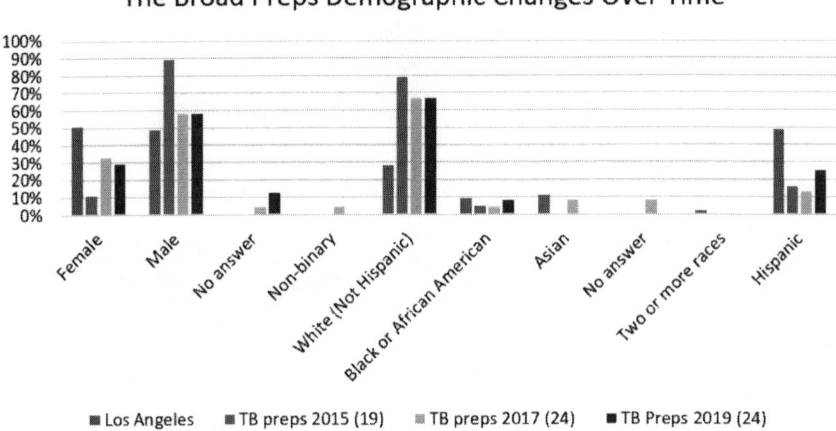

Figure 7.1. The Broad Preps Demographic Changes over Time.
Courtesy of The Broad

In late 2017, The Broad was awarded the IMLS National Leadership Grant for Museums to expand and formalize the DAP to help address the lack of diversity of museum staff. For more information on DAP, see box 7.1.

BOX 7.1. THE DIVERSITY APPRENTICESHIP PROGRAM

George Luna-Peña

The Diversity Apprenticeship Program (DAP) is an unprecedented initiative by The Broad museum in Los Angeles to provide job-training opportunities and career pathways for people from underrepresented communities—BIPOC, women, immigrants, lesbian, gay, bisexual, transgender, queer/question, intersex, asexual+ (LGBTQIA+), those formerly incarcerated, and foster youth—in the often-overlooked area of art handling and preparations.

Originating with an Institute of Museum and Library Services National Leadership Grant, the DAP was launched by The Broad in Los Angeles in 2017 with two primary goals: first, to train a yearly cohort of eight apprentices in art handling and preparations and, second, to develop a replicable model to drive industry-wide change and create a climate of equity, opportunity, and respect for art handling.

The DAP brings together eighteen partner organizations of varying sizes, sectors, and types—from small and large nonprofits to university and college galleries to commercial companies and government institutions. Partners host apprentices for hands-on experience, serve as members of the DAP's advisory group, and participate in the evaluation and improvement of the program. Many of our partners have also continued to provide career pathways for apprentices in the field by hiring them at the conclusion of their apprenticeships.

Each cohort of apprentices participates in a full-time, paid apprenticeship for nine months. During this time, apprentices receive full benefits, 160-hours of paid technical training, and more than twelve hundred hours of paid hands-on work experience at partner sites across the city. Throughout the program, apprentices receive personalized support from mentors who are professionals in the field. Apprentices also participate in career development workshops (e.g., resume, cover letter writing, mock interviews) and career chats with professionals across the industry.

Apprentices build confidence, skills, best practices, and the network to create a lifelong opportunity for themselves and their families. The

DAP has a 100 percent graduation rate and 94 percent of program participants have found employment in the field after their apprenticeship. As one graduated apprentice shared, "I have options and that's not something I'm used to telling myself."

The program also impacts partner organizations. Hosting an apprentice is a commitment on the part of the partner institution. It requires a new way of mentoring and working. Partner institutions are often pushed into a space where they are encouraged to confront the often uncomfortable realities that have made the field an exclusionary space for too many for too long. In that sense, the DAP serves, in real time, as a springboard for partners to move toward more equitable practices and policies.

Some partners have made concrete changes: adding gender-inclusive language to their employee handbooks, implementing a living wage for all staff, changing their interview processes during hiring, and creating gender-inclusive bathrooms.

As the program has evolved, we have come to understand that equity does not happen on its own. We must be intentional in the ways we center equity, and this is especially true in the work we do with our partner organizations. All partners and mentors are required to participate in a series of antiracism trainings and dialogue spaces that touch on topics like microaggressions, building inclusive workplace practices, and unpacking white supremacist work culture.

To share the DAP model and approach more widely, we have published the *DAP Toolbox* (thebroad.org/dap/toolbox). The *DAP Toolbox* is a groundbreaking free publication. It serves as both an introduction to the history and structure of the DAP and a toolbox to share best practices, lessons learned, and tools and resources for art handling and to help install similar programs at institutions nationwide.

Ultimately, the DAP is impacting the lives of apprentices and their families while also setting a strong example of a successful and inclusive model for the museum field.

CONCLUSION, TAKEAWAYS, AND RECOMMENDATIONS

We came together to support each other and brainstorm additional DEAI work we could do. This resulted in a small action team we launched with HR and leadership to continue to discuss all aspects of DEAI in our museum. Stacey played a key role in inviting the organization Race Forward to lead a racial justice training for all staff. She was also a founding member of the employee engagement and equity team, which has since evolved into two entities, the engagement team and the equity team. These teams ensure greater transparency and connection among staff across the organization and sustained efforts toward antiracism and equity.

Although we have both moved on from The Broad, our initial efforts impacting hiring practices laid the foundation for initiatives that continue at the museum and are shared with other museums as models of best practice. Julia continued her work on the DAP as an advisor from her position at the LACMA, a key partner on the DAP. Part of that work was to coauthor the DAP Toolbox[18] with DAP program director at The Broad, George Luna-Peña, and deputy director of The Broad, Stacy Lieberman. The toolbox is a free publication designed to help individuals and organizations in their efforts to achieve greater diversity, equity, and inclusion. Julia has also partnered with HR at LACMA to implement some of the equitable hiring processes listed in this chapter, including developing skills tests for hiring art handlers.

The data has shown that museum staff members do not represent our communities. Only about 10 percent of museum leadership comprises people of color, whereas 37 percent of Americans are people of color. We can all change our workplaces for the better. We encourage you to make antiracism and equity work something that you regularly talk about with friends and colleagues at other museums, organizations, and throughout your life. Ask yourself what you have control over and what you can personally change. Baby steps are still steps forward.

We can all make a difference. Don't underestimate your own power to influence change; change can be initiated from anywhere in the institution. Small actions lead to big shifts.

NOTES

1. Bunch, "Flies in the Buttermilk."
2. Westermann et al., "Art Museum Staff Demographic Survey 2018."
3. Morey Group, *The Broad 2019 Annual Visitor Survey Report*, 3.
4. Vankin, "What's Drawing Millennials to Downtown LA's Broad Museum?"
5. Mullainathan, "Racial Bias, Even When We Have Good Intentions."
6. Research shows that we all have unconscious bias that affects our decision-making, including during hiring (Banaji and Greenwald, *Blindspot: Hidden Biases of Good People*, 49, 52, 148, 160, 161, 195–97, 206, 229, 230).
7. Tulshyan, "How to Reduce Personal Bias When Hiring."
8. Harvard University, Project Implicit, "Preliminary Information."
9. MTV, "MTV's Look Different Campaign."

10. Bailey-Bryant, "We're Not that Hard to Find."

11. Ernst & Young LLP, and Royal Bank of Canada, *Outsmarting Our Brains: Overcoming Hidden Biases to Harness Diversity's True Potential.*

12. Cain Miller, "Is Blind Hiring the Best Hiring?"

13. Knight, "7 Practical Ways to Reduce Bias in Your Hiring Process."

14. Dattner, "A Scorecard for Making Better Hiring Decisions."

15. Newton and Bristoll. *Spatial Ability Practice Test 1.*

16. Webb, "How to Alter Your Hiring Practices to Increase Diversity."

17. Knight, "7 Practical Ways to Reduce Bias in Your Hiring Process."

18. The Broad, "Diversity Apprenticeship Toolbox."

Part III

ASSESSMENT AND ACCOUNTABILITY

Chapter Eight

Using Data to Inform Diversity, Equity, and Inclusion Strategy at the Minnesota Historical Society

Chris Taylor

Data, Data, Data. When I worked as the chief inclusion officer for the Minnesota Historical Society (MNHS), we used data to project revenue, gauge audience and attendance, track donors, and develop the exhibit schedule. When I joined MNHS in 2005, data informed decisions and strategy in most facets of the museum, except for our diversity, equity, and inclusion (DEI) work. Meanwhile MNHS had been implementing DEI initiatives within its education division for decades. In 2012, inclusion and diversity became one of four strategic priorities at MNHS.[1] Yet, we had been basing decisions and strategy on trends or best practices rather than data, and we could not effectively measure our progress.

Early DEI efforts at MNHS consisted of community engagement and outreach and several exhibits that spotlighted specific communities. In 2014, MNHS created the department of inclusion and community engagement (DICE) within the education division. However, the director of education and I envisioned DICE as an institution-wide resource. One of the goals for DICE was to develop a strategy for DEI work at MNHS.

MNHS, the largest historical society in the country, had developed a stellar reputation in the field of museum work.[2] I think this reputation worked against us in terms of our diversity work. Many of our staff believed in an internal narrative that positioned the museum as a destination employer. Although this may have been true for white colleagues, it was not true for many of our staff from various BIPOC communities. I often had confidential conversations with BIPOC staff about their experience at MNHS. These conversations confirmed that, like so many other similar institutions,[3] the organizational culture at MNHS proved problematic for these individuals. Whether they had encountered negative experiences with interactions with supervisors, promotions and reclassifications, recognition for work, or other facets of the culture, these staff members felt excluded and often felt oppressed.

MNHS leadership realized that having a diverse workforce was critical to becoming an inclusive institution. Informal assessments of staff retention over the previous five years indicate that, proportionately, BIPOC staff left MNHS voluntarily at a higher rate than white colleagues. BIPOC staff often confided that the culture of the organization, specifically lack of influence in decision-making and repeated microaggressions, precipitated their decision to leave.

In 2014, DICE worked with our evaluation team to develop a tool to measure staff perceptions of inclusion within the organizational culture at the museum. This survey helped us gain a deeper understanding of staff needs and provided direction to DICE while the department developed a strategy for DEI work. In this chapter, I describe the need for the survey at MNHS, how the survey was developed, a summary of findings, and lessons learned as we went through the process.

DEVELOPING THE SURVEY

The aforementioned informal assessments of staff retention and anecdotal information about staff experience led DICE to recognize the need for a formal survey tool to collect data from all staff to assess perceptions of organizational culture.[4] Prior to the development of this survey, MNHS had neither regularly measured staff experience nor collected metrics to better understand whether staff felt valued and included. Although we designed the survey specifically to help us gain an understanding of how staff experienced the organizational culture at MNHS, we used the term *engagement survey* to describe the tool because that term was more familiar to our leadership.

Drawing on Bernardo M. Ferdman's "The Practice of Inclusion in Diverse Organizations: Toward a Systemic and Inclusive Framework," my team identified characteristics of an inclusive organization and grouped them into fourteen areas: diversity and inclusion as a strategic priority; community relationships; respect for diversity; communication and information sharing; orientation and values alignment; supervisor engagement in inclusion; employee recruitment and retention; workgroup appreciation; workgroup involvement;

workplace authenticity; organizational culture of inclusion; decision-making; safety; and continuous learning.[5] The survey included a number of prompts per area and respondents could choose from among five response options using a Likert scale.[6] We also included several demographic questions in the survey that allowed us to disaggregate the data to get a better understanding of the experience of particular groups of staff. We also provided an open-ended comment section for each area that gave context to the quantitative findings in the survey and provided concrete examples that illustrated the perceptions of staff.

When developing survey questions, we referred to our museum's strategic plan, created in 2011, which called out "inclusion and collaboration" as an institutional value and "diversity and inclusivity" as a strategic priority. We included questions to gain insight into the ways in which DEI related to individuals' work duties and to gauge staff perception of the level of alignment between the institution's actions and the diversity and inclusivity strategic priority.

We disseminated online and paper versions of the survey, distributing the latter to staff who did not have regular access to an MNHS email account.[7] About 30 percent of MNHS staff responded to the survey.

SURVEY FINDINGS

Key findings from the survey relate to eight of the fourteen characteristics of an inclusive organization.

Diversity and Inclusion as a Strategic Priority

In the strategic plan, MNHS stated that staffing should reflect the diversity of the state. More diverse teams within the institution would lead to more creativity and innovation, which would, in turn, result in programs and services more reflective of the inclusion and diversity valued by MNHS. When we analyzed responses to survey questions related to workforce diversity, we discovered that many staff perceived that the institution lacked effective recruitment strategies. In addition, only about one-third of the respondents felt that MNHS prioritized retention of diverse staff, and only about one in five respondents felt that MNHS successfully retained a diverse staff. Responses to the statement that MNHS, "Clearly articulates the contribution of diversity within the workforce" indicated that, while MNHS stated workforce diversity as a value, leadership had not articulated why it was important. Although the lack of diversity within the workforce was visibly evident, the data helped us better understand perceptions of the effectiveness of recruitment and retention practices as well as the level to which staff understood the value that diversity brings to the organization. Moreover, our analyses of open-ended comments revealed an important attitude related to hiring: of those that left comments, nearly one-third felt that to successfully hire a more diverse staff, the museum would need to lower or dilute our hiring standards.

Community Relationships

In another section of the survey, we sought to assess the museum's efforts to build community relationships. Community engagement is an effective component of an inclusion strategy when institutions seek to create lasting, sustainable, and mutually beneficial relationships with communities. In this section, we asked participants to respond to prompts related to community collaboration, the ability to address challenges experienced by historically marginalized groups in Minnesota, recognition of employees for their community work, and internal and external communication. For each of these areas, less than 60 percent of respondents indicated a positive perception of the museum's ability to build community relationships. The significant number of respondents that answered "Don't Know" in this section highlighted a lack of communication about the community engagement work that *was* happening.

Alignment of Organizational Values and Behavior

Organizations too often state their values rather than live them.[8] Values are meant to guide the daily actions and work of an organization. Leadership should clearly state expectations for how employees internalize values and apply them to their behaviors and interactions. The DICE survey asked if MNHS reinforces staff behaviors that align with organizational values. Only a little more than one-third of respondents agreed. Comments in this section indicated that staff felt that MNHS invested quite a bit of time in stating that inclusion is a value but did not clearly articulate actions or intended outcomes. One respondent wrote, "despite the many forums and emails concerning our organizational commitment to a culture of diversity, it's often difficult and abstract to apply the info directly to one's daily work life." Data from this section made it clear that the institution was talking the talk but struggling to walk the walk regarding its stated value of inclusion.

Supervisor Engagement in Inclusion

In this section, we provided statements about how supervisors support an inclusive environment for their teams in terms of respect ("My supervisor respects my expression of diverse beliefs"), decision-making ("My supervisor engages me in decision making"), and accountability ("My supervisor holds me accountable for creating an inclusive culture"). Overall, the comments in this section demonstrated that supervisors across the institution engage staff in decision-making and respect their team's diverse beliefs. However, one staff member outlined a concern that I had heard from several other staff members in offline conversations: "As a person of color my expression of diverse perspectives are welcomed more often when I am 'speaking for my race' than when I am expressing my opinions as an individual. This is frustrating." This comment indicates that instances of tokenism are happening within interpersonal interactions between supervisors and staff in some areas of the organization.

Respect for Diversity

We felt that it was incredibly important to understand the level of respect experienced by BIPOC staff. The results were not wholly surprising. In the aggregate, most respondents felt that they were treated fairly without discrimination. Overall, respondents also felt that they could be transparent about their social identities and that their colleagues noticed and valued diversity of all types. One interesting finding in this section related to respondents' perceptions of the institution: statements in this section that began with "I" or referred to an individual's actions tended to be perceived positively. For example, in response to the statement, "I am treated fairly, without discrimination or barriers based on my identities," most survey respondents selected "Always" or "Almost Always." In contrast, respondents primarily indicated "Sometimes" when posed with statements that referred to actions made by the institution. The prompt that stated, "at MNHS, we address differences in ways that lead to mutual learning and growth" received significantly more "Never" or "Almost Never" responses than the others. We saw this distinction between individuals and the institution throughout the survey. We inferred that although individuals at MNHS highly respected diverse identities, the staff felt that the institutional culture of MNHS was not grounded in that same type of respect. One respondent commented: "I am never directly discriminated against because of my race, but the culture makes me feel as if it is most appropriate to 'assimilate' into the dominant culture (socially and professionally)."

Organizational Culture

Retention of a diverse workforce hinges on an organizational culture where everyone feels valued and engaged.[9] However, predominantly white organizations tend to center white cultural norms and practices, while regarding any other work practices as undesirable or unacceptable.[10] We designed a section of the survey to investigate the level to which staff felt that MNHS cultivated inclusion through policies and procedures, opportunities to learn about and build relationships with people from different cultural backgrounds, and other aspects of the institutional culture. Although respondents tended to agree that MNHS encouraged an environment of respect within the workplace, results were less favorable when the survey prompts included words like "culture of inclusion," "diversity," and "identities." For example, only about one-third of respondents felt that MNHS utilized organizational policies to create a culture of inclusion. When disaggregated by race and ethnicity, we found that staff who identify as BIPOC displayed significantly more negative perceptions than white staff regarding the extent to which MNHS integrates diverse perspectives into decision-making, examines its practices to ensure consistency with diversity goals, provides formal opportunities for employees to learn about its diversity and inclusion values, and provides staff opportunities to explore the impact of personal identity on organizational culture.

Workplace Authenticity

Noninclusive cultural norms often cause BIPOC staff to feel uncomfortable expressing their authentic selves in the workplace. In other words, people from outside of the dominant culture feel as though they must assimilate or hide parts of their identity to be more accepted. This inability to be authentic diverts time, effort, and energy away from work activities and creates an emotional burden that staff carry with them beyond work.[11] Knowing that workplace authenticity is important for staff to feel a sense of inclusion, we asked staff in this section to respond to statements about the ability to be themselves at work. Overall, the results showed a high level of comfort, until we looked at the disaggregated data. On three of the four prompts in the section, responses by BIPOC staff showed a difference of at least 10 percentage points relative to white staff in regard to how included they felt in MNHS culture. For example, in response to the statement, "I need to conceal or distort valued parts of my identity, style, or individual characteristics," white staff members were 30 percent more likely to select "Never" or "Almost Never" than BIPOC staff. These findings served as even more evidence that the organizational culture of MNHS may be a barrier to a more diverse workforce.

Work Group Involvement

This section of the survey provided information about the impact of the lack of inclusion in the MNHS culture, such as the level to which staff felt "part of the same team," supported, and that they could succeed. The aggregate data seemed to indicate a supportive and inclusive culture. Even when we disaggregated the data, there weren't as many significant differences as other sections. However, one statement did show a significant difference. In response to how often they identified with the statement, "I cannot succeed here because of my identity," only about half of BIPOC staff members indicated "Never," whereas more than 80 percent of white staff indicated "Never." This is significant because when a staff member feels like they cannot achieve success in an organization, they are more likely to leave.[12] The disproportionate amount of BIPOC staff who felt they could not succeed, therefore, suggests an impact on staff retention and the ability of the organization to gain overall increases in workforce diversity.

THE BIG PICTURE

The disaggregated data shows that MNHS's purportedly inclusive culture was a myth. Staff perceptions that they cannot be themselves or succeed in the organization because of their identity reveal a huge red flag about the culture. Those results clearly show a misalignment with the strategic priority for diversity and inclusion and the organizational values espoused by MNHS. Moreover, the institutional priority and values seemed to be more performative than substantive; the museum publicly states commitment without following through with implementation.

The widespread perception that MNHS had not developed a strategy for recruitment or retention spoke volumes to the performative nature of the work at MNHS. In addition, the lack of policies or accountability measures to promote inclusion within the workplace hinted at a lack of understanding of how to create inclusion. The organization was not providing staff with opportunities to learn about diverse cultures and practices and build skills to increase levels of cultural competence.

While analyzing the survey results, we understood that the demographics of the majority of survey respondents may skew the data. The demographic breakdown of respondents to the MNHS survey was as follows: 80 percent of respondents identified as white, 14 percent declined to identify their race or ethnicity, and 12 percent identified as BIPOC. Anecdotally, I know that some BIPOC staff did not indicate their race or ethnicity due to fear of identification. The overwhelming majority of white respondents working in a predominantly white institution meant that the aggregate data may skew more toward a favorable perception of organizational culture. For instance, in the "Respect for Diversity" section, survey responses pointed to an overall positive perception about the way marginalized identities were respected within MNHS. However, we also received a comment from an individual who felt the need to assimilate into the cultural norms of the organization. Collecting data on race and ethnicity allowed us to disaggregate the data and compare answers from POC staff with answers from white staff. When examined this way, the data showed discrepancies between the lived experience of staff. We especially found differences in the categories of organizational culture of inclusion and workplace authenticity. One important outcome of the survey was the disruption of the internal narrative of MNHS as an incredible place to work. Clearly, the makeup of staff identities impact their experiences of workplace culture at MNHS.

DATA-INFORMED DEI STRATEGY

The data gathered through this survey provided a pivot point for our DEI strategy at MNHS. Although we still considered an external focus on community engagement and audience development to be important, we were struggling to value members of our own staff that came from the very communities that we were hoping to engage.

As a result of the survey findings, the museum launched a number of internal initiatives. We increased opportunities for staff to learn about DEI concepts and skills. We conducted our own workshops on topics like intercultural competence and unconscious bias and connected those concepts to departmental work carried out throughout the institution. This helped to disrupt normal patterns of practice and shift to more inclusive work styles. We also worked really hard to develop more employee resource groups that provide spaces for staff to come together, learn, and advocate for change within the institution.

Having the data was a game changer for us in DICE; it not only brought legitimacy to the lived experience that we often talked about in the institution, but it also disrupted the narrative about the culture of MNHS. We determined that there were actually several cultures within the organization and the workplace culture worked better for those with dominant identities. The data we gathered proved critical to developing a strategy for a sustainable increase in levels of inclusion. Much like any other function of the organization, data allowed us to set goals, determine outcomes, and measure progress toward those goals.

We learned a lot in the process. First of all, our survey was too long. We were excited to measure perceptions of inclusion within the culture of the organization and tried to squeeze too many indicators into one survey. I think a shorter survey would have elicited more responses. We also needed to have clearer messaging with greater transparency about the purpose of the survey and how we intended to use the results. More importantly, we needed to specifically state who would have access to the raw data (only myself and the two-person evaluation team). Clarifying this information prior to sharing the survey would have helped increase the number of participants.

We readministered a more streamlined version of the survey in 2018. We decreased the number of questions by looking for any redundancy in the survey and combining statements. We also worked with an organization to help us test the reliability and validity of the survey. Even though the instrument slightly changed (for the better), we were still able to compare data between the surveys to measure progress.

All in all, this was an incredibly helpful process that resulted in significant changes at MNHS. In a culture that places high emphasis on data, the survey results provided the type of evidence that was critical to validating staff member perceptions and establishing a clear direction to guide DEI work at MNHS.

NOTES

1. The other three strategic priorities at MNHS are educational relevance, Minnesota's historic resources, and sustainability and stewardship.
2. For example, MNHS received the 2003 MUSE Award, the 2007 MUSE Award, and the 2016 MUSE Award from American Alliance of Museums.
3. Paquet Kinsley and Wittman, "Bringing Self-Examination to the Center of Social Justice Work in Museums," 40–45.
4. A similar version of the original survey can be found in the MASS Action Toolkit. See MASS Action, "MASS Action Toolkit," 209.
5. Ferdman, "The Practice of Inclusion in Diverse Organizations: Toward a Systemic and Inclusive Framework," 3–54.
6. A Likert scale measures strength of response on a scale. For our survey, most Likert scales included the following options for responses: Always, Almost Always, Sometimes, Almost Never, Never, and Don't Know.
7. We discovered that not all staff that worked for MNHS had email accounts so a paper version of the survey was essential. Furthermore, the staff that worked in shifts, such as seasonal interpreters or gift shop staff, did not regularly check email before or after shifts at the time of the survey.
8. Schein, *Organizational Culture and Leadership.*
9. Winters, "From Diversity to Inclusion: An Inclusion Equation," 205–28.
10. Sue, *Microaggressions in Everyday Life.*
11. Yoshino, *Covering: The Hidden Assault on Our Civil Rights.*
12. Sue, *Microaggressions in Everyday Life.*

Chapter Nine

Polishing the Mirror

Reflections on the Equity Audit Developed and Conducted by the Corning Museum of Glass

Katherine Larson and Lianne Uesato

Like many museums, the Corning Museum of Glass, located in upstate New York, is reckoning with its historical legacy of inequality. Although beginning prior to 2020, our efforts took on new significance and enhanced visibility after the murder of George Floyd and resulting national attention to racial and social justice. As an organization, we are committed to prioritizing diversity, equity, and inclusion (DEI) and measuring our progress. To that end, the organization has been reorienting to make a fuller commitment to the work of equity and social justice. In 2019, the Corning Museum completed an internal equity audit, which was the first major institutional step in undertaking deliberate DEI work.[1] In this chapter, the two authors, who were members of the team who led the audit process, "polish the mirror" by reflecting on the process and outcomes of the audit, itself a reflection of a moment in time. Our goal is to share our experiences with other organizations who may be considering conducting a similar assessment.

WHY DID WE CONDUCT AN EQUITY AUDIT?

A cross-departmental DEI team was first formed several years ago. Members of the DEI team, typically numbering around fifteen, are self-nominated staff members who are committed to and passionate about DEI work. The DEI team strives for representation from as many departments as possible across the museum. One member of the museum's leadership team serves as liaison between the DEI team and museum leadership, but the DEI team itself is chaired (or co-chaired) by a nonleadership member or members. Team members undertake DEI work in addition to their regular job responsibilities.

DEI work began in earnest in February 2018, when the DEI team participated in an intensive planning retreat with consultant Maketa Wilborn. With Wilborn's guidance, we used the multicultural organization development model to evaluate the cultural fluency of the museum.[2] We identified ourselves as a monocultural organization, which maintains the privilege of those who have traditionally held power and influence. In accordance with recommendations from Wilborn, the DEI team decided to undertake an organizational assessment of our institutional readiness for DEI work, a process and report which came to be known as the equity audit. The goals of the audit were to establish a baseline for the museum in our journey toward equity and inclusion, to evaluate awareness among staff of DEI issues, and to begin to generate a vision for the museum to become a more equitable, diverse, and inclusive organization.

In conducting the equity audit, the DEI team recognized the need to benchmark the organization's current practices and discover what we were already doing well, where we were not living up to our ideals, and what the obstacles were. In the process of conducting the audit, we wanted to identify strengths and weaknesses in our current organizational practices and begin to craft a vision for a more diverse, equitable, and inclusive environment.

HOW DID WE CONDUCT THE AUDIT?

The process of developing and conducting the equity audit took about fourteen months, with the bulk of the work occurring in fall 2018 and winter 2019. Wilborn provided a preliminary set of questions to guide the content of the audit; however, the DEI team had to determine what information would be most relevant for our organization and how best to collect the information. The team also wanted to ensure that the audit process involved collecting information, opinions, and experiences from individuals across the institution and not just those on the DEI team. The DEI team had found success with subteams to focus on particular initiatives, and we decided to use the same strategy for the audit. Members of the audit subteam were the two authors (a curator and conservator), Jen Kuhn (hot glass programs, and a contract staff member), Cordelia McBride (information technology), and Michelle Padilla (digital media). This combination of skills, relationships, and perspectives turned out to be highly advantageous.

The audit subteam built the audit process and questions based on publicly available resources from many other organizations.[3] We eventually settled on three methods of gathering information:

- *External Benchmarking.* Fall 2018 DEI and education intern Alice Carvalho-Bonilha collected census data about demographics of our local area, along with benchmarking information from other nonprofits in the community and museums nationwide. This data helped us identify how our staff demographics related to the local community and compared with other museums and arts organizations. The Mellon Foundation Art Museum Staff Demographic Surveys of 2015 and 2018 were particularly relevant.[4]
- *Interviews with Departmental Representatives.* Twenty-three people responsible for various museum operations answered a series of questions about funding, resources, plans, and limitations about DEI work within their departments. The primary goal of this effort was to document DEI initiatives already taking place, identify possible areas of growth, and capture possible obstacles for this work. We sent the questions in advance (see figure 9.1) and encouraged interviewees to speak to other staff in their departments about their responses. Interviewees had the option of participating in a verbal interview or responding in writing. Verbal interviews were recorded and transcribed.

Are DEI elements currently included in your departmental projects, programs, activities, work plans, strategic planning, and budgets?

Are there any best practices or standards related to diversity, equity, and inclusion you are currently following or want to follow?

Do you and/or your staff belong to any professional organizations that are doing anything with regards to DEI work?

Is your department working with any external organizations or communities that a) represent communities of color or other historically underrepresented groups, or b) are also trying to diversify?

How do you and your staff see your department growing in DEI related matters? What would you like to do more in the future, and, if so, what resources might you require?

Do you and your staff members feel equipped to approach your area with a focus that considers a wide spectrum of diversity? If not, could you explain the obstacles? How can the DEI team help?

What would DEI success look like in your area?

Do you collect demographic data on non-staff groups (e.g., Visitors, Group Visitors, Volunteers, Interns, Docents, Youth Programs, or Board Members)?

Is there anything else you would like to share?

Figure 9.1. Questions from interviews with department representatives. We also asked for examples of successful work.
Image Courtesy/Copyright of Authors

Who We Think We Are

- The museum has a diverse staff in regard to race and ethnicity
- The museum has a diverse staff in regard to economic background.
- The museum has a diverse staff in regard to gender identity.
- The museum has a diverse staff in regard to sexual orientation.

How We Engage with DEI

- I value the strategic priority for diversity, equity, and inclusion.
- I believe diverse, inclusive, and equitable organizations are higher performing and more successful.
- The museum has well-defined values and policies related to diversity, equity, accessibility, and inclusion.
- Museum leadership supports diversity, equity, and inclusion efforts.
- The museum communicates its organizational values to employees on a regular and ongoing basis.

How We Relate to our Communities

- The museum effectively communicates, enriches, and engages with diverse communities.
- The museum treats its visitors fairly on the basis of gender, sexual orientation, race, ethnicity, disability, and economic background.
- The museum adequately serves a racially diverse audience.
- The museum adequately serves an economically diverse audience.
- I believe our workforce should better reflect the communities we serve.

How We Work

- My supervisor promotes a respectful, diverse, and inclusive environment.
- Employees are treated with respect regardless of position.
- I feel I can advance my career at the museum regardless of my race, ethnicity, gender identity, sexual orientation, age, or disability.
- I need to conceal or distort parts of my race, ethnicity, gender identity, sexual orientation, age, or disability at work.

How We Deal with Conflict

- The museum has well-defined non-discrimination and harassment policies.
- The museum effectively enforces its policies against discrimination, harassment, and retaliation.
- I have personally witnessed discrimination of any type at the museum.
- I have been on the receiving end of discrimination of any type at the museum.
- I have personally witnessed sexual harassment at the museum.
- I have been on the receiving end of sexual harassment at the museum.

Where We Want to Go

- The museum provides sufficient resources to help members of underrepresented groups feel included.
- I think diversity, equity, and inclusion training should be mandatory for museum staff.
- I would like to have additional training or resources on diversity, equity, and inclusion.
- What diversity, equity, and inclusion work do you think should be a priority for the museum?
- Is there anything else you'd like to share with the DEI team?

Figure 9.2. Staff Engagement Survey Questions. Depending on the question, response options were: "Strongly Agree, Agree, Disagree, Strongly Disagree, or Don't Know", "Yes, No", and "Always, Almost Always, Sometimes, Almost Never, Never, and Don't Know" options. All questions also had an open text field in which participants were invited to add comments.
Image Courtesy/Copyright of Authors

- *All Staff Surveys.* We conducted two all-staff surveys, intended to capture information from all individuals in the organization. A seven-question demographic survey asked staff to self-identify age, race, gender, sexuality, (dis)ability, and economic status. A longer thirty-nine-question staff engagement survey asked people about their specific perceptions of and experiences at the museum (see figure 9.2).

WHAT OBSTACLES DID WE FACE?

The audit subteam faced a variety of challenges, from organizational structure and logistics to building trust and ensuring buy-in. Defining and including "all staff" proved to be one of our most complex tasks. The Corning Museum has three categories of staff members who work on our campus: permanent staff, employed directly by the organization; contract staff employed through external contract agencies; and permanent or contract staff who are employed through Corning Incorporated, which provides culinary, housekeeping, and security services to the museum. To make the process as inclusive as possible, we felt it was especially important to include the perspectives of people employed in nonpermanent positions. Although many of these employees have worked at the museum for years and are highly visible to the public, they are rarely involved in organizational initiatives and decision-making.

Obstacles to including contract employees and staff employed through Corning Inc. proved numerous and many layered. First, the audit subteam had to secure permissions and buy-in from the employer to include those employees. The support of museum leadership in securing Corning Inc.'s permissions was critical, as several meetings and messages of endorsement were needed to communicate the intention and potential impact of the audit. Second, the subteam had to determine which employees would be eligible to complete the survey.

We encountered resistance from some museum staff that some of the temporary, contract staff, and Corning Inc. employees may not "know" the institution well enough to provide "valuable" feedback. We countered that all people who work within the museum's groups are representatives of the institution, and each individual has experiences that are meaningful and valuable. Working with human resources and museum leadership, the audit subteam determined that any employee who averaged at least twenty hours a week of work on-site in the month prior to when the survey was conducted would be eligible.

Another obstacle we faced was the mechanics of administering the survey, specifically surrounding concerns about privacy and inequitable access to computers. During the time of this survey's creation, the museum was just introducing the Microsoft Office 365 suite. We considered using Microsoft Forms to administer the survey, which was available within this software. However, when testing Microsoft Forms, we felt the platform was not yet positioned for staff information to remain totally anonymous. Moreover, we were concerned that staff might think their responses could be traced back to their Office 365 user accounts. We did not want concerns about privacy to deter people from participating in the survey. Instead the team decided to use

SurveyMonkey, a low-cost survey tool for which we already had an organizational account. SurveyMonkey provided an easy and intuitive interface to develop the questionnaire, share the link to the survey, and analyze and visualize the resulting anonymous data. Because we took these steps and used this platform, we were better able to reassure staff of the survey's anonymity.

Our second solution was to offer staff the option to fill out a paper survey. This resolved any lingering concerns about computer-based tracking and also allowed those who do not have regular computer access at work to take the survey. The team distributed blank surveys at team meetings and in break rooms and requested responses be returned via interoffice mail. We received seventy completed paper surveys (31 percent of all responses). The team then manually entered paper responses into SurveyMonkey after the survey period had closed, so all data could be aggregated using SurveyMonkey's tools.

Privacy concerns also governed the team's decision to divide the survey into two parts, one collecting demographic information including gender, race, and sexual orientation and the other about attitudes and experiences. The team knew we were sacrificing some information by organizing the survey in this way. We would not be able to determine, for example, how staff identifying as BIPOC or lesbian, gay, bisexual, transgender, queer/questioning+ (LGBTQ+) experienced the institution differently from staff who identified as white or heterosexual. However, because so few people in our organization identify as nonwhite, we felt it was critical to ensure their identities remained anonymous to ensure authentic responses.

The DEI team spread word and built trust around the all-staff survey and equity audit process in a variety of ways, recognizing that people across the organization had nonequitable access to information. In addition to making announcements at all-staff meetings (which not all staff, as we defined it, attend) and posting on the museum's intranet site (to which not all staff have access), members of the DEI team conducted a grassroots campaign in which a member of the team personally spoke with every permanent staff member, encouraging them to take the survey and answering any questions or concerns they had about it. Although it wasn't logistically or practically possible to speak with every contract or Corning Inc. employee, we attended their departmental meetings and posted information in break rooms. During this part of the engagement effort, we became even more convinced of the importance of having a long-term contract employee on the audit subteam. This employee was crucial in helping us understand the contract employee experience, build trust among other employees in that employment category, and determine the best ways to engage them.

Our efforts to build buy-in and ensure participation in the survey were highly successful. The survey was open for the first two weeks of November

2018. Our overall survey response rate was 72 percent of employees across all three employment categories. Participation was highest among permanent museum employees (88 percent of 162 eligible) and lowest among Corning Inc. employees (35 percent of the seventy-five eligible).

HOW DID WE REPORT ON THE AUDIT?

With the data from external benchmarking, departmental interviews, and all-staff survey in hand, the audit subteam began to compile our findings into a coherent report. We built our report around a series of questions: who we are (benchmarking information); what we do (departmental interviews); and what we think (survey results). The final result was an eighty-three-page report, which included an executive summary, a graphic at-a-glance, and a how to read this report section. Because the document was intended to serve as an ongoing resource and reference, we included as much information as possible about our methodology, decision-making, and underlying research.

We knew that much of the information in the report was sensitive, and not everyone would react well to its contents. The DEI team first presented the report and key findings and recommendations to the museum's leadership team, which is the main decision-making body of the organization. To our deep appreciation, they asked very good questions, provided further suggestions and recommendations to improve the quality of the report, and showed a high degree of engagement with the process. They did not require us to edit or redact any information.

In anticipation of the release of the report to all staff in spring 2019, we launched a communication plan with a multipronged internal communication strategy (all staff meetings, intranet, and break rooms) as well as a more informal grassroots campaign to connect with every member of staff in the weeks after the release of the audit to answer questions and receive feedback.

HOW HAS THE CORNING MUSEUM USED THE RESULTS OF THE EQUITY AUDIT?

Findings from the audit revealed a widespread desire for more institutional accountability, DEI training and initiatives, and transparent communication within the institution. To address DEI concerns raised in the audit, the institution embarked on several direct actions. The DEI team and leadership team formed a joint team to work on an institutional equity statement. The resulting equity statement, detailing the museum's DEI commitments, was released in May 2020 and is featured prominently on the museum's website and on-campus messaging. This joint team structure has proved highly successful, and a follow-up roadmap team is currently meeting to develop a long-range plan for the institution.

In addition, the museum committed to DEI training. Since 2019, staff training plans have included mandatory DEI training on topics such as identity, privilege, and bias. Members of the DEI team responded creatively to the challenges of 2020 by offering discussion groups about the equity statement, and the board of trustees and the leadership team began designating a portion of regular meeting time to continuing DEI education.

The DEI team now serves as a research hub for the museum at large by evaluating best practices in the field, bringing resources to the museum, and serving as a consultant to staff. Staff can highlight departmental initiatives through an online DEI success form. The DEI team uses the information collected in these forms to document institutional work, connect people, and provide feedback and support. Smaller groups of the DEI team are focused on different projects, including generating an annual report and updating staff via all-staff meetings, intramuseum blog posts, and word of mouth. The ambassador group, an extension of and recruitment pipeline for the DEI team, supports the team's mission, facilitates communication about our work across the museum, and coordinates DEI-related activities.

HOW DO WE REFLECT ON THE AUDIT?

The DEI team had hoped that the audit would help the organization see itself more clearly in the individual anonymous reflections. No one on the audit subteam was a professional statistician or social scientist; therefore, we had to modify our expectations for definitive results and view the audit as part of an iterative process. The institution will need to consistently gather staff feedback on progress toward organizational DEI goals regularly to see itself clearly as it changes. In this section, we, the authors, reflect on the audit process and raise questions that should have been considered more deliberately at the time. In this way we polish the mirror, in hopes of improving processes for assessing future work.

Working within a predominantly white culture, the DEI team was aware that a document that converts people into data is a tool that could cause harm. We chose to structure the survey questions around institutional values for relevance, leaving space for individual expression in the comment sections. The personal way we spoke about the audit with staff built trust, and we felt accountable for carrying that trust in the way we synthesized their responses.

Working within an organization that was just beginning to undertake DEI work meant that we as a team also encountered challenges despite our desire to create an inclusive process. We found that there are as many "right" ways to conduct an equity audit as there are people on a DEI team. Though reflection was part of the audit process, enough time has passed for us to step back and evaluate. The following questions may help create a framework for consideration in future projects. Although some of the following questions were considered at the time, we should have been more explicit in addressing them for ourselves and for readers of the report to balance numbers with nuance both during and after the audit.

- Drafting the audit survey
  - Do these questions align with institutional values?
  - Are the questions inclusive?
  - Are we ensuring anonymity?
- Honoring the answers
  - Are we interpreting the results honestly?
  - How do we balance quantitative data and qualitative comments?
  - How can we tell the truth while maintaining confidentiality?
  - What can we learn from negative feedback?
- Setting realistic team expectations
  - How should we handle conflict?
  - What are the power dynamics within the team and between its members and staff?
  - How will we ensure all members, particularly BIPOC members, are heard?
- Making decisions as a team
  - Are the deadlines for discussion, review, and feedback clear and realistic?
  - Who is making decisions?
  - Do all team members understand the rationale?

As we reflect on the equity audit now, three years after we first started planning and two years after we completed the report, we recognize that the real outcome wasn't the eighty-three-page document, the recommendations, or even the survey results, although certainly those are important documents to understand our institution's DEI journey. Issues raised in the audit responses continue to prompt cycles of important discussions and gradual change. Institutional commitment to hearing and incorporating feedback from all staff will continue to encourage DEI work. The successes of the equity audit extend beyond specific DEI initiatives: the audit process initiated conversations across the organization, encouraged more curiosity and proactive ownership of equity initiatives beyond the DEI team, and helped lay the groundwork for a culture of inclusion that better acknowledges the contributions of all employees.

NOTES

1. The equity audit was a major cross-organizational effort, requiring the support and full engagement of numerous museum staff members. We especially acknowledge the contributions of the 2018–2019 DEI matrix team: Bryan Buchanan, Jane Cook, Jonathan Heath, Elizabeth Hylen, Olivia Khristan, Jennifer Kuhn, Katherine Larson, Cordelia McBride, Michelle Padilla, Siyao Peng, Alexandra Ruggiero, Troy Smythe, Jessica Trump, Lianne Uesato, Diane Webster, and Kris Wetterlund, as well as Alice Carvalho-Bonilha (DEI and education intern, fall 2018) and Karol Wight (president and executive director).

2. Jackson's model, as adopted by Wilborn, asks organizations to identify themselves along a spectrum of inclusivity, from exclusionary, monocultural organizations, through compliance, and ultimately to culturally fluent (acknowledging the work is never done). See Jackson "Theory and Practice of Multicultural Organization Development," 175–92.

3. We particularly looked to and are grateful for the Readiness Assessment and Toolkit (MASS Action, October 2017, https://www.museumaction.org/resources/); Unrealized Impact: The Case for Diversity, Equity, and Inclusion, especially questions from the Staff Experience survey (Promise54, 2017, http://www.unrealizedimpact.org/); the California Endowment, Diversity, Equity, and Inclusion Audit Report (the California Endowment, August 2017, https://www.calendow.org/diversity-equality-inclusion-audit/); and Marjorie Bequette and Evelyn Ronning of the Science Museum of Minnesota (personal communication, winter 2019).

4. Westermann et al., "Art Museum Staff Demographic Survey 2018."

Chapter Ten

From Awareness to Action

Developing Your Diversity, Equity, and Inclusion Strategy through Racial Healing

Regina N. Ford

I was hired as the new vice president of human resources at Pacific Science Center in Seattle, Washington, in September 2019. I brought more than ten years of experience leading major diversity, equity, and inclusion (DEI) initiatives across large Fortune 500 companies, and I was charged with continuing the organization's DEI work, expanding their efforts in new ways. Prior to my arrival, the Pacific Science Center had been using a formalized approach to DEI efforts since 2016. Over a four-year period, we had appointed the most ethnically diverse board of directors in our organization's history; created an internal committee focused on inclusion, diversity, equity, and access (IDEA committee); analyzed our employee representation data across all levels of the organization to proactively increase diversity through hiring; and implemented science education programs that brought free or low-cost science education to Title I schools, rural communities, and children experiencing homelessness or in foster care. The summer of 2020 brought into blatant clarity that what we were doing was not enough. The civil rights movement spreading across the globe demonstrated the full scope of the task at hand when tackling racial inequality. As organizations operating within the United States, we are subject to the civil laws, public policies, and mechanisms of power and control that our country upholds. The Center for American Progress describes the contradictory nature of these laws and policies:

> The United States is a contradiction. Its founding principles embrace the ideals of freedom and equality, but it is a nation built on the systematic exclusion and

> suppression of communities of color. From the start, so many of this country's laws and public policies, which should serve as the scaffolding that guides progress, were instead designed explicitly to prevent people of color from fully participating. Moreover, these legal constructs are not some relic of antebellum or Jim Crow past but rather remain part of the fabric of American policymaking.[1]

For Pacific Science Center, we came to the realization that the scope of the challenge before the United States to uproot our systems of racism mirrored the scope of our challenge as a science museum to ensure DEI across all aspects of our organization. It occurred to me that this challenge of the nation is the challenge of Pacific Science Center. Forming committees, analyzing employee data, and diversifying the board of directors were reactive topical treatments to a disease that was cellular. To create antiracist systems that truly support equity across our organization, we had to involve participants from all levels of the institution in a process that generated, assessed, implemented, and tracked antiracist goals.

RACIAL HEALING

On June 16, 2020, I organized the Pacific Science Center's first open conversation on racial equity (CORE). My aim was to begin reengaging our DEI work by starting with a process of racial healing, a process through which parties recognize their common humanity, acknowledge the truth of past wrongs, and build the authentic relationships capable of transforming communities and shifting our national discourse on race.[2] Due to the mandated closure of the science center's facilities because of COVID-19, sixty-nine employees from different business units were available to attend our first conversation on race. The experience was cross-departmental and cross-hierarchical, and it included both former employees and current employees (all employees participating through their personal choice). There was a single topic: race.

- How has race impacted your life personally?
- How do those experiences influence how you show up at work?
- What do you think about Black Lives Matter, George Floyd's murder, and what's going on in the world today regarding race?

To create a safe space to discuss topics related to race, I shared the following ground rules or agreements:

- Commitment to considering Black people and the impact to their community.

- Speak from your own experience.
- Make space for others when they are sharing their experience.
- Take space for yourself and feel safe in the conversation.
- Ask why you are talking at this moment or not.
- Silence is OK.
- Feel free to disagree (and to explain why).
- Do not attack—no cursing or pointing fingers.
- Personal stories remain confidential, not recorded.

By collectively agreeing to these guidelines, participants felt comfortable sharing personal details about their experiences with racism. Some employees shared how their family members brought them up with racist views, including people of color whose older family members made them feel ashamed for having dark skin or features associated with being nonwhite. Others discussed racist comments they had experienced at work, in bars, in interviews, and at school. It was an extremely powerful and difficult conversation; however, we were able to begin our antiracism work where it needed to start—with authentic examples of the destructive impact of racism on individuals and why it is worth fighting every day to make Pacific Science Center an antiracist organization.

Following our first CORE discussion, we established four foundational principles from which we would create our DEI strategy:

1. Racism negatively impacts everyone, not just people of color. We all have a stake in eliminating it.
2. Racism is pervasive throughout every part of our lives: when we apply for housing, eat at a restaurant, and go to school, church, social events, and work.
3. The impacts of racism last a lifetime. Therefore, we shouldn't expect that employees who have dealt with racism will not bring those experiences to work—nor should we expect our customers won't bring their thoughts and experiences around race to our premises.
4. Racism is so pervasive that it may appear in subtle and sometimes unconscious ways, resulting in an unearned advantage to a specific group and an unearned disadvantage to others. For example, systemic racism and bias may impact the items we choose to sell in our gift shops or the photos we use to market our programs. We might see biases reflected in social media posts, customer comments, signage on property, and music selections. We may also witness microaggressions during team meetings or employee interactions. The examples are endless.

AWARENESS TO ACTION

Pacific Science Center has launched many programs to address a lack of racial diversity among its employees and its senior leadership. In December 2015, a new CEO, Will Daugherty, was selected by the board of directors due largely to his commitment to DEI and organizational change. In the first four years of Daugherty's tenure, the institution increased the ethnic and gender diversity of the board of directors, appointed the first ever Black chair to the board, and promoted the first ever Black employee to serve on the executive leadership team (VP of science engagement and outreach). Although these changes were appropriate and helpful, Daugherty and the executive leadership team realized after the first CORE conversation that their approaches lacked the depth and breadth of scope that would be necessary to uproot institutional systems and remove racial bias as much as possible.

This was a crucial moment of clarity for Pacific Science Center's leadership. Like all organizational leaders who want to implement policies that undo systemic racism, the question remained—how? The racial healing conversations in our CORE meetings helped to uncover some answers to these questions. Among the angst, anger, fears, and hopes expressed in those conversations were also recommendations for change. Participants in the racial healing conversations made comments such as, "The world does things this way. We could do this way instead," and "Why do we accept these HR policies as standard and required? There are other options."

I quickly realized that the ideas emerging in our racial healing conversations provided a road map to building our most effective DEI strategy. I decided to create opportunities to brainstorm a vision for our future and discuss the changes we need to make to mitigate racism in our society, workplaces, and local communities—and do so without boundaries. If we start with an open field of possibilities and ideas for improvement, we can then figure out how to build the future we want to see together through a more formal planning process that ties our assessment of where our organization leaves room for bias, to accountable actions and task owners for removing or greatly reducing that potential for bias.

Open Brainstorming—No Idea Is a Bad Idea

In the next stage of our process, I facilitated a meeting to brainstorm changes we could make to remove racial bias and support antiracism at the Pacific Science Center. Having previous experience facilitating courses, focus groups, and executive discussions on racism, racial healing, and DEI, I was equipped to lead these highly sensitive and often emotional conversations on racial equity. I highly recommend that organizations hire an external facilitator who is experienced in conducting sensitive racial healing conversations if they do not have someone on staff with this real-life experience.

In our online CORE meeting, the complete group of former and current Pacific Science Center employees from across all departments and all levels of the organization gathered to discuss any and all ideas for removing or reducing racial bias from the Pacific Science Center. To ensure there was a consistent flow to the conversation, I asked that staff refrain from evaluating any ideas during the first brainstorming session. As a result, there was absolutely no debate about the quality or potential efficacy of any of the ideas. The first brainstorming exercise was purely and intentionally focused on presenting ideas. At the end of our brainstorming session, the staff had pitched a total of seventy-five ideas.

Bringing Science to the Brainstorm

Once we had our list of seventy-five ideas to support antiracism, we needed to select which ideas to put into action first. We believe that the only way for an organization to implement a credible process for developing an antiracism plan is to involve all levels of the organization in identifying the problems and prioritizing actions to address those problems. A top-down approach would only replicate a system of power we were seeking to eliminate. This process was one of the most challenging parts of our antiracism journey.

We decided to prioritize ideas on the basis of two factors: (1) the potential positive impact of the idea and (2) how much effort (in terms of time, money, resources, etc.) would be required to implement the idea. Although we were committed to addressing all initiatives that we believed were valuable to our antiracism commitment, we decided to deprioritize ideas that would take more money, resources, and time to implement to focus on "low-hanging fruit" that we could tackle immediately with little lead time.

An Idea Priority Matrix

To help us consider and rank the ideas and eventually determine who will be best placed to implement them, we grouped the ideas into seven categories (see table 10.1). We then focused each of our deep dive conversations on one of these seven organizational categories. In advance of each meeting, we described the topic and encouraged participants to post links to any reference materials related to the meeting topic (articles, videos, books, etc.) in the calendar invite for the meeting.

Table 10.1. Categories for Identifying Antiracist Initiatives

Core Focus Group Topics	*Function*	*Examples*
1. Community Engagement	Review partnerships with community organizations and look for opportunities to advocate for antiracism	Join the Washington Employers for Racial Equity coalition; work with local sports teams on antiracism programming; host guest speakers at our facilities
2. Science Museums and Cultural Institutions	Identify ways that we can partner with other science museums and cultural institutions to elevate antiracism and advocate for DEI together	Create exhibits on antiracism and DEI; review current exhibits, displays, signage, websites, and so on to remove inequities and bias
3. Science Discipline (Westernized Sciences and Non-European Ways of Knowing)	Evaluate the historical ways in which science has advanced racist and eugenicist views and develop ways to dismantle those racist constructs in science education and the discipline of science itself	Hire more BIPOC science educators; review all science education curriculum to remove bias and include more BIPOC scientists/inventors; name camps and facility spaces after BIPOC scientists/inventors
4. Organizational Policies, Processes, and Procedures	Review Pacific Science Center policies (hiring, discipline, code of conduct, employee handbook, etc.), processes, and procedures to remove bias and advance diversity, equity, and inclusion	Translate employee handbook in multiple languages; add our antiracism commitment to all job descriptions, offer letters, employee handbook and performance expectations; discuss our antiracism commitment and CORE conversations as the first order of business at all board meetings; all vendor agreements and contracts

Core Focus Group Topics	*Function*	*Examples*
5. Colleague Engagement	Identify ways in which we can create a clear sense of our antiracism commitment and a strong sense of belonging and DEI in our work environment	Add antiracism commitment to all meeting agendas and hang in all meeting rooms; create meetings and open spaces specifically for colleagues to discuss racism, bias, inequities, both internally and externally
6. Customer Offerings	Evaluate how we can promote antiracism, diversity, equity, and inclusion through the products and services we sell to our customers	Create exhibits representative of BIPOC scientists, experiences, and interests; partner with BIPOC artists and companies for gift shop paraphernalia; partner with BIPOC caterers and chefs for our cafe items; hold community conversations with BIPOC guest speakers on topics of racial equity in public policy
7. Customer Engagement	Examine the ways in which we interact with individual customers on the physical premises and online and seek opportunities to explain our antiracism commitment and advocate for racial equity, diversity, and inclusion	Add our antiracism commitment to our website, ticket receipt, and confirmation emails; create signage for standing boards and electronic boards with antiracism and inclusive messages (e.g., "Science Thrives with Diversity")

Live Polling Feedback

After discussing the main topic, we conducted live polling via Zoom and asked participants to score each idea related to the topic based on its level of perceived impact and amount of effort required to implement the idea. After seven weeks of deep dive conversations and polls to help us rank all seventy-five ideas produced during the initial brainstorming session, I partnered with the CEO and chief of staff to plot the ideas on a priority matrix. As illustrated in figure 10.1, we placed impact scores on the vertical axis and effort scores on the horizontal axis. This matrix allowed us to identify twenty-five ideas with high impact scores and low effort scores. These ideas are represented in the top right corner of the matrix.

ACCOUNTABILITY FOR ACTION

After seven weeks of brainstorming and scoring ideas, a plan emerged. Our organization was now armed with a list of seventy-five ideas produced from an open and inclusive forum of employees at all levels as well as a priority list of twenty-five ideas to tackle first. For organizational change to last long term, it must be protected, upheld, and advocated by its executive leadership team (ELT), comprising team members at the VP level or above, and the entire organization should be held accountable to execute the ideas.

In the next phase of the development of our DEI strategy, we convened seven working groups of fifty-seven staff charged with deriving action plans

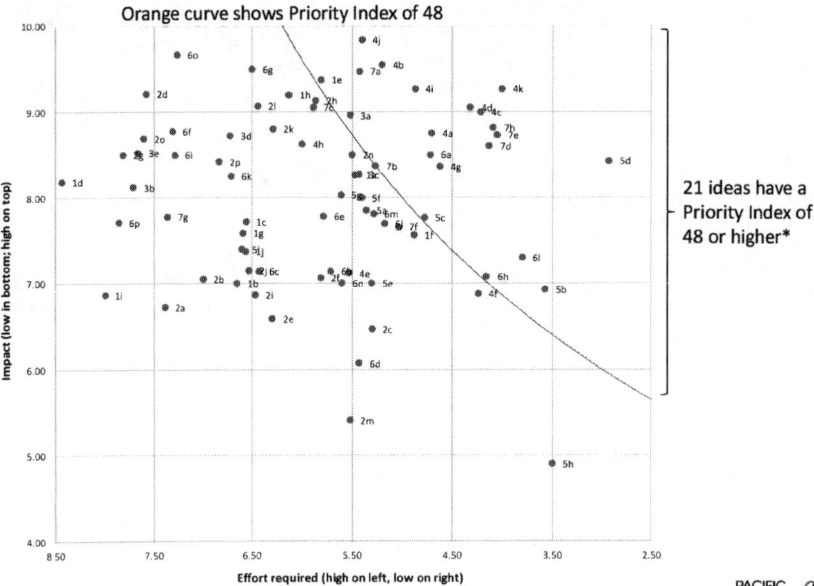

Figure 10.1. Prioritization Matrix graph plotting the group ranking of DEI ideas by projected impact against effort to implement.
Courtesy of Pacific Science Center

for implementing the ideas under each of the seven organizational categories of change. For each of the seven focus group meetings, two ELT members volunteered to facilitate the conversations. The ELT members all had previous experience facilitating difficult conversations and were committed to being accountable for outcomes of each focus group.

The seven groups met biweekly to create action plans for implementing the subset of the top twenty-five ideas that fell within their organizational category. Two of the top twenty-five ideas that garnered the highest scores from participants included having community discussions on antiracism hosted by trained DEI facilitators on our campus and creating a community board listing a multitude of grassroots organizations to help us tell the stories of BIPOC communities through Pacific Science Center communication channels.

Finding practical ways to implement the ideas required external research, so a library of subject-matter documents, research papers, articles, TED Talks, and videos were created in a shared CORE resource using Microsoft Teams SharePoint (see bibliography). SharePoint was a useful tool for this type of sharing because it allowed both internal organizational emails and external emails to be used so that both current and former employees could share.

In addition to reviewing resources available on the internet, we engaged other museums and cultural institutions to learn how others were approaching challenges similar to those reflected in the twenty-five ideas we were seeking to implement. We invited speakers from local museums and cultural institutions to join our CORE meetings and become part of a community-based conversation on antiracism. Speakers from the Seattle Art Museum, Northwest African American Museum, the Museum of Flight, and many other local cultural institutions joined our conversations on antiracism and helped support our efforts. Several board members joined our CORE meetings as well, including the board chair and chair elect.

By September 2020, three months after our initial racial healing conversation in June, we had a holistic DEI strategy with clear goals and priorities; action plans for all seven organizational areas of change; and roles and responsibilities for all the DEI work. In addition, we had ongoing timelines for implementation; success metrics to confirm what good looks like for seven organizational change areas; and tracking mechanisms to give visibility across the entire organization as to how we are performing against our DEI goals.

To ensure our DEI strategy would continue to be executed and not be confined to a document used for performative purposes, we embedded accountability into all seven organizational change areas. We appointed roles to lead each of the seven organizational change areas to ensure that continuity is guaranteed regardless of shifts in staffing. These group leader roles are accountable for (1) tracking progress of all DEI goals until completion; (2) facilitating monthly focus group meetings to enact action items within their group; (3) requesting additional resources or support from other working groups or the ELT to accomplish the group's goals; and (4) reporting out in monthly organization-wide CORE meetings on the progress of each action item.

This accountability structure has successfully ensured that across the entire organization—from hiring to talent management to separation; in every policy and procedure; in every product, program, and service we provide a range of customers—all employees are reminded to consider DEI in everything they do.

CONCLUSION

The Pacific Science Center was in a cloud of emotion in June 2020. Like most every other organization in the United States, it was clear the need for racial equality was stronger than ever, but the road toward that goal was uncertain, daunting, and precarious. Our choice to start with those raw emotions of how racism impacts individuals and the world at large and then move toward an action plan for progress—instead of the opposite approach of attempting to apply a process on top of a problem inextricably tied to emotion—proved to be a powerful mechanism for developing a unique DEI strategy designed to attack racism at the roots of our institution. By starting with honest, painful, raw, and emotional racial healing conversations, we were able to move from personal proof of how corrosive racism is; to the cathartic process of brainstorming ideas for formative change; to an analytical method of prioritizing those ideas; and finally, to creating a structure of accountability to ensure high-priority ideas are implemented.

More than a year later in September 2021, the seven working groups focused on organizational change continue to meet monthly. These meetings are still led by ELT members who are held accountable for ensuring the group fulfills its goals. The working groups report out at monthly CORE meetings with complete organizational transparency. Current and former employees of the Pacific Science Center continue to attend, as well as local civic leaders, representatives from various local cultural institutions and for-profit corporations, board members, DEI practitioners, and recognized advocates for racial equality. Pacific Science Center was the first nonprofit organization to join the Washington Employers for Racial Equity (WERE) coalition, and we are active members to this day—helping to define ways to track progress toward racial equity for all its members and to build coalitions to change public policy around housing, education, transportation systems, homelessness, and so on across the state of Washington that will improve racial equality outcomes in these areas. We have updated our entire interview and hiring process; on-boarding procedures; supplier outreach process; employee handbook language; marketing review requirements; meeting engagement protocols; DEI training; and list of resources on DEI to push all employees at every level to think deeply about how we can further DEI in everything we do.

By starting with racial healing, employees at the Pacific Science Center developed a deep awareness that something fundamentally different needed to be done to address racial inequality. From this space of healing, we were able to generate a detailed DEI strategy that has moved us toward our goals of creating a more just and equitable organization.

NOTES

1. Solomon, Maxwell, and Castro, "Systematic Inequality and American Democracy."
2. W. K. Kellogg Foundation, "Restoring to Wholeness—Racial Healing for Ourselves, Our Relationships, and Our Communities."

Chapter Eleven

Holding Ourselves Accountable to Antiracist Work at the RISD Museum

Lily Benedict, MJ Robinson, and Kajette Solomon

RISD Museum employees are holding ourselves accountable to antiracist practice, which requires clear definitions of our antiracist goals, an organizational structure that fits new modes of working, and the ability to measure our progress. Acknowledging that the practice of antiracism is necessarily collaborative, RISD Museum staff members' relationships to one another became the strong, interdependent threads holding the museum accountable to our collective goals. In this chapter, we weave together our perspectives, descriptions of processes, and short quotes from our colleagues, revealing emergent patterns in our institution's evolving journey in antiracist work.

We, the authors, share a vision of museums as exciting, accessible, and liberatory spaces. We all began our work at RISD as educators supporting school and group visits. We bring our facilitation skills and abilities to engage with diverse audiences to the work we elucidate further in the coming pages. Lily is a white, cisgender, able-bodied woman who uses her privileged positionality to push the museum to better serve the young people she works with as a K–12 educator. She brings her own curiosity and joy of learning to her work and strives to spark that spirit in others. MJ is a white and class-privileged person who celebrates their genderqueer identity and their neurodivergence for leading them toward a life challenging oppressive power structures with the tools they know best: art and play. As a Black, Jamaican immigrant, cisgender, and able-bodied woman, Kajette believes in the power of museums as dynamic spaces to explore, experiment, and innovate. Because the worlds of art and history often exclude those who share her background, she is committed to building equitable, diverse, and inclusive museums for all through collaborative educational programming and antiracist pedagogy.

LAYING THE FOUNDATION: ALL-STAFF DIALOGUES

In 2017, four junior RISD Museum staff—including the three authors of this chapter—worked with the approval of senior staff to launch all-staff dialogues, an internal, cross-departmental discussion series focused on issues of power, racism, and social equity in museums. Instead of bringing in external facilitators, we facilitated these conversations ourselves. Although this new initiative lay outside of our official job descriptions, we felt we had the skills, capacity, and passion to move the program forward. Amber Lopez, the museum's former Nancy Elizabeth Prophet Fellow, first proposed the idea of all-staff dialogues. In her words,

> the initial goal was to have loosely facilitated conversations, by and for staff, using current issues in the museum field to address internal staff biases and gaps of knowledge. We wanted to create a space for staff to engage in "difficult conversations," to consider the limitations of their own positionality, and to learn how best to represent the objects, artists, and cultures present in the collection.[1]

Some of our early questions included: "What is the museum's responsibility when exhibiting artwork that may offend?" and "What does it mean to decolonize the museum?"

By 2018, to make this program sustainable and more integrated into our institutional culture, we began training other staff members to become facilitators, expanding the all-staff dialogues team from four to thirteen members who each brought their own perspectives and topics to the table. This team of volunteers became our first antiracism working group. All-staff dialogues were a key first step to fostering personal accountability to antiracist work among our staff by creating a forum for us to learn and grow together. In our experiences, practicing vulnerable conversations and active listening built trust and open communication into our work culture. In the words of database manager Kiku Langford McDonald,

> [I appreciated] having those conversations in a safe space. . . . I could practice putting my words together and putting my thoughts together. Also, it's given me allies. Without the staff dialogues, I wouldn't necessarily know what kinds of things different people are passionate about or knowledgeable about. [After these] open discussions with each other, I have a better sense of what people's

> backgrounds are, so that if I'm faced with a situation, whether at work or outside of work, I know who I can turn to and talk through those ideas with.[2]

The all-staff dialogue initiative became the foundation for the museum's antiracist action plan, codeveloped in 2020 by all-staff dialogue facilitators with former director John Smith.

CREATING AN ANTIRACIST ACTION PLAN

Our progress toward creating an antiracist action plan in 2020 was catalyzed by individual and collective staff responses to global movements addressing systemic racism. On-call educator and artist MJ Robinson offers their perspective on the political context leading up to the process.

MJ's Reflection

After a cascade of COVID-19 planning meetings at the RISD Museum on March 12, 2020, I received a call that a white family member had been murdered by police in a no-knock raid. I froze, crumpled on the sidewalk in front of the laundromat, and could hardly breathe. The next day would be our last in-person workday. I masked my panic, spritzed sixty pencils with sanitizer, taught a group of sixth graders, washed my hands, and left work early to try to catch my breath.

By June 5, I was mourning and moving, a metallic thread in a tapestry of more than ten thousand neighbors marching through Providence. Black Lives Matter. Defund the police.

> Our museum director at the time, John Smith, released a statement and Black Lives Matter homepage banner in response to the political uprising against police violence and systemic racism following the murders of George Floyd, Breonna Taylor, and countless other Black people at the hands of police. Staff mobilized to ensure that his words, which we believed in, didn't end up ringing hollow like similar statements by organizations and corporations filled with well-meaning white faces but not backed by action.
>
> I bring my experience as an artist and as an antiracist, prison abolitionist, and lesbian, gay, bisexual, queer/questioning, intersex, asexual, two-spirt+ (LGBTQIA2S+) community organizer and facilitator to my work with all-staff Dialogues at the RISD Museum, a program that has powerfully shifted our work culture to be more vulnerable, collaborative, and antiracist. With other facilitators our founding crew had trained over the years, we were able to put together an emergency all-staff dialogue on Zoom on Tuesday, June 9. We spent time in small breakout rooms with the prompt "What immediate and long-term steps

can we take as an institution to actively disrupt racism, and how do we communicate these and hold ourselves accountable?"

Director John Smith consolidated staff ideas from the meeting on June 9 into a key takeaways document. The breakout-dialogue group facilitators became the de facto plan makers, meeting with John about twice a month from June through October to expand staff thoughts into what became our antiracist action plan.[3] We used the SMART goals framework, creating goals that are specific, measurable, actionable, realistic, and time-based. As chief curator and curator of ancient art, Gina Borromeo explains, "throughout the [antiracist action plan] writing process, we were asking each other: 'How can we measure this? What are the actual steps?' So assessment and accountability were integrated into the plan's creation."[4]

The resulting plan includes three main sections, each with specific action items, as follows.

Confronting Ourselves Together

- Openly acknowledge the museum's Eurocentricity and complicity in white supremacy culture; actively work to redress its colonial foundations through reinstallation and reinterpretation of the collection in our galleries, programs, publications, website, and other platforms.

From the inside out

- Require ongoing antiracist development for every museum board member, staff member, volunteer, intern, and fellow.
- Use every available opportunity to hire, support, and retain museum staff with a diverse range of identities and backgrounds, particularly for leadership and decision-making roles.

At the top

- Implement a plan to develop the RISD Museum's board of governors and fine arts committee to equitably and inclusively reflect our communities.

We shared the antiracist action plan with the museum's board of governors, on our website, and to all museum staff, and continue to share it with new job applicants. It is periodically updated to reflect work that has been accomplished and goals that have shifted.

NEW ROLES FOR ACCOUNTABILITY AND ASSESSMENT

At the same time that we were finalizing our antiracist action plan, education program coordinator Kajette Solomon was ruminating on her experience as one of few Black people on staff at the RISD Museum. Seeing a need for a full-time role focused on antiracist work, Kajette advocated for changes to her job description and was ultimately promoted to a newly created position: social equity and inclusion (SEI) program specialist. Kajette elaborates on the process that led to her promotion in the following description.

Kajette's Reflection

In June 2020, I was thinking about my future at the museum and what I wanted to contribute. With all the uproar in museums and calls for accountability in their responses to the Black Lives Matter protests, I asked myself: What could my career trajectory look like as a Black woman in a predominately white institution? I knew I wanted a path to a position that involved shaping our organization and being a part of decision-making. I attended all the meetings where we solidified our antiracist action plan. As questions and concerns were posed about who would shoulder some of these new responsibilities, I began to see a need that I could fulfill.

That summer, I also represented the museum on several panels, sharing our all-staff dialogues program as a model for other institutions to begin the internal work of confronting systemic racism and shifting work culture. I quickly realized that my previous role no longer aligned with the work I was doing and wanted to continue developing. Subsequently, I met with a colleague in human resources at RISD. I discussed my aspirations and they guided me on what to do next. I then explored other museum SEI position descriptions and spoke to colleagues at other museums with similar roles. When I brought a proposal for a role I could see myself in to my supervisor, interim director Sarah Ganz Blythe, she was excited and supportive. Sarah recognized that this was a "stretching moment, a moment of growth." As a leader, she took responsibility for removing procedural and financial obstacles "to let that growth happen."[5]

> I could imagine my future at the museum just like our antiracist work imagines the future of the museum. That was poignant for me. A few drafts of my current job description took shape, the new role made its way through the position review committee (to solidify a title and equitable compensation), and after three months my promotion to museum SEI program specialist was finalized and announced to staff.
>
> Being a facilitator in our all-staff dialogues from the program's inception, I saw holistically what our values were as an institution and how we do and don't

> relay that to the public. What does care look like in practice, for both staff and for our visitors? While my role is to keep us on track, meeting the goals set forth in the antiracist action plan, we are all also holding each other accountable because we've built the systems to do so.

As SEI program specialist, Kajette develops and maintains a structure to reach goals in the action plan and to ensure that the museum is collecting the data needed to measure its progress. Kajette acts as an accountability partner to staff by supporting, coordinating, and tracking RISD's social equity and inclusion work. Before her role was created, no one staff member or department was specifically responsible for overseeing SEI work at the museum, although RISD, catalyzed by student activism, created a Center for Social Equity and Inclusion in 2017 that works mostly with students and faculty.[6] Kajette meets monthly with staff at the center for SEI to align initiatives across the larger institution.

Another key document currently informing Kajette's work is our museum's report from our participation in the Museum Assessment Plan (MAP)'s Community and Audience Engagement Assessment track in 2020–2021. In the report, MAP is defined as "a national, voluntary program which helps museums strengthen operations, plan for the future and meet standards through self-study and a consultative site visit from an expert peer reviewer."[7] Our peer reviewer conducted cross-departmental internal interviews, questionnaires, and surveys to investigate and provide recommendations toward our goals to reach different communities and audiences and address barriers to participation. One of the primary suggestions, for example, was to create a communication platform to present our revised policies resulting from our antiracist action plan.

In coordination with the museum's interim director, Sarah Ganz Blythe, and based on the needs identified in MAP and the antiracist action plan, Kajette created twelve task forces that she supports. Kajette generates task force meeting agendas and keeps groups focused on action items and timelines for meeting goals and ensures that different task forces' work is aligned but not redundant. She first presented the task forces during a full-staff meeting, explaining that some staff members would be assigned to task forces based on their roles or areas of experience. Kajette also encouraged others to volunteer and requested that supervisors support participation in this critical work. The terms of commitment are flexible: staff can join any task force and communicate with Kajette if they choose to leave or switch task forces. Brief descriptions of each task force are listed as follows:

- Accessibility: Share internally about current in-progress physical and digital accessibility improvements, such as our wayfinding signage, website, and databases.

- Administration: Create a "policies and key information" hub that is accessible to staff from across departments. Create an antiracist resources handbook.
- All-staff dialogue: Continue to hold at least three all-staff dialogue sessions per year, led by rotating teams of staff facilitators.
- Americas research initiative: Continue work to research and repatriate American Indian funerary objects, sacred objects, and objects of cultural patrimony. Share evolving land acknowledgment.
- Collections management: Update collection management policy through an antiracist lens. Conduct an initial audit and improve systems to track the identities of makers for works exhibited, cared for, and taught from.
- Communication–Deaccessioning: Deaccession with a clear, antiracist strategy. Use funds from future deaccessioning to ethically acquire and care for works by BIPOC makers.
- Communication–Web/Media: Use our web and media outlets to communicate out our antiracist work.
- Community partnerships: Identify and tend to internal and external relationships with community stakeholders.
- Museum board of governors: Establish and implement a plan to develop the RISD museum's board of governors and fine arts committee to equitably and inclusively reflect our communities.
- Sustainability/Climate emergency: Research our carbon footprint, create resources, best practices, and policies for sustainability and climate justice.
- Training and SEI development: Provide regular internal and external SEI training and education for staff, docents, on-call educators, and interns.
- Visitor experience: Prioritize visitor and user experience throughout the museum's physical and virtual spaces.

In response to MAP recommendations around improving communication about our work, task forces share their progress at monthly full-staff meetings. Task forces will submit progress reports three times per year with regular board sessions and the museum will continue improving how we keep the public informed about our SEI and antiracist work via our website and other digital platforms. Task forces clarify who is responsible for work and open a path for staff who have historically been excluded from decision-making to share their ideas. According to Kris Samuelson, museum preparator and collection care specialist:

> My [SEI] work [used to be] more about being out in the community or in discussions, but not really as focused with my peers at the museum. It was more outside work. . . . [Now,] if I have any great ideas, I feel more invited and able to share them because of the task forces and [share-outs at] full-staff meetings.[8]

MAKING OUR WORK VISIBLE

From all-staff dialogues to Black Lives Matter statements, antiracist action plans to new staffing structures and reporting measures, we, at the RISD Museum, continue to grow in antiracist practice. Several months into her new role, Kajette offers insights into the impact of these shifts on staff and workplace culture.

Kajette's Reflection

On a whole, I've seen staff become more active in exhibiting passion for what is just and equitable and more apt at seeing how antiracism directly impacts their day-to-day work and decision-making. Our entire staff stewards this work together.

> As an accountability partner with all departments of the museum, I'm experiencing the challenges of managing the goals of each task force and the implementation of our antiracist action plan. It's difficult juggling several simultaneous projects, but our entire staff is deeply invested in the practice of antiracism and accomplishing our goals. We understand that the future of our institution and the museum field depends on us making changes toward equity, reparation, and inclusivity. I've made a point to ground myself in why these efforts are important. I've also built support across campus to ensure I'm not working alone, but in alignment with RISD's institution-wide SEI initiatives. I expect ebbs and flows in momentum, but there are constant signs of progress at meetings, in revised policies, in how we report our work, and in the operationalization of SEI initiatives across RISD demonstrating that buy-in is strong.
>
> I've had to clearly articulate my new job responsibilities and continuously clarify my role to avoid being tokenized. I have created and redefined some personal and professional boundaries to honor the emotional toll these changes bring and to avoid burnout. I try to remain hopeful and confident that the RISD Museum will grow into the vibrant, responsive, welcoming place we are well on our way to becoming. I am grateful to be a part of this shift at this place and at this time.

We are learning more about the strong connection between transparency and accountability and how critical they are for the process of becoming that Kajette describes. We have found that waiting until the work is done to tell others about it does not create true accountability—too often that approach hides failures and makes successes seem self-congratulatory. For example, in 2018, protesters demanded the RISD Museum return a Benin bronze sculpture, a head of an Oba, to Nigeria in solidarity with affected communities' calls for restitution and decolonization. Following the protests, we invited the group's organizers to a conversation with all RISD Museum staff to share that for more than a year, curators were conducting extensive provenance research with the goal of disowning and repatriating the work.[9] Had we opened up our internal work to the public sooner, there could have been a deeper understanding of the museum's existing commitment to the long, complicated, and sensitive work of repatriation. By publishing our antiracist action plans as they evolve, we hope to encourage the public to continue holding us accountable alongside our board members. We are becoming transparent in the ways we communicate this work.

Measuring progress in our antiracist work will mean changes to both our structure and our current measurement systems. The RISD Museum assesses our work by many different metrics—number of visitors, exhibitions, programs, objects in the collections, and qualitative measures, including exhibition reviews and staff performance reviews. Embedding antiracist goals into our work systems has given us new benchmarks against which to measure success. We are currently gathering demographic data from our board members and program partners in conjunction with a visitor experience survey. Evaluating these specific data points will help us learn if we are representing the needs of our community and shape how we can then measure steps toward fundamental changes to serve all our constituents better.

If our institution is a length of cloth, it certainly has edges frayed by white supremacy, stained by colonial history, and sloppy patches of prejudice that any conservator would frown at. RISD Museum staff are driven to continue weaving and mending the cloth in new ways. We will continue collaborating, incorporating different materials, and trying new techniques. We hope our process inspires you, too.

NOTES

1. Benedict et al., "Confronting Ourselves Together: All-Staff Dialogues at the RISD Museum."
2. Kiku Langford McDonald, Zoom interview with authors, March 26, 2021.
3. RISD Museum, "RISD Museum's Anti-Racist Work."
4. Gina Borromeo, Zoom interview with authors, March 31, 2021.
5. Sarah Ganz Blythe, Zoom interview with authors, March 29, 2021.
6. "RISD's SEI Action Plan, Rhode Island School of Design," accessed September 13, 2021, http://sei.risd.edu.
7. American Alliance of Museums, "Museum Assessment Program: About MAP."
8. Kris Samuelson, Zoom interview with authors, March 30, 2021.
9. Raicovich, "One Museum's Complicated Attempt to Repatriate a 'Benin Bronze.'"

Part IV

STAFF LEARNING AND TRAINING

Chapter Twelve

Elements of Friendship

An Approach to Internal Community Building

Ashanti Davis, Mel Harper, and Marissa Volpe

When you think of friendship, what words come to mind? We think of warmth, laughter, and joy, as well as feeling seen, heard, and safe. Now think of your workplace. What words best describe the culture there? Do you notice any overlap or disconnect between the two?

Within institutions where we devote 35 percent or more of our waking hours,[1] it can be difficult to bring our authentic selves to work—especially for marginalized groups in historically white institutions. We may fear microaggressions, discrimination, or being stereotyped or excluded. We may feel pressure to assimilate into white-dominant culture to be accepted and promoted. These fears could lead employees to hide their authentic selves, keep their heads down, and simply do the work and then go home.

Working on diversity, equity, accessibility, and inclusion (DEAI) initiatives encourages us to question dehumanizing models of productivity and transactional relationships and instead see the humanity in our colleagues. For those of us working toward DEAI in museums, the professional *is* personal. We can't ensure that staff's unique identities and cultures are honored in the workplace without getting to know each other personally as individuals.

To accomplish this, we propose a radical reimagining of museum work culture toward a space of acceptance and authenticity, where staff can feel seen and heard in an authentic way and know that they are *among friends*. We offer the elements of friendship as a framework for fostering belonging and inclusion at any institution.

We authors work at three different museums with different focuses—science, visual art, and history. When we began collaborating on this chapter, we compared our practices and looked for commonalities that unite our work. It became clear that all three of us incorporate elements of friendship into our internal community building. Ashanti Davis coinstigated the people and culture group at the Fleet Science Center in 2018 as a space for all interested members of the organization to share, discuss, and cocreate positive change in support of the organization's mission. Since 2017, Mel Harper has co-led the National Gallery of Art's Inclusion Roundtable, a self-selecting group of staff who gather informally to unpack issues of DEAI affecting the museum field. Marissa Volpe has led History Colorado's DEAI work since she joined the museum in 2018. When the protests in support of Black lives and against police brutality occurred in the summer of 2020 after the murder of George Floyd, she and a group of staff across departments came together to build on the statement History Colorado put forth regarding antiracism, and they continued to meet monthly to put antiracist values into practice.

Across each institution, we incorporate three elements of friendship—trust, truth telling, and time—in our internal community-building. We believe this "elements of friendship" framework can help guide community-building work at any museum—or any collaboration for that matter. Indeed, this framework proved to be integral in our collaborative approach to coauthoring this chapter.

ELEMENTS OF FRIENDSHIP: ESTABLISHING TRUST

What is trust and how do we begin to establish it between people who are vocal about championing change in an organization? Trust is a foundation for the friendships and the relationships that exist both inside and outside of our organizations. Merriam Webster defines trust as "assured reliance on the character, ability, strength, or truth of someone or something or one in which confidence is placed."[2] Take a moment to reflect on colleagues in your organization with whom you place confidence. What stands out about them? How do you work with them? What do you know about them that has assured you of their character, ability, or strength? What have you been able to achieve professionally or personally with them? Now take a moment and think about the people outside of your organization whom you really trust. Who are they to you? What relationship do you have? Do you consider them a friend? Trust is a foundation for our working relationships and friendships, but what would it mean for trust to also be a foundation for our collective change work?

Although it may seem more purposeful to jump into the planning and shifting of organizational cultures, it is necessary to take a step back and begin to develop trust among the group of individuals with whom you will be collaborating on DEAI initiatives. We may have worked in our organizations for many years, but that does not necessarily mean that we have a sense of trust with our colleagues. At the Fleet Science Center, our people and culture group began building trust with simple activities that allowed us to gain insight and a better understanding of one another. For example, we participated in a game called "Would You Rather,"[3] which involves asking participants to select one of two choices, such as "Would you rather eat broccoli or carrots?" or "Would you rather watch *Star Trek* or *Star Wars*?" These questions seem basic and trivial, but when used with intention, they allow us to discover common and divergent interests among colleagues. Starting with questions about pop culture preferences and food can lead to deeper conversations about what we are grateful for, how we express gratitude, where we gain inspiration, and even how we manage conflict or stress. These questions allow us to build trust by better understanding our coworkers and their values and applying empathy on a regular basis. Most importantly, these conversations create spaces of psychological safety, which are necessary when having challenging conversations about white supremacy culture, equity, systems of oppression, and how we as cultural institutions must change.

Case Study: Establishing Trust at the National Gallery of Art

Mel Harper

In 2019, staff at the National Gallery of Art were preparing for a temporary installation of Richard Mosse's immersive video work *Incoming*. For *Incoming*, Mosse photographed events along two major pathways into Europe using a thermal radiation surveillance camera that obscured individuals' identities. Education staff in particular were hungry for professional development sessions to learn more about international migration and wondered how best to serve visitors who had been impacted by it, especially K–12 students. We realized that migration, the movement of people from one place to another, is ingrained in the human experience. Many National Gallery employees have personal stories of migration or are close to people who do. How can we ever hope to serve audiences impacted by migration without acknowledging the first- and second-generation immigrant experiences and other cultural connections within our own staff? However, before we could even begin to approach conversations so core to our personal identities, we had to build a foundation of trust.

To begin to build trust, the National Gallery of Art's Inclusion Roundtable invited staff to a gathering to start to unpack the topic of migration together in community. The roundtable is a self-selecting group of staff who gather informally once a month to discuss issues of DEAI affecting the museum field. My fellow education colleague Rachel Trinkley and I organize the group, which began in 2017 within the education department. Since its founding, the roundtable has expanded to welcome staff from all divisions of the museum, including curators, conservators, security officers, librarians, lawyers, and more.

Our gatherings often include first-timers as well as returning participants, so we incorporate trust building and group norms into the planning of the agenda. Each gathering focuses on a different emergent topic that is suggested by participants or in response to urgent issues going on within the museum or out in the world. Group norms (sometimes referred to as community agreements) are a list of ground rules that guide the way we interact with each other during discussions. The list of roundtable norms is short and includes reminders like, "Do not freeze people in time"—a commitment to honoring each other's capacity to grow and change over time.

Gatherings incorporate interactive experiences to support participants in the intellectual, social, emotional, and physical nature of DEAI work as well as reduce hierarchies—all in attendance can collectively engage in the experience. On site, this might look like drawing activities, stretching or mindfulness exercises, or thoughtful icebreakers. At Zoom gatherings during the COVID-19 pandemic, participants can contribute to a communal whiteboard in response to a prompt or add words and phrases that resonate with them during discussions in the Zoom chat. Activities like these make participants' thinking visible in a virtual environment and highlight areas of connection, which is a step toward building or strengthening trust.

During the roundtable gathering that focused on migration, we invited participants to share about their family history via story circles, a methodology created by artist and activist John O'Neale.[4] Often understood as reflecting indigenous traditions,[5] story circles structure community dialogue by empowering each participant to share their voice if they desire. Cultural worker and organizational development practitioner Jessica Solomon adapted a model for using story circles in virtual meetings.[6] Solomon recommends creating a graphic with participants' names arranged in a circle to guide the order of sharing. For our in-person session leading up to the opening of Mosse's *Incoming*, roundtable participants organized themselves into groups of six to eight, seated in a circle. One by one, participants had the opportunity to share the story of their own family's arrival to the United States, as best they understand it. Each person took turns sharing in the order of where they were seated around the circle, and anyone could pass if they did not want to share.

When introducing the concept of story circles, we emphasized the importance of actively listening and giving each story one's full attention rather than planning your own story in your head.

After a round of story circles, roundtable participants were struck by the atmosphere of trust fostered within each small group, how much more connected they felt to colleagues, and how supported and affirmed they felt as they shared the story of their family. The increased trust among the group had a positive impact on program planning discussions: staff were more inclined to assume good intent from colleagues as they discussed the complicated issues surrounding global migration and felt more confident that their own contributions would be heard and appreciated.

As a self-selecting, drop-in group, the composition of the roundtable is ever-changing, but by intentionally providing opportunities to build bonds each time we gather, we holistically strengthen trust among all staff, one personal connection at a time.

ELEMENTS OF FRIENDSHIP: TRUTH TELLING

> Truth is an everlasting conversation about things that matter in a spirit of discipline and compassion.[7]
>
> —Parker Palmer, PhD

The concept of friendship may conjure up notions of warm-heartedness and understanding, but another critical aspect is accountability. As institutions wrestle with how to move beyond transactional relationships toward those that are generative and healing-oriented, truth telling, shared vision, action, and responsibility are vital when building and nurturing inclusive workplace communities.

Friends who courageously speak the truth to one another often have flourishing relationships oriented toward growth. Herein lies the opportunity for museum professionals to offer insights and invitations to our colleagues as we work toward inclusion and belonging. But what does truth telling look like in a professional setting? And furthermore, how do we model truth telling at both the institutional and interpersonal levels?

Case Study: Truth Telling in History Colorado's Antiracism Group

Marissa Volpe

History Colorado is a state-run network of nine historical properties and museums. In addition, we house the State Historical Fund, the largest grant-making organization for historical preservation in the nation along with the Office of Archaeology and Historic Preservation. Institutional racism and inequities are pervasive in historical societies, and our institution is no exception. The histories that institutions choose to remember, preserve, and share have reinforced dominant narratives that have persisted to this day.

After Floyd's murder in the summer 2020, a group of staff came together to advocate for institutional accountability and concrete actions. Stemming from this work, the group developed History Colorado's grounding virtues, which serve as the north star to guide all antiracism work at the institution. These guiding virtues have been approved by board leadership, incorporated into all employee and volunteer applications, and will be incorporated into staff performance evaluations as a means for continued conversations around antiracism at History Colorado.

The small group that led the work shared a vision for a better institution. We had trust in each other and our leadership and believed that we could build a different kind of institution together. We followed an open process model in which a small working group designed and facilitated monthly meetings and provided all staff access to planning documents, shared Google drives, and opportunities for feedback. In doing so, we were able to offer all staff a year's worth of reflection, capacity building, and truth telling at the institutional level.

In working together as a staff community, we realized that to flex our truth-telling muscles in a way that was generative and life-giving, we needed fruitful ways to talk to one another. We needed a common language that would help us come back to our common vision if we began to stray.

The first of three offerings that helped us on our journey was the development of a words matter guide, cocreated across departments and shared with all paid and unpaid (volunteer) workforce members. This language guide is formed and revised through an ongoing conversation about how our words create an inclusive workplace environment. The guide also includes helpful suggestions for offering feedback.

Second, we've created intentional spaces to pause and reflect. We've introduced and practiced the concept of "calling in" and "calling out." In our understanding, calling in aims to preserve relationships and sees the long view in accompaniment work over time. Calling out, however, aims to address immediate harm and make prompt repairs.

And lastly, we've begun to unpack and understand the principles of nonviolent communication, which focuses on identifying and meeting unmet needs in relationships. By practicing naming needs that are not met and requesting alternatives, colleagues begin to interrupt pervasive systems of oppression and dominance. We began to learn this process with the help of an outside facilitator who accompanied small groups of History Colorado staff interested in increasing interpersonal skills. We were able to see how nonviolent communication was modeled in real life and to practice this process in partnership with designated "empathy buddies." In the end, we formed stronger connections with the techniques of nonviolent communication and offered staff a means to enter into growth-oriented, albeit challenging, relationships.[8]

For History Colorado, our antiracism journey has been neither easy nor smooth and we recognize that this is an ongoing process of learning and unlearning. For History Colorado staff, friendship and truth telling has meant directing institutional accountability and action through an open process for all staff to examine their personal and departmental commitments to antiracism. Additionally, it has meant looking inward toward interpersonal exchanges. At the core of this work is a dedication to growth and concrete, accountable work actions.

ELEMENTS OF FRIENDSHIP: SPENDING TIME ON COLLECTIVE CARE

After meeting and building a foundation of trust with a friend, a friendship deepens and matures as you care for each other over time. Spending time together is one of the most treasured aspects of friendship. Spending time with friends brings joy and laughter and creates lasting memories.

Time is considered at a premium within most workplaces, including museums. We rush from deadline to deadline, squeezing in "getting to know you" ice breakers at the beginning of some meetings, anxious to move on to what we consider the *real work*. Time is money. That is what the trap of capitalism tells us. Corporate models of productivity[9] and white-dominant culture[10] weaponize a sense of urgency to maximize profits at the expense of the staff experience. If we continue to follow these models, we will never move cultural institutions toward our DEAI goals.

The only way to do DEAI work well is by slowing down, making space for staff to engage in collective care consistently over time, and creating opportunities for colleagues to show up for and support each other during impactful moments. When a big life event or transition happens in a friend's life, you show up. Because you care for your friends, you take the time to care for them. Over time, this demonstration of care has the cumulative effect of deepening and strengthening relationships and creating solid networks of community support.

By prioritizing community care consistently over time, whether in virtual meetings or in person, we create networks of support that will endure throughout and beyond the pandemic or any other significant event affecting the museum.

Case Study: Time for Collective Care in the Fleet Science Center's People and Culture Group

Ashanti Davis

Like most museum employees across the country, the staff at the Fleet Science Center transitioned to working from home in March 2020 and then endured more than a year of crises impacting health, the economy, and society as a whole. We encountered the challenges presented by a new way of working, whether we worked at home alone or navigated sharing space with roommates, partners, or children. We may have experienced the loss of loved ones due to COVID-19 or the pain of not being able to attend funerals, offer hugs, or be hugged in return. We may have experienced xenophobia due to the hate speech and actions directed at Asian communities or watched news that replayed over and over the murder of Black people and other people of color by civilians and police officers. Some of us may have experienced all of these challenges and others were less impacted, but we were all still expected to maintain some form of work productivity. With the convergence of these crises, there was a clear need to come together to be seen and heard.

The people and culture team at the Fleet Science Center, which had started two years prior to the pandemic, shifted priorities to make the space and time for staff to feel seen and be heard. We set aside time in our monthly group conversations to check in with folks, encourage vulnerability, and invite anyone to share beyond stating the obligatory, "I'm okay." At first, there were moments of awkward silence, but these meetings soon became vulnerable spaces of connection where staff shared the pain of losing a family member or friend or described feelings of exhaustion and fear.

We were able to build on existing levels of trust and create a psychologically safe space to welcome personal truths that are often uncomfortable to express out loud. By safeguarding time to express and share in our humanity, we enacted a crucial element of friendship: spending time on community care. We also demonstrated that the institution should not maintain the same expectations of work productivity while significant events are happening in our communities or country. In January 2021, when white supremacists attempted a siege of the US Capitol, staff began messaging one another in real time on the all-staff Teams channel expressing their concerns. By midday, these conversations had prompted the creation of a virtual convening for staff to express the real thoughts and feelings that were interfering with work productivity.

This moment and the moments that led up to this acknowledgment of our humanity shed light on the importance of not maintaining the status quo for the sake of productivity.

CONCLUSION

One lesson learned during the COVID-19 pandemic is that the lines between staffs' personal and professional lives are tenuous at best, and none of us can predict when an event will cause the lines to blur. In response to the racial reckoning of 2020, many institutions have doubled down on the existing tendency to "corporatize" DEAI, such as "one-and-done" antibias trainings and jargon-filled press releases. But to make a true, holistic shift toward approaching museum work with equity and empathy, we must move beyond checking boxes and waiting for experts to fix us from the outside. We must look internally and change ourselves, thereby transforming our museums.

Embracing the elements of friendship can help museums shift to becoming people-centered institutions. This isn't nepotism or favoritism; it is an acknowledgment that there is no way to do this work well without developing authentic relationships.

At the National Gallery of Art, staff have acknowledged the positive impact of getting to know each other in an authentic way. When collaborating on exhibition and program planning work, it is much easier to assume good intent from colleagues and to respect each other's diverse areas of expertise when there's already a foundation of trust and more knowledge of each other's personalities. Various project teams have noted the difference in ease of working with staff who have the shared understandings gained from participation in the roundtable group versus those who have not. Several colleagues have expressed a strong desire to expand the group and open up the experience to as many people as possible to increase mutual understanding and trust within the staff.

History Colorado's small inclusion impact groups of twelve to fifteen staff across departments provided a space of trust, intimacy, and shared purpose, which then formed the foundation of the institution-wide antiracism work that started in 2020 and continues today. As new colleagues join the institution, especially during virtual working conditions, dedicated staff continue to prioritize creating spaces for colleagues to be seen, heard, and connected and to feel a sense of belonging.

At the Fleet Science Center, the elements of friendship have begun to ripple into staff conversations about an organizational culture that we aspire to create. Building on the work of people and culture as well as staff-centered inclusion and engagement data, we have begun to conceptualize an aspirational culture that will require us to first create spaces for staff to build trust, share truths, and take time to strengthen our community.

Our experience of coming together from different types of institutions to coauthor this chapter demonstrates the widespread efficacy of the elements of friendship as a framework for DEAI work. While cowriting this chapter, we navigated the elements of friendship to share our experiences, stories, and personal backgrounds across three different time zones to formulate this approach to building internal communities at any museum. We hope that these elements of friendship can move your organization forward. Build trust. Tell the truth. Take time.

NOTES

1. Thompson, "What Percentage of Your Life Will You Spend at Work?"
2. *Merriam-Webster*, "Trust."
3. Cultural Competence Learning Institute, "Would You Rather?"
4. Junebug Productions, "Story Circle."
5. US Department of Arts and Culture, "People's State of the Union."
6. Solomon was trained in Story Circles in the tradition of John O'Neale via Alternate ROOTS, a southern artist collective for social justice. Art in Praxis (@artinpraxis), "Facilitator Tips for Virtual Meetings 1: Turn that Grid into a Circle."
7. Palmer, *The Courage to Teach.*
8. Rosenberg, *Nonviolent Communication: A Language of Life.*
9. Garton and Mankins, "The Pandemic Is Widening a Corporate Productivity Gap."
10. National Museum of African American History and Culture, "Whiteness."

Chapter Thirteen

Embracing Our Complexities in Arts Spaces

Implicit Bias Training and Trauma-Informed Approaches

Sue Bell Yank and Theresa Sotto

Arts and cultural organizations that support social justice movements too often broadcast their support for equity and inclusion externally, especially through social media,[1] without asking their own staff how best to create an equitable and inclusive internal culture. Meanwhile, arts workers who are at the forefront of pushing for equity and inclusion in their institutions are faced with the emotionally laborious challenge of promoting change internally while communicating with a range of publics who may or may not be aligned with the same goals. An essential component in the fight for racial justice is to acknowledge how collective histories and systemic power imbalances impact staff and may inform how staff interact with various publics. Staff and community training in antiracism, trauma-informed approaches, and implicit bias can be a key part of improving accountability and justifying a culture shift within institutions.

In this chapter, Sue Bell Yank formerly of 18th Street Arts Center in Santa Monica, California, and Theresa Sotto, formerly at the Hammer Museum in Los Angeles, California, discuss their experiences with trauma-informed and implicit bias trainings within their organizations. Though trauma-informed training is more prevalent in the health-care field (often referred to as trauma-informed care), and implicit bias training is just starting to gain popularity in cultural institutions, they are both important steps in preparing art workers to do the difficult, daily labor of cultivating a more antiracist society. These trainings encourage us to embrace the complexities of each human experience and acknowledge the collective histories and systemic power imbalances that may inform how staff and publics interact. This foundational knowledge and empathic understanding is necessary for racial justice.

These two types of trainings fit together in supportive ways, and can be combined with antiracism, conflict resolution, and restorative justice training as well. As white culture workers reflect on the biases within the United States that have also shaped their own personal perspectives, they may encounter hard truths about themselves and how they operate in the world that are complicit with a white supremacist, ageist, patriarchal, ableist, and heteronormative society. BIPOC culture workers may discover some of this same complicity or be confronted with reliving the instances of racism and bias that they have experienced. This can be profoundly traumatic, and a trauma-informed approach gives us the tools for self-compassion, empathy, boundaries, and facilitation to help us navigate this journey together and in support of one another.

Ultimately, building this common understanding together while embracing our deeply personal contexts will help give us the collective agency to act in contradiction to our system, and create a culture of understanding, empathy, dialogue, and justice.

CULTURE WORK WITH A TRAUMA-INFORMED LENS

Sue Bell Yank

As 18th Street Arts Center, an artist residency and community center with a mission to support artists at all stages of their careers, first embarked on our Culture Mapping 90404 cultural asset mapping project in 2015, we didn't know what we would uncover about our local neighborhood. Culture Mapping 90404 is a community-led cultural asset map and collection of oral histories designed to serve as a platform and memory-keeper of "cultural treasures" deemed important by our local community.[2] We were motivated to embark on a cultural asset mapping process to build institutional memory around stories, community partnerships, and relationships formed over our more than thirty-year history. As we dug deeper, we learned about the traumatic displacements of the working-class Pico neighborhood with the building of the 10 Freeway that affected three thousand largely Black and brown residents. We learned of "ghost sites" (a category of local assets we began using in our map), treasured local businesses, corner stores, parks, and theaters that had succumbed to eminent domain, displacement, and gentrification. We spoke with residents who had difficulty buying homes because of racially restrictive covenants, and who had promised their Japanese American neighbors that they would watch their valuables as they were shipped off to internment camps. As we centered voices that had been traditionally decentered in Santa Monica, we learned of the deep collective traumas that still affected the neighborhood and its political empowerment today.

This map has proved to be fertile ground for artists, and the culture mapping process has given birth to several deep and ongoing partnerships with local community organizations, a neighborhood advisory council, and new educational programs. Yet this work often triggers personal and collective traumas that leave our participants and partners vulnerable. We realized that as a staff, we often lacked the capacity or training to address the individual and collective traumas our artists or publics may be bringing with them and are triggered as they participate in our programs.

To understand the kinds of trauma that our 18th Street Arts Center communities might be facing, I found the pair of ACEs "tree" developed by the Building Community Resilience (BCR) initiative directed by Dr. Wendy Ellis of George Washington University to be particularly helpful, and have continued to use it as a contextual framework in my practice as an educator and facilitator. The first ACE stands for adverse childhood experiences that have long-term health and behavioral impacts, such as food insecurity, housing instability or a mother grappling with depression. These personal or familial traumas are represented by the leaves on the tree in figure 13.1. However, we must also acknowledge the societal soil in which these traumas take root, which leads to the second ACE, adverse community environments. As Ellis writes, "The tree is planted in poor soil that is steeped in systemic inequities robbing it of nutrients necessary to support a thriving community. Adverse community environments such as a lack of affordable and safe housing, community violence, systemic discrimination, and limited access to social and economic mobility compound one another creating a negative cycle of ever worsening soil."[3] These collective traumas are endemic to our society and may be experienced by those who never had an adverse childhood experience, simply because of their race, class, gender identity, sexuality, or neighborhood environment growing up. The traumas inflicted on residents of our local Pico neighborhood and reflected in our culture map may be indicative of broader social traumas. Part of addressing systemic inequity holistically is to acknowledge its impact on our communities, and to be proactive in providing safe and equitable environments without participating in retraumatization.

Without resources or tools, we can easily contribute to trauma without recognizing what we are doing. Although we can't fully understand the depth of what each person is grappling with, we can support our staff with the capacity to acknowledge traumas and design situations that prevent retraumatization. It is necessary for racial justice and equity to provide tools to embrace the

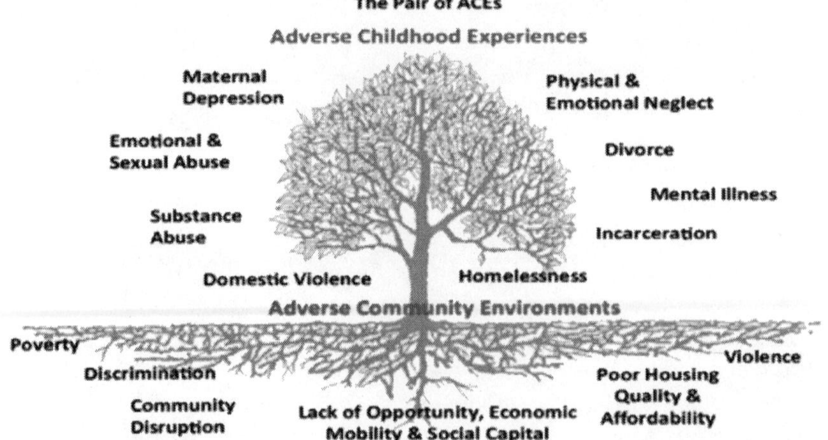

Ellis, W., Dietz, W. (2017) A New Framework for Addressing Adverse Childhood and Community Experiences: The Building Community Resilience (BCR) Model. Academic Pediatrics. 17 (2017) pp. S86-S93. DOI information: 10.1016/j.acap.2016.12.011

Figure 13.1. The Pair of ACEs "tree" developed by the Building Community Resilience (BCR) initiative directed by Dr. Wendy Ellis of George Washington University is a tool to understand community trauma. The first ACE stands for Adverse Childhood Experiences that have long-term health and behavioral impacts, and the second ACE—Adverse Community Environments—represents the societal soil in which these traumas can take root. Ellis, W., Dietz, W. (2017), "A New Framework for Addressing Adverse Childhood and Community Experiences: The Building Community Resilience (BCR) Model." *Academic Pediatrics*. 17 (2017) pp. S86-S93.

complexity of each community member, each visitor, each artist; to question essentializing stereotypes and our own judgments, to empower communities we work with in their own self-determination, and to meet the challenges of an unjust system proactively.

Six Guiding Principles for a Trauma-Informed Approach

As an organization moves toward becoming trauma-informed in their approach, the leaders and staff must be willing to shift power dynamics both internally and externally to support the needs of our communities and the staff responding to these needs. Trauma can manifest in many ways—not only through the adverse childhood experiences or adverse community environments (the pair of ACEs) but also through vicarious or secondary trauma (i.e., a profound shift in worldview after prolonged exposure to traumatic materials or the traumas of others) and compassion fatigue (i.e., becoming desensitized to the traumas of others). As we open our cultural organizations to a more trauma-informed approach for our stakeholders, we must recognize the traumas our staff will also be confronted with, and provide them with the support they need to achieve well-being and self-compassion[4] in both work and life.

The good news is, you can recalibrate an organization and train staff to become trauma-informed without everyone needing to become a therapist. For example, at 18th Street Art Center, we send out an agenda in advance of our community meetings to help our time together feel safe and predictable. We take time to discuss how we agree to communicate with one another at the start of more participatory programs, creating a safe space for folks to open up and share. We call out if someone is making others feel unsafe and take time to return to the agreements we created together. Figure 13.2 is a resource from Echo,[5] an organization that provides trauma and resilience training for families that illustrates some of the strategies organizations might employ. These techniques are founded on a few basic principles I'll describe. Each organization will need to work through what this means for their organization and that reflective process is often the catalyst for more systems-wide change.

How to Support Someone
Who Has Experienced Trauma
Predictability
Everyone loves surprises! Not. Trauma survivors often prefer predictability because that feels safer.
Attribution
Don't refer to the person's 'upbringing, problem, issues, behavior.' Call it for what it is - trauma.
Space
Allow time for the survivor to calm down and take perspective. Trauma survivors often have difficulty regulating emotions and take longer to calm down.
Perspective
Be aware when 'past is intruding into present.' Don't take responsibility for what is not yours... gently.
Reciprocity
Give what you also need to receive: listening, empathy, and empowerment.
Support
Be kind, loving, patient... but empathetically set limits - you have needs too!
Recalibration
Rid 'over-reacting', 'over-sensitive', or 'over'-anything from your vocabulary.
Choice
It can be a big trigger when a survivor is denied choice and control. Confer, collaborate, and cooperate.
©2018 Echo
echo

Figure 13.2. A resource from Echo, an organization that provides trauma and resilience training for families (https://www.echotraining.org/), that illustrates some of the strategies organizations might employ to provide a trauma-informed environment.

Power Over/Power With

The first overarching task is to examine the power dynamics at work within the institution, which translates to the staff's relationships with everyone external to the institution. Two power paradigms particularly predictive of an ineffective or effective trauma-informed approach are the Power Over and Power With dynamics. Originally defined by Mary Parker Follett, a pioneer of feminist organizing theory, Power Over (or coercive power) reflects a more traditional mode of transactional power, in which a person or organization in a position of authority is exercising control over others based in coercion or fear, followed by the dispensation of rewards or punishment. When working with artists, the contracts and agreements we make (paying or not paying, demanding certain intellectual property rights) can be coercive in some cases. When we work with communities, using their stories, plights, or traumas for artistic or audience development purposes without mutually beneficial outcomes, can be a way we leverage our power inequitably.

Power With (or coactive power) involves the sharing of responsibilities and rewards within a power structure, in which the leadership values and facilitates cooperative relationships throughout the organization toward accomplishing intrinsic goals that everyone buys into. In arts organizations, this might look like cross-departmental teams that innovate new ways to create accessibility in public programs; advisory councils working with curators to identify relevant cultural content; long-term community partnerships that accomplish shared goals; or training museum guards in visitor engagement and educational techniques. A Power With structure necessitates that leaders support their teams in achieving their goals and facilitate a decision-making process that holds everyone (including the leaders) accountable. This can be a lengthy process of education, training, and support that may sometimes feel like "giving up" or differently distributing institutional power—not always an easy prospect.

Once a cultural organization is attuned to practicing a coactive Power With structure internally, the foundation is laid for beginning to practice the six guiding principles for a trauma-informed approach. For 18th Street Arts Center, this meant instituting a neighborhood advisory council that would determine the direction and focus of aspects of our programming; cocreating a restorative justice process to handle conflicts within our community of artists; and putting in place both core values[6] and a process to hold us accountable to them. These six principles were originally intended to increase emergency responder awareness of the impact that trauma can have in the communities where they work, but they have implications for any organization working with diverse publics.

- *Safety:* Throughout the organization, staff and the people they serve feel physically and psychologically safe.

- *Trustworthiness/transparency:* Organizational operations and decisions are conducted with transparency and the goal of building and maintaining trust among staff and the publics they serve.
- *Peer support and mutual self-help:* These methods are considered integral to the organization and are key vehicles for building trust, establishing safety, and empowerment.
- *Collaboration and mutuality:* There is recognition that healing happens in relationships and in the meaningful sharing of power and decision-making. The organization recognizes that everyone has a role to play in a trauma-informed approach.
- *Empowerment, voice, and choice:* The organization aims to strengthen the staff and visitors' experience of choice and recognizes that every person's experience is unique and requires an individualized approach. This builds on what visitors, staff, and local communities have to offer, rather than responding to perceived deficits.
- *Acknowledging cultural, historical, and gender issues:* The organization actively moves past cultural stereotypes and biases, offers culturally responsive services, leverages the healing value of traditional cultural connections, and recognizes and addresses historical trauma.[7]

For most cultural organizations to truly adopt a trauma-informed approach inside and out is challenging. The power dynamics of cultural institutions have historically been notoriously opaque, with those in power making decisions about what is culturally important to society and replicating an unapproachable veneer of elitism. When our organizations share power with local communities, empower their visitors, and collaborate, it is often within the siloes of education or visitor engagement departments rather than emanating from throughout the institution. Shifting the paradigm requires a strong commitment from the institution's leadership. By inviting more voices, we may hear criticisms that we really don't want to acknowledge. Some staff or donors in positions of authority may feel that they are losing power, influence, and legacy. The payoff, however, can be transformative: a trauma-informed cultural institution that is strongly trusted and supported by its visitors, a place of safety and transparency and empowerment.

MITIGATING IMPLICIT BIAS AT THE HAMMER MUSEUM

Theresa Sotto

Trainings focused on raising awareness of implicit biases, similar to trauma-informed approaches, are intended to cultivate a safe environment and acknowledge cultural, historical, and gender inequities. Implicit bias trainings can help raise awareness of how systemic inequities influence individual behaviors, equip staff with tools to be more effective in confronting bias, and ultimately create a safer environment for both staff and the public. At the Hammer Museum, I had been facilitating trainings on implicit bias for staff for several years, and the trainings increased in frequency after a regrettable incident demonstrated the urgency of this work.

In 2017, a group of BIPOC teens and young adults visited the Hammer Museum for an educator-led tour. Following the tour, the group had time to explore the galleries on their own but they chose not to and instead lingered in the courtyard until it was time for their bus to depart. That evening, the organizer of the trip emailed the museum to express dismay about the group's experience. She stated that the group received excessive security scrutiny and felt so uncomfortable that they did not continue exploring the museum after the tour was over. I was horrified that this group had such a painful experience. I contacted the organizer to see if the group would be willing to share their experiences in person over lunch at a local restaurant of their choice, paid for by the Hammer. I wanted to apologize on behalf of the museum and learn from their feedback. During lunch, the group articulated specific instances when they felt they were being intensely watched and described being told not to touch the artwork in a stern tone, whereas other visitors who were standing closer to paintings were not reprimanded. One student directly stated, "I felt discriminated."

Sadly this is a scenario that is all too common in museums. Staff who work with the public, especially those whose jobs require them to enforce rules, often need to act quickly to prevent injury or damage to artworks or property. Unfortunately, the decision to act isn't always grounded in behaviors and may be rooted in bias. Regardless of any egalitarian values we may hold, the forces of systemic racism take root at an early age[8] and, over time, influence our attitudes and actions, often without our conscious awareness.

Following the lunch with the group, Hammer staff in our internal cross-departmental diversity and inclusion group (DIG) (see chapter 5) discussed how we could foster a climate in which all visitors feel welcome and safe. In my role overseeing educational programs at the Hammer Museum, I had already led implicit bias trainings for educators in my department. With the support of museum leadership and DIG, I began leading trainings for all staff in the visitor experience and gallery operations departments.

Although many existing implicit bias trainings are rooted primarily in scientific research, the training I developed stemmed from fifteen years of gallery teaching practice. While sharing subjective insights about art, sometimes individual biases come through—whether intentionally or not. I grew to realize the potential for museum objects as powerful vehicles for purposefully increasing bias awareness. I developed a series of activities, three of which I detail here, that are designed to increase awareness of our own biases and privileges, which sociologists say is the first step in mitigating bias.

Activity 1: Privilege Inventory

Privilege inventories offer a generative way of understanding how our backgrounds and identities shape how free we are to move through the world without being subject to bias. In my trainings, I use a privilege inventory designed for the context of the museum space[9] and include questions such as: Do you see your race or gender represented in this gallery? Do you think your race or gender is respectfully represented? Were you able to take the stairs to the gallery? Are the gallery labels written in the dominant language spoken in your home?

I preface this activity by stating that participants do not need to share their responses to the inventory, nor should they feel like they need to definitively choose "yes" or "no" for questions that elicit a more nuanced response. In this way, the inventory serves as a vehicle for individual reflection rather than an exercise in public shaming.[10] Moreover, the questions are not solely designed to increase awareness of an individual's privileges; they also point to examples of institutional bias. After participants complete the inventory and tally up their "privilege score," individuals often reflect on ways that the museum has been exclusionary and consider how they might use their privilege to be better allies for others.

Activity 2: Associating Words and Images

The inherent quality of art to evoke a range of personal associations offers an opportunity for viewers to reflect on how these associations were shaped by their lived experience. When we consider a work of art beautiful, for example, where does that notion of beauty come from—is it rooted in biases about stereotypical gender roles, cultural norms, or the media? For this activity, I share a selection of words that have the potential to be associated with dominant groups or stereotypical norms, such as *valuable* or *powerful*. For each word, participants select a work of art that they most associate with the word. I ask the group to make selections quickly, increasing the likelihood that the decision is rooted in unconscious bias. Without fail, more than one individual will select the same work of art for two opposing words or two different works are selected for the same word. For example, individuals have selected Rodney McMillian's *Chairs and Books* (2004)[11] for the words *valuable*, *safe*, or *poor*, depending on which associations are strongest for each person. McMillian's work consists of two found armchairs that are worn and missing seat cushions and that flank a stack of dozens of books. Do individuals more strongly associate books with value or safety as opposed to, for example, an image of an affluent home? Did they grow up in homes with chairs that are in pristine condition and therefore associated this image with the word *poor*? These differences provide fertile ground for reflections on how various identity categories, such as race, gender, ethnicity, education, and class, have shaped personal associations and may bias how we interpret what we see.

Activity 3: Manage Bias with CARE

When faced with an insensitive or downright racist comment, I offer a framework designed to handle the situation productively: CARE, an acronym that stands for Clarify, Assess, Recontextualize, and Elevate (see table 13.1).[12] The CARE framework allows museum staff working with the public to balance professionalism and safety concerns while also taking the opportunity to provide contextual information that aims to expand an individual's biased perspective. For example, if a museum visitor states that they're looking for "real art, such as the European paintings" we may aim to counter their understanding of what defines "real art" by expanding their definition with non-European examples.

Throughout all of the aforementioned activities, I intersperse reflective discussions about how these activities relate to museum jobs, ideally referring to specific scenarios that have happened in the museum.

Embedding Implicit Bias Trainings across the Institution and Beyond

Over time, due to word of mouth, I began leading this training for coworkers across departments in addition to frontline staff as well as for several other arts institutions. I believe that one reason for its effectiveness is the use of works of art as sites for both self-reflection and for developing a deeper understanding of colleagues' backgrounds so that we can be better allies for one another. As art museum professionals, we take pleasure in engaging with works of art. This comfort level and feeling of enjoyment lays the foundation for a more open-minded discussion and productive self-reflection than if everyone were being lectured about social science research about bias. Aspects of this training have been effective with external audiences as well, especially

Table 13.1. Managing Bias with CARE

Use this framework to address biased, insensitive, or racist comments and steer difficult conversations into productive learning opportunities.

1. CLARIFY	What makes you say that? If I understand you correctly, your assumption is . . . What I'm hearing you say is . . .
2. ASSESS	Reflection questions: • How am I feeling in this moment? Am I in a frame of mind to have a productive conversation? • How are others reacting? • Am I in a safe environment to respond? Questions to ask out loud: • Can someone share another opinion? • How do others feel?
3. RECONTEXTUALIZE	Experts have said that . . . Others in this group have shared different opinions . . . According to [select from the following list] . . . • the artist(s) • the curator(s) • several news sources • studies on this topic In this museum, we use the term . . . I think we can all agree that . . .
4. ELEVATE	Thank you for listening to my perspective. I'm really glad we had this discussion. I'm thankful that we can be honest and open-minded with one another.

Activity 2, which I have incorporated in collaborations with the UCLA David Geffen School of Medicine in an effort to reduce bias in the medical field.[13]

Findings from post-training surveys have demonstrated that most participants' awareness of their implicit biases increased. For example, following a session for psychiatry residents, nine out of eleven survey respondents strongly agreed or agreed with the statement, "I increased my awareness of my implicit biases"; and following a training for museum frontline staff, 87.5 percent of the survey respondents indicated that the training increased awareness of their implicit biases. Such findings point to the promise of works of art in providing a vehicle for raising awareness of our own biases across a range of internal and external audiences. Of course, one training on implicit bias will not eradicate a lifetime of categories reinforced by the media, pop culture, and our own institutions; however, raising awareness is the first step in the right direction.

CONCLUSION: UNLOCKING THE POTENTIAL FOR SWEEPING CHANGE

For both implicit bias trainings and trauma-informed approaches, it is important to note that we are swimming upstream against deeply rooted systemic inequities, biases, and behaviors imprinted into us from our culture, upbringing, and lived experiences. It can be a long and difficult process to disentangle ourselves from how we are used to acting, and even more challenging for staff operating within a hierarchical structure to be vulnerable or speak hard truths. When you are unraveling systems, you sometimes catalyze chain reactions that either lead to systemic change, or willful deflection. During these trainings, we may start hearing things that we don't necessarily want to hear. It is of utmost importance to create a safe space for these discussions to occur and to recognize that the process will, at times, be uncomfortable. We also need to be willing to put our money where our mouth is; real systemic cultural change will not happen when there are resource pressures and incentives to maintain the status quo (i.e., it will be too expensive, it will take too much time, or this is not part of my job). The process may be lengthy, and the learnings will constantly need to be refreshed. Through it all, leadership must both support staff through the changes that may be catalyzed, and emphasize the importance of this work together.

If complete executive-level approval is not realistic from the inception of these trainings, we recommend starting the conversations with like-minded, cross-departmental colleagues, verbalizing the positive benefits of staff trainings, and continually looking for opportunities to gain support across leadership positions. Grassroots efforts can have a ripple effect as more and more colleagues become convinced of the impact of this work on workplace culture and audience satisfaction. Ideally, however, the leadership of your cultural organization would be deeply invested in change and willing to listen to truths that may not reflect well on how the organization has been operating thus far. The payoff of this investment can be transformative: greater staff investment in the organization, an impact on overall health and wellness, greater community cohesion, and the increased loyalty of visitors and patrons. Trainings that focus on trauma-informed approaches and implicit bias are just one piece of the puzzle toward a truly antiracist, equitable, and just organizational culture; but they help lay the foundation for sweeping change.

NOTES

1. Artforum, "'We Can Do Better,' Claim US Museums Criticized for Hollow Signs of BLM Solidarity."

2. 18th Street Arts Center, "Culture Mapping 90404."

3. Moving Healthcare Upstream, "When a Picture Tells the Story: The Pair of ACEs Tree."

4. Self-compassion is related to self-care. Whereas self-care comprises the strategies one might employ to cope with stress and achieve a sense of well-being, self-compassion is the acceptance and kindness you show to yourself through times of failure or difficulty.

5. Visit ECHO at https://www.echotraining.org/.

6. 18th Street Arts Center, "Core Values."

7. These definitions are adapted from the Centers for Disease Control and Prevention's Office of Public Health Preparedness and Response (OPHPR), in collaboration with Substance Abuse and Mental Health Services Administration's (SAMHSA) National Center for Trauma-Informed Care (NCTIC). See Trauma Informed Oregon, "Guiding Principles of Trauma-Informed Care," for more information.

8. Four-year-old children exhibit racial bias, according to Perszyk, Lei, Bodenhausen, Richeson, and Waxman, "Bias at the Intersection of Race and Gender: Evidence from Preschool-Aged Children," 1–2.

9. Many thanks to Weiwen Balter, a Hammer Student Educator from 2015 to 2019, for collaborating on this inventory.

10. In contrast, an exercise called a "privilege walk" begins with everyone standing in a line and individuals step forward for every form of privilege stated aloud. Those with the least privilege are left behind and, therefore, may experience feelings of shame and defensiveness. See Ehrenhalt, "Beyond the Privilege Walk."

11. See "Rodney McMillian, *Chairs and Books*" in *UCLA Artists in the Hammer Museum Collections.* https://hammer.ucla.edu/collections/ucla-artists-in-the-hammer-museum-collections/art/chairs-and-books.

12. This framework was inspired by and adapted from "Facilitating Difficult Conversations" worksheets created by the Museum of Tolerance and the Los Angeles County Museum of Art, 2017.

13. Castillo, Scott, and Sotto. "Building Community and Structural Competency through Art: An Art Museum and Psychiatry Partnership."

Chapter Fourteen

Sustaining Antiracism Education in Museums

Advice from Antiracism Facilitators

Marit Dewhurst and Keonna Hendrick

In summer 2020, calls for assistance in navigating workplace conversations about race, racism, and antiracism surged. As people stepped bravely out of pandemic city shutdowns to protest the murders of Ahmaud Arbery, Breonna Taylor, George Floyd, and countless others, many colleagues within museums and cultural organizations began to break the silence around racism to imagine institutional changes toward antiracism. In the year that followed, many museums began some of their first official forays into exploring antiracism,[1] often led by external facilitators who guide museum professionals through discussions and activities on reducing racial harm within museum practices.[2] According to our own experiences and other facilitators in the field, these sessions at times receive positive anecdotal reviews from participants; however, there can be significant resistance to ongoing institutional change driven by antiracism. We have worked with a number of colleagues across institutions and have learned that the process of instituting antiracism in all aspects of museum operations is ongoing work that requires leadership to set antiracism as an institutional priority, which is then supported by departments and individual staff members across the organization. If institution-wide adoption of antiracism is the goal, then the implementation of leadership pledges must extend beyond the scope of work of any individual, including diversity officers and executive directors, into collective action by staff and board. Antiracism education is, at its heart, the work of building community, affirming our interdependence, and committing to a practice of equitable distribution of power.

Reflecting on our experiences as diversity and inclusion facilitators in the field, this chapter highlights common pedagogical approaches, potential pitfalls, and specific strategies for nurturing antiracist employee education in museums. In naming key approaches, challenges, and opportunities for antiracism education within museums, this chapter also offers museum professionals with guidance for how they may initiate antiracism education for staff and to nurture museum spaces as sites where equity, inclusion, and access inform all aspects of institutional operations.

OUR ROOTS AND PERSPECTIVES

In 2014, as community activists protested the murder of Michael Brown, many museum workers began to challenge the notion of institutional neutrality and more openly question how #museumsrespondtoferguson.[3] We began offering a series of workshops for New York City–based museum educators to encourage people to consider how their racial identities[4] informed their professional work in museums. Since those early discussions, we have worked with a diversity of cultural organizations across the United States to facilitate workshops about cultural equity, antiracist teaching, and inclusive practices in the arts. As both a Black American woman and a white American woman, we have experienced the work of facilitating antiracism workshops within museums differently, and yet, we have learned much about the persistent and pervasive nature of racism in our field. We have also seen real possibilities for both individual transformation and institutional change.

From the outset of our work together, we have always approached teaching about equity and inclusion through the lens of community building. Originally trained as youth workers and cultural workers, we center our workshops on the belief that we must work collectively to dismantle racism. Our approach focuses on building and nurturing community—a lens that shapes the advice we share in this chapter.

NURTURING ANTIRACISM WITHIN INSTITUTIONS

When working with museum leaders and arts administrators, we often find that many people are eager for a checklist of actions to implement and avoid to dismantle racism within their work and institutions. Sole reliance on prescriptive lists for antiracist practices runs counter to building depth of knowledge of inclusivity and responsiveness to inequities in disparate contexts. Instead of transactional models that fail to challenge learners to interrogate racism, transformative approaches to antiracism education provide opportunities for all stakeholders to think critically and benefit from extended practice to talk and work across differences without avoiding controversial topics. Education on racial equity serves as an empathetic act. In our workshops we aim to give space to all stakeholders and community members to discuss often ignored equity concerns to encourage increased inclusion of racially minoritized individuals and audiences.

At the same time, we recognize that many people—especially white people in the United States who are not taught to think about race and racism—are eager for clear guideposts to steer their work. In this chapter, we have organized our reflections around four key actions required of any museum interested in engaging in antiracism and cultural equity work: *clarifying* the need for antiracism education within the museum; *initiating* antiracism education with a foundation of enthusiasm, trust, and collectivity; *supporting* antiracism work once it has begun; and *sustaining* equity and antiracism as core values and embedded practices within our institutions.

Clarifying the Need for Antiracist Education: Recognizing Positionality and Purpose

We have been heartened by the surge in interest in diversity, equity, accessibility, and inclusion (DEAI) initiatives broadly, especially within museums;[5] and yet we have often seen that without careful consideration about the shape of this interest, many antiracism initiatives can derail quickly. We urge museum leaders to take the time to clarify the specific needs for antiracism education within their institutions and communities. Transformative learning requires deep individual and collective critical reflection on how our racial identities shape our experiences. Without a consideration of their own internalized consciousness, museum leaders will be ill-equipped to effectively shepherd antiracism education. Many diversity and equity facilitators will require this reflection as part of their initial proposal process; therefore, we suggest that museum leaders consider the following ideas to clarify their intentions.

Reflect on biases and assumptions: Knowing our own biases and perspectives about race, racism, and our racial identities is integral if we are to invite diverse—and sometimes conflicting—experiences and opinions to the table. As Melissa Crum and Keonna Hendrick suggest, we must unearth and analyze our individual racial identity stories to better understand how racism has shaped who we are and who we believe ourselves to be in relation to each other.[6] This work must be habitual; we must spend regular time reflecting both individually and collectively using informal (social conversations, shared experiences with works of art, etc.) and formal (question prompts, guided activities, etc.) reflection strategies about how racism informs our views of ourselves, our professional lives, and our relationships with each other. Without this necessary understanding of how pervasive ideas about white supremacy have limited our views of ourselves and each other, we are more likely to fall into patterns of harm as we learn to talk across our differences.

Identify your power and points of leverage: Anyone who has critically reflected on their identity and has facilitation skills[7] can begin a conversation; however, those conversations will take starkly different forms based on the position and agency of those leading the way. Museum leaders must recognize what positional power, decision-making capacities, and access to levers of institutional power they have to determine the best strategy for building collective action. For those in positions of power, we encourage leaders to seek opportunities to listen to colleagues with less agency to clarify the needs of DEAI education (see box 14.1). For those with less positional power, we advise colleagues to reflect on their experiences of inequity in the museum and to document and share those experiences to further underscore the need for institutional change.

BOX 14.1. CLARIFYING DEAI PURPOSE: QUESTIONS TO ASK YOURSELF

- Has my racial identity enhanced or limited my power in the museum?
- How do I define *racism*? Does the museum have a shared definition?
- How does racism manifest, if at all, in the museum? What examples have I witnessed, experienced, or perpetuated?
- How does racism impact my colleagues? My supervisors? Myself?
- How does racism impact the audiences we serve?
- What biases do I hold that influence my comfort in addressing these issues? How might my biases impact my approach to communicating concerns to others?
- What agency or sphere of influence do I have in this organization?
- How might I introduce DEAI concerns to colleagues who can support me in developing a strategy for informing leadership? What are the risks and benefits of calling attention to these issues?

Initiating Equity Education

Whether prompted by a governing strategic plan, a manager's vision, a committee or task force's recommendations, or an outside group's challenge to act, the initiation of any move toward antiracism within long-standing institutions can be jarring for museum professionals. Reticence to change is often tied to fear, which can come in many flavors, including questions and concerns about mission alignment, job stability, institutional relevance, limited finances, public missteps, and the possibility of causing harm. These fears and many others will be ever present throughout any institutional change. To mitigate their effect on antiracism work, museum leaders can seek opportunities to cultivate collective action and invite colleagues into reimagining their work in light of equity.

Relate equity and inclusion to the museum's mission and values: DEAI education must be tied to the museum's mission to uplift it as a core element of the institution's work, rather than a passing add-on. Ideally, museum leadership teams can articulate how DEAI education is a key component of the vision for the future of the museum and communicate how inclusion and equity are tied to the success of the museum community.

Connect to shared motivations: Many of us come to work in museums for similar reasons: we believe that cultural organizations are vital community assets, we care about engaging with public audiences, or we have had powerful experiences with art, science, history, and culture. We are fascinated by the many stories we can learn about ourselves, each other, and the world. Although people within museums might work on different elements of the collection, conservation, interpretation, and exhibition, developing shared motivations can help lay a foundation for the challenging work of moving toward equity and inclusion. We relate these reflections to the ultimate goal of creating spaces where all visitors and colleagues have the freedom to access and engage with museums in ways that are significant to them. In doing so, equity work can be viewed as a way to fortify their own shared motivations, rather than as an add-on to our work.

Build buy-in: All too often we have witnessed excited museum leaders rush hopefully into initiating DEAI work without building the necessary systems of support. Due to the challenging and occasionally destabilizing nature of conversations about race and racism, it is imperative that museum leaders build consensus about the need for DEAI among museum staff. This work cannot rest solely on the shoulders of one or a few individuals; if it does, then it no longer seeks to be transformational but risks being transactional and dictative. Shifting institutional culture requires buy-in and staff investment on many levels including intentionality in messaging, coalition-building, and timing. Museum leaders who are sensitive to the existing culture of their organization may, for example, consider framing DEAI work as opportunities to learn within a community of colleagues, rather than implement diversity trainings, which are often considered didactic or guilt-inducing. When framing workshops as community building, we emphasize the importance of collective action toward antiracism and the value of full staff participation in shaping institutional culture. This framing signals that the institution is prepared to have brave conversations about its history, current practices, and policies, and seeks strategies for addressing challenges and promoting institutional (and individual) accountability.

Start where people are: Any DEAI education work must begin with the specific context and culture of the museum as it is in this moment in time. This means understanding the unique dimensions of race and racism embedded within the people, the museum's history, and the surrounding community. Although some museum leaders will want to immediately begin with a deconstruction of white supremacy, this can be quite jarring and alienating for some museum staff, potentially resulting in fracturing among the staff. Questions such as those in box 14.2 can provide a starting point for individual reflection or small group conversations to analyze what ideas, knowledge, and awareness everyone may be bringing to the table. It is critical to note that the moment museum leaders begin posing such questions, there will likely be a range of responses, some of which may be surprising. All responses and reflections should be considered as valid and worthwhile; these responses should shape the form and focus of the DEAI education.

BOX 14.2. INITIATING DEAI EDUCATION: QUESTIONS TO ASK YOURSELF AND YOUR COLLEAGUES

- How does antiracism work relate to our mission?
- How does racism manifest in the museum (e.g., in collections policies, exhibition practices, education or public programming, audience interactions)?
- What do I (we) value in terms of equity, inclusion and diversity? What do other colleagues value? Where do values intersect?
- What biases, assumptions, or presumptions are happening around DEAI work in the museum?
- What messages are being communicated about the need for DEAI education?
- What potential obstacles or resistance might arise as we introduce antiracism? How are we prepared to navigate these challenges?

Supporting Equity Transformation through Staff Education

After one workshop we had facilitated for a museum, a colleague poetically described the aftermath as akin to having someone come into your house and open all of the cabinets, rummage through them, and then leave them ajar for those at home to clean up. It was an apt description for how many museum professionals feel once the work of antiracism has begun. For some the experience is exhilarating, empowering, and affirming. Meanwhile, for others it can feel uncomfortable, destabilizing, and scary. Museum leaders must recognize that colleagues will experience the work of antiracism in different ways and be prepared to support colleagues as they move toward an ever-deeper commitment to antiracism and equity. In box 14.3 we share a set of questions that can be used informally or in more structured surveys throughout any DEAI education initiative.

BOX 14.3. SUPPORTING DEAI EDUCATION: QUESTIONS TO ASK YOURSELF AND YOUR COLLEAGUES

- How are we emphasizing the importance of nurturing a collective sense of community?
- What tender areas or sticky points are arising in our DEAI education? How can we provide extra support and time to address those?
- How are we reminding colleagues of the shared purpose of our work together?
- How are we encouraging a sense of joy and collegiality in our work together?
- How are we making transparent the ways in which each person has a specific sphere of influence within the institution and that those spheres are all connected?
- What tools for discussion can we use to practice antiracist forms of communication? How can we embed these tools into our daily policies, procedures, and protocols?

Emphasize community building and relationships: If antiracism workshops are effective, then they can transform how people understand the relationships between themselves, their colleagues, their sense of purpose, and their roles within the museum. As such, museum leaders should acknowledge these changes and seek opportunities to emphasize that all equity work is fundamentally about building community among collective actors working toward building antiracist institutions. Museum leaders can encourage colleagues to find the joy in their collective work perhaps through viewing, sharing, or making art, celebrating institutional milestones, eating meals together, or even engaging in non-museum social activities. Since antiracism work cannot be done alone, we must pay attention to nurturing the community connections that will enable us to enter into difficult conversations and transformations with greater trust in our relationships.

Identify spheres of influence: Museums are complicated ecosystems. It is quite common for a silo effect to create communication gaps between various departments; those who work in the store may never cross paths with those who work in conservation or curatorial offices. These gaps result in cloudy visions of who has power and agency, especially when it comes to DEAI work. Often we will hear from colleagues who believe that DEAI education has little to do with their daily work within the museum. To create more open opportunities for sharing and learning together, museum leaders can support staff in articulating the choice points or decision-making powers held by each person within the organization. As colleagues begin to understand and name their own spheres of influence and how they overlap with those of their colleagues, they will be better equipped to work toward collective DEAI action. The colleague in visitor services might realize that *how* they greet visitors is directly linked to visitors' sense of inclusion in the museum. Likewise, the colleague in procurement might see that they can set policies for bringing in more vendors from underrepresented communities. And a conservator might ensure that community members with cultural expertise contribute to conversations about how artworks and artifacts are collected and researched.

Use the tools: Few of us are taught how to have complex conversations about race, racism, and our own relationships to white supremacy, let alone in professional settings. Without practice having these conversations, many museum professionals worry about saying the wrong thing, harming colleagues or their own job security, alienating relationships, being silenced or misinterpreted, among many other anxieties. Creating and using set guidelines for communication can alleviate some of this fear and apprehension. Akin to Robert's Rules of Order or other meeting organization formats, discussion protocols can guide colleagues through challenging conversations to enable us to delve more deeply into the topics we too often ignore with colleagues. Most antiracism workshop facilitators will introduce guidelines for discussion or community agreements,[8] as well as other practical step-by-step discussion guides. Museum leaders can work with colleagues to adapt these guidelines for the particulars of their own institution and then embed them in regular meetings to make them a part of the museum's mode of communicating.

Sustaining Equity for the Future: Translating Education to Practice

Once your organization has started down the path toward equity and inclusion work, you cannot stop. Stopping equity education can be tremendously harmful because it communicates the idea that it does not require constant nurturing and investment. In many ways, to stop is to support the status quo. Although we close with this section, museum leaders must plan for the sustainability of DEAI education from the outset. We've included some questions in box 14.4 that can be used to guide planning for the future based on what emerges in DEAI education. It should go without saying that true sustainability will require museum leaders to embed DEAI education into common work protocols, exhibition timelines, orientation plans, and budget allocation processes. DEAI education takes time, money, and willingness to shift former ways of working; real change needs constant and consistent attention.

BOX 14.4. SUSTAINING DEAI EDUCATION: QUESTIONS TO ASK YOURSELF AND YOUR COLLEAGUES

- What were the goals of the staff education workshop? Were the goals achieved?
- What were some challenges to achieving the goals?
- How will teams adapt the content of the workshop to their practice?
- What accountability measures can you and your colleagues commit to implementing?
- What blind spots or challenges did you notice while implementing DEAI education?
- What questions did the process raise for you about how you and your colleagues navigate conversations about antiracism?
- What knowledge or skills are required to advance you and your colleagues beyond conversation to action? How will they be obtained?
- Where can you create feedback loops in your action plan that involve internal and external stakeholders?
- What long-term strategies might alleviate or prevent the patterns or examples of racism you identified in your institution?

Commit to shared principles: We encourage museum leaders to collaboratively identify shared values that can guide practical DEAI work throughout the institution. Values such as transparency, collaboration, or sharing power often emerge from DEAI education and can serve as starting points to discuss shared concepts. This focus on values can involve all stakeholders within the museum and enables museum staff to create a framework for action, rather than a to-do list.

Embed into daily work: Once a museum has a set of shared principles for ongoing DEAI work, the task is to bring those principles to life. Working in departmental teams, colleagues can spend time applying different values to their everyday tasks and job responsibilities. For example, a curatorial team might consider how to shift toward transparency in their acquisitions protocols. This can be a move toward equity in making clear any historical patterns of preference and clarifying goals for more racially equitable and accountable acquisition plans. Using shared principles as lenses through which to reimagine daily tasks can empower colleagues to see DEAI work as embedded in their job responsibilities, rather than an additional task to complete.

Gain feedback from staff throughout and after DEAI education: To further root DEAI approaches into the museum, communication is key. Museum leaders should consistently collect insights, critiques, and questions from all participants. This not only can build trust and a sense of inclusion but will also inform future opportunities for continuing professional development. One popular possibility is to conduct a DEAI audit,[9] which can allow all stakeholders to share experiences, insights, and feedback in a formalized manner for both documentation and ongoing analysis. A feedback loop will also communicate that DEAI work is an ongoing process, requiring constant iteration and refinement to meet the evolving needs of the museum as it grows.

Clarify accountability: Any effort to sustain DEAI education requires concerted accountability; it is far too easy to slip back into comfortable patterns of behavior that reinforce the status quo. Moving toward cultural and social equity and inclusion requires us to be on our toes and leaning into new and sometimes uncomfortable actions at all times. To this end, museum leaders can create systems of support to encourage ongoing commitment to DEAI learning and transformation in a range of formats. Accountability partners, regular agenda items devoted to DEAI, annual reviews, collective reading and action groups, and structures for sharing successes and pitfalls are all options to help hold each other to the challenging and empowering work of equity and inclusion.

CLOSING THOUGHTS

In the past year, we have been overwhelmed by a palpable hunger for change in museums. Although some fear this moment may pass, we have seen real shifts in how museum colleagues are initiating DEAI education within their institutions. We have talked with graphic designers who have developed marketing strategies that rely less on tokenizing images of visitors of color. We have witnessed docents sharing how they had subconsciously avoided showing artworks by artists of color and have since changed their entire strategy for teaching from their museum's collection. We have read revised orientation materials that explicitly support diverse gender expression in the workplace. And we have seen trustees put additional financial backing behind DEAI education initiatives. While it is rarely easy, we have also seen the joy that can come from colleagues learning how to have frank and compassionate conversations with each other and what happens to the depth of our collegial relationships when we really listen, affirm, and respond to each other's lived experiences. Although the task of learning about racial equity can be challenging, it can also help us deepen our relationships, strengthen our communities, and reimagine how we engage with our institutions. In other words, racial equity education offers a chance to instill a sense of purpose, joy, and collaboration in our professional lives as we seek to uplift more just and equitable museum experiences for ourselves and our audiences.

NOTES

1. In our workshops and throughout this chapter, we define antiracism as the active interrogation and dismantlement of racism, with the intention for equitable redistribution of power. An ongoing process that considers the economic, sociological, historical, and political frameworks enabling racism. This is based on our definition of racism as when a person or group *unconsciously* or *consciously* builds power or affirms the belief that one group and their cultural practices are superior to other racial identities.

2. See Finkel, "Meet the Experts Who Root Out Racism and Exclusion in the Arts," and Li, "American Museums Are Going Through an Identity Crisis."

3. In 2014, Aleia Brown and Adrienne Russell created the hashtag #museumsrespondtoferguson, setting conversations about the responsibility of US museums to engage with police brutality against Black and brown people and other contemporary racial equity issues. Colleagues such as Porchia Moore, Aleia Brown, Adrienne Russell, La Tanya S. Autry, Radiah Harper, Melissa Crum, Joni Acuff, Laura Evans, Cathleen Lewis, Therese Quinn, Monica S. Montgomery, Stephanie Cunningham, Elisabeth Callihan, Alyssa Greenberg, Chris Taylor, Mike Murawski, Omar Eaton-Martinez, and many others urged museums to consider how the legacies of racism and white supremacy continue to inform US museums.

4. In this chapter, we focus on our racial identities as an entry point to discussing the interconnected nature of all the layers of our social identities. Our racial identities are not separate from other aspects of who we are.

5. We facilitate our workshops within the framework of antiracism, though there are many different frameworks for DEAI education (i.e., disability justice, feminist frameworks, etc.). We focus on antiracism here, though our work is often referred to more broadly as a part of "DEAI" education or professional development within museums. Because DEAI work typically requires similar approaches to initiation, support, and sustainability regardless of the guiding framework or focus, we use DEAI and antiracism education interchangeably in this chapter.

6. Hendrick and Crum, "Multicultural Critical Reflective Practice and Contemporary Art," 271–98.

7. Although entire books, workshops, and degree programs are dedicated to developing facilitation skills, we prioritize some of the following skills and dispositions in our own work: extensive knowledge of the oppressive systems and the involvement of museums in them, problem-solving skills, understanding of museum operations, ability to connect theoretical frameworks with practical applications, active listening, willingness to be vulnerable, trust in the process, community-building, capacity to connect multiple ideas together, patience, compassion, humility, humor, joy, and a deep belief in everyone's capacity to grow and change.

8. There are many resources for these online. We often include some of the following: Remember that learning is a process; acknowledge that we are all growing. Call people in. Create space for all to participate as they are able. Lean into discomfort; it's where learning happens. Focus on consequences, not just intentions. Confidentiality.

9. See Mass Action for resources: https://www.museumaction.org/resources.

Part V

ENGAGING GROUPS BEYOND STAFF

Chapter Fifteen

Redefining Consultation

The Burke Museum Native American Advisory Board

Rex Buck Jr., Polly Olsen,
Sumathi Raghavan, and Julie K. Stein

We dedicate this chapter to our co-author and esteemed Wanapum Elder, Rex Buck, Jr., whom we lost in February 2022. Rex's lived practice embodied the words, "One heart, one mind. Be patient, move forward." His teachings, leadership, and love for the community inspire us to continue his work.

In October 2019, the Burke Museum—the state museum of Washington—celebrated the grand opening of the "New Burke." This new building and museum represented more than a decade of work, a transformative project that enabled the Burke to carry its natural history and culture collections safely and sustainably into the future. In planning and development, we sought to make the collections—and the research, education, and programs they make possible—truly a resource for *all* the communities we serve, in accordance with the Burke's mission of caring for and sharing "natural and cultural collections so all people can learn, be inspired, generate knowledge, feel joy, and heal." Visitors to the new museum find a physical structure built on an inside-out model where the traditional back of the house, available only to those who knew to ask, is now the house, a place where all can observe and engage with the objects and people, and see the daily work that gives the Burke relevance and meaning. On any given day, visitors may encounter fragile Native American baskets being cleaned in the culture workroom, students rehousing archaeological fragments in the collections area, or researchers carefully removing rock from recently discovered fossils in the prep lab.

Coordinated by the museum's leadership in partnership with the Burke's Native American Advisory Board (NAAB) and tribal liaison, preparations for the opening of the new museum created space and opportunities for tribal consultation and input, resulting in the incorporation of ceremonies and protocols intended to ensure the people, objects, ancestors, and buildings were honored and protected during the transition to the new facility. These included fortifying cedar brushings for staff and volunteers; a pre-groundbreaking blessing of the project, conducted by tribal elders representing all four regions of Washington state; and a solemn send-off ceremony for ancestors returning to their homes after being cared for at the old Burke.

The week of the grand opening itself featured an Indigenous Preview Day during which we welcomed nearly eight hundred members of local tribes, religious ceremonies honoring diverse Native beliefs, and public performances and demonstrations by area carvers, weavers, dancers, and musicians. The ribbon used for the formal ribbon-cutting ceremony was woven by University of Washington (UW) students from the cedar that is so central to the Native tribes of this region. Guests for the ceremony included not only UW, state, and local officials but also the leaders of multiple tribal nations and an honor guard of Indigenous veterans representing diverse parts of Washington state and all of the various branches of military service.

The Indigenous perspectives found in the lead up to and throughout the grand opening festivities are the result of decades of efforts by the Burke to authentically engage with Native American communities and audiences. These efforts were built on the work of anthropologist Erna Gunther, director of the Burke from 1929 to 1967, and on the dedicated relationships cultivated by Bill Holm, curator emeritus of Northwest Coast Indian Art.[1]

This chapter will trace the more recent evolution of the Burke's relationship with the Pacific Northwest tribes, specifically examining the transformative effects of the introduction of the NAAB and tribal liaison. A concluding discussion of lessons learned through this process can offer broader guidance for other institutions hoping to engage in stronger, more authentic, reciprocal consultation with their communities—Native American and otherwise—with the creation of advisory boards and the dedication of staff to proactively connect and listen.

THE EARLY HISTORY OF THE NATIVE AMERICAN ADVISORY BOARD

The creation of the NAAB was unique for its time. Like many of its peers, the Burke was founded on and has been sustained over the years by a colonial mindset that favored curatorial, academic expertise over community-centered knowledge. As recently as the 1980s, community members' involvement in the life of the museum was limited to the roles of volunteers and docents, largely as a result of what was, as former curator of ethnology Jim Nason (Comanche) explains, the mistaken belief that they could not "usefully contribute to museum exhibition and educational projects."[2]

This state of affairs began to change in the late 1980s, during preparations for a well-funded, year-long celebration of the Washington state centennial. The Burke was selected to host the state's major exhibit on Native American peoples of Washington—*A Time of Gathering: Native Heritage in Washington State*—with a focus on the period from 1775 to 1989. A temporary nine-member Native advisory board was created by now-emeritus curator Robin Wright in mid-1987. This board assisted the Burke in the planning, object selection, and outreach process.

In 1993, a Native American advisory committee (NAAC) was reconstituted under the leadership of Jim Nason. Although the initial mandate was broad, the NAAC's efforts were focused primarily on repatriation, due to the 1990 federal enactment of the Native American Graves Protection and Repatriation Act (NAGPRA).[3] Although this work was vital to the tribes involved, the NAAC's role at the Burke remained largely responsive through these years, becoming more of an ad hoc group that was contacted when staff needed advice on specific projects or circumstances.

In 2006, the NAAC voted to rename itself the Native American Advisory Board (NAAB), a change intended to convey the fact that the group was an official, permanent part of Burke leadership. Nevertheless, elements of the NAAB's previous, less formalized nature remained. Interactions with the Burke lacked substantive consultation or collaboration and were largely limited to status updates on repatriation, education, and the activities of the Bill Holm Center, a highly regarded center for the study of Native arts of the Pacific Northwest established in 2003.

A significant shift in the NAAB's role at the Burke occurred in 2009, when planning for the New Burke began in earnest. As the design process got underway, museum leadership—motivated by the community and curatorial input—required the architectural firm to attend a NAAB meeting to share information with members, and to get their feedback on design ideas at this early stage. Features of the new Burke reflect the integration of the priorities and values of the architect, Tom Kundig, the NAAB, and the museum. These features include a Coast Salish-style shed roof[4] and an exterior composed of durable exterior Kebony siding that calls to mind forests across the Pacific Northwest and will, like cedar or fir, silver with age. Stairs once planned for the exterior were moved inside to create a more welcoming experience for elders.

In addition to consultation with the NAAB, the Burke's executive director and government relations staff also traveled to tribal communities around the state for advice and input on the inside-out concept, the artist studio, and other interpretive approaches. In the process, they identified an ongoing need for a staff member who would be responsible for managing the museum's government-to-government relations with its sovereign tribal partners, which would continue well beyond the opening of the new Burke.

This need would be taken up and carried forward in 2016, when the Burke's government relations manager was wrapping up her efforts to secure state funding for the new Burke and advocating to have her position evolve into that of a tribal liaison, held by a Native person. She found support for this proposal with curators, who had experienced the need firsthand while consulting with tribes about the new Burke exhibits. A comprehensive job description was written and presented to the NAAB for their suggestions. Funding for the role came in part from resources reallocated from the government relations position, the NAGPRA coordinator assigned to the Burke's archaeology department, and a contribution from UW. The establishment of a full-time position, paid for by the museum, represented a strategic and ethical commitment to ensuring that authentic tribal consultation remained central to the Burke going forward.

THE ARRIVAL OF THE TRIBAL LIAISON

In June 2017, Polly Olsen (Yakama) joined the Burke as its first-ever tribal liaison. An enrolled member of the Confederate Tribes of Yakama Nation, she brought fifteen years of valuable, diverse experiences working with leaders in government, university, and tribal settings. Before joining the Burke, Polly had served as an advisor to the UW's Intellectual House project, creating an "elder engagement model" that later was a key part of the new Burke blessing ceremony. The relationships she built with these elders, some of whom were NAAB members, supported a smooth transition onto the Burke team.

In her role as the museum's tribal liaison, Polly works with both internal and external constituencies:

Staff: Polly serves as a resource across the museum, providing information on tribal histories, treaties, sovereignty, self-governance, protocols, customs and traditions, natural resources, and cultural properties. She identifies and develops potential museum-tribe partnerships around research, exhibits, educational offerings, fundraising, and communications.

Native American Advisory Board: Polly coordinates the twenty-six-member advisory board's operations, planning and facilitating virtual and in-person meetings that accommodate travel distance, weather conditions, and other potential accessibility conflicts.[5]

THE NAAB AND THE TRIBAL LIAISON IN PARTNERSHIP

The tribal liaison's internal support strengthened the NAAB's capacity to guide the Burke in ways that in turn strengthened the museum and its relationship with the broader Native community. One notable shift was the expansion of NAAB members' areas of expertise to include cultural knowledge keepers, cultural heritage specialists, educators, museum professionals, natural resources professionals, and tribal leaders. NAAB members must be members of a Washington State, Oregon State, Idaho State, or federally recognized tribe or Alaska Native Corporation. Recommendations made by the executive director and tribal liaison (with input from curatorial staff) are presented to tribal leadership for review and approval before final appointment per NAAB approval. Each NAAB member may serve up to three 3-year terms.

In addition to expanding and formalizing NAAB membership, Polly led the NAAB through a review and refresh of the group's key documents—its mission statement[6] and statement of guiding principles—and later coordinated the formation of an executive committee, chaired by Rex Buck, Jr. (Wanapum), who has served on the NAAB since the late 1990s.

Polly's leadership has brought new cohesion to the NAAB, as the stronger connection to museum staff has increased awareness of opportunities for consultation and identified areas where the NAAB's voice and authority were needed. The NAAB's higher profile is evident in decision-making across the museum, in ways not seen before, as detailed as follows.

Organizationally: In 2017, when the museum began modifying its mission statement, NAAB members raised the possibility of adding healing and joy to our list of desired goals so that the mission would better reflect the museum's impact on community relationships. Their guidance was crucial in shaping the final mission: "The Burke Museum cares for and shares natural and cultural collections so all people can learn, be inspired, generate knowledge, feel joy, and heal." Similarly, when the Burke went through its most recent strategic planning process, the NAAB was a key participant. The NAAB and the museum's fundraising board, the Burke Museum Association, are now treated as coequal parts of the leadership structure; members now serve together on the search committee identifying candidates to succeed the museum's executive director when she retires in 2022.

Programmatically: The tribal liaison and the NAAB have worked to connect the community with the scientific work taking place at the Burke by expanding access and research opportunities within Indian Country, in particular for Native youth interested in STEM careers. The museum's education department consulted heavily with NAAB members as part of the recent revision of the onsite and offsite curriculum in alignment with the state's Since Time Immemorial standards.[7]

Institutionally: Working with the NAAB, the tribal liaison promotes communication and collaboration between the Burke and Washington state Indian tribes, particularly with an eye to creating reciprocal, two-way exchanges where tribes are informed about the Burke's work and the Burke understands tribes' priorities and opportunities.

As an example, the Burke's land acknowledgment reads: "The Burke Museum stands on the lands of the Coast Salish Peoples, whose ancestors resided here since time immemorial. Many Indigenous peoples thrive in this place—alive and strong." This powerful, deceptively simple expression represents nine months of careful consultation between the tribal liaison and area tribes. The early drafts were conceptualized as a welcome from tribes to museum visitors. As conversations proceeded, the NAAB members observed that this was not meant to be a statement from them, but rather a statement from the Burke to the visitor about our relationship with the tribes. The statement changed in voice and tone to represent this new perspective. The current statement represents the diverse Indigenous people of the region and better aligns with the Burke's role as the state museum.

REFLECTIONS ON AUTHENTIC COLLABORATION

In considering the Burke's history with the NAAB and the tribal liaison—the successes and failures, the moments of tension and moments of joy—a few key lessons stand out:

1. *Successful community collaboration means involving those communities early in the process while plans are still being made.* Examples of such collaborations include the well-received and meaningful ceremonies planned for the opening of the new Burke, as well as the new Burke itself, for which consultation with the tribes began at the stage of architectural, exhibit, and interpretational planning, resulting in a building, galleries, and programs that appropriately balance the priorities of the museum with those of Indigenous communities. The visitor-centered, inside-out interest in transparency and access to collections is tempered by Native concerns that not all information should be available to all visitors.

   When consultation doesn't take place early enough, there can be a rush to create the appearance of collaboration and that speed can create problems. For example, the new Burke outdoor spaces feature a camas meadow, which honors the traditional role this plant has played in Indigenous food and medicine in the region. The camas seedlings were grown in plastic tubes and cared for at a nursery until they were ready to be planted onsite. The NAAB was not involved in this process, but later was invited to celebrate a First Foods ceremony before the planting, during which Polly discovered that the fact that the plants had been grown through artificial methods was deeply painful to the tribal elders present and was considered a violation of religious beliefs. The lack of early consultation about the camas resulted in real damage to the Burke's relationship with the Native community, even while it was part of an effort to do the opposite.

The hiring of the tribal liaison was similarly not without complications: The new Burke project began in 2010, yet Polly was hired in 2017. This gave her only two years to create cultural practices and work with curators and community in exhibit consultation, as well as educate Burke staff and leadership about meaningful tribal inclusion, while accommodating the diversity of tribes, science, cultural specialists, museum professionals, and departments involved. Creating an unnecessary sense of urgency overlooks the crucial fact that undoing systemic inequities developed over decades or even centuries takes time and is not subject to a simple, quick fix.

To avoid similar outcomes in the future, the NAAB, the tribal liaison, and the Burke staff seek to ensure that consultations take place early in the development of museum collections, exhibits, events, and programs, so that community voices are considered integral parts of the planning effort and not, in the words of NAAB executive committee member Yellowash Washines (Yakama), "just cosmetic, not window dressing, [but] active participants, [part of] meaningful consultations."

2. *At institutions like the Burke, with long histories and entrenched power structures, creating a cultural shift requires patience and diligence.* Adding a tribal liaison requires significant advance work to get buy-in from existing staff beyond the theoretical notion of a "great idea." Although there was widespread agreement at the Burke that a tribal liaison was needed, there was not equal agreement about the parameters of that role, and because these conversations took place *after* the hire was made, the Burke experienced moments of discomfort—and sometimes, real conflict—as everyone adapted to new ways of doing things. In hindsight, several questions could have been raised internally, in parallel to the external process of hiring a tribal liaison:
   - As the tribal liaison and the NAAB become more involved in the life and processes of the institution, how can or do staff members partner with them? Does this involve letting go of existing tribal contacts? What happens if various staff get contradictory advice from various tribal contacts?

- What is the pathway for decision-making when the tribal liaison, NAAB, museum staff, and other leadership do not agree about a way forward?
- What are the specific boundaries of the tribal liaison's authority?
- How do Native individuals who are already on staff understand their relationship to the work of the tribal liaison?

As the Burke has sought to address some of these issues retroactively, we have employed several strategies. First, while the tribal liaison position was originally conceived of as reporting to the director of external affairs (communications/marketing), the role now reports directly to the executive director and attends directors' meetings. Secondly, we are shifting away from a model that elevates educators, curators, scientists, and researchers as experts above all others toward one that sets all knowledge holders side-by-side, to achieve the goal of equitable cocuration and co-ownership. Third, instead of disrupting or diverting existing relationships, we now emphasize transparency in all dealings with tribal advisors, artists, cultural specialists, and knowledge keepers.

3. *Trust above all.* For self-evident reasons, tribes historically do not trust institutions like the Burke, which have neglected their interests, acquired their treasures, and erased their cultures. Yet as Yellowash Washines (Yakama) notes, "there can be no healing without trust."

The Burke's current approaches to building trust rest on the foundation created by the centennial exhibit *A Time of Gathering*, and even more on the hard work that began with the 1990 federal enactment of NAGPRA. Together, the Burke and tribal members joined together in the difficult, often painful consultation needed to send ancestors and funerary objects back to their families of origin. Perhaps the best-known of these events is the story of The Ancient One (Kennewick Man),[8] who was discovered along the banks of the Columbia River in 1996 and transferred to the Burke in 1997, before eventually being returned home to the tribes.

The presence of a director-level tribal liaison who is herself Native also contributes significantly to trust between the museum and tribes. As a museum representative who is both willing to sit and listen patiently to expressions of the real hurt that the Burke has inflicted on Native people, but who—as a member of the Yakama Nation—has also experienced that cultural trauma, Polly can communicate each side's perspective in ways the other can understand. The museum hears the grief created by its historical treatment of Native communities, who in turn hear the Burke's sincere intention to do better, one aspect of which is the presence of the tribal liaison herself. The trust built in this manner paves the way for a new, healthier, more equitable relationship.

4. *One person can't do it alone.* It is not an *easy* job. We don't want the world to think you hire a tribal liaison and the relationships are going to be golden, easy, and some box you can check as diversity.

> The emotional labor and historic trauma is real.
>
> —*Polly Olsen*[9]

The addition of a tribal liaison to the staff marked a pivotal moment in the Burke's history with Native communities. As a sign of the Burke's commitment to healing its relationships with tribes, and as a real individual responsible for that work, the role of tribal liaison holds a great deal of promise, which in turn carries a great deal of pressure.

Those considering creating a tribal liaison position must recognize that the toll such deeply emotional and empathic work takes on a person in that role requires extra self-care, as well as deep understanding on the part of supervisors and peers in the museum. Serving as the point of connection between two large, complex organizations offers challenges because each has its own internal political intricacies and conflicts that must be understood and navigated. Balancing the colonial practices of museums and academic institutions with a multiplicity of Indigenous values and worldviews is not simple, especially when the tribal liaison herself has been shaped by both environments. And finally, because the tribal liaison assumes responsibility for the well-being of both the museum and the Native community, the stakes can feel higher and mistakes and missteps more painful.

Proper support of a tribal liaison—and relatedly, the NAAB—requires an investment of financial resources that allow for additional dedicated (and preferably Native) staff to reduce the burden placed on any one individual; equally important is the establishment of an environment offering cultural safety where space for mistakes, reflection, and reconciliation makes it possible to conduct sometimes difficult negotiations between museum and Native stakeholders.

CONCLUSION

In its 2018 publication, *Facing Change: Insights from the American Alliance of Museums' Diversity, Equity, Accessibility, and Inclusion Working Group,*[10] they articulate the need for "empowered, inclusive leadership" at all levels of an organization.

This chapter lays out one museum's approach to meeting this goal, tracing the evolution of the Burke's NAAB as it has become more integrated into museum leadership and more empowered to shape museum practice. Working with Native communities has offered numerous challenges, given the paternalistic, colonial lens through which museums have often viewed tribes and their culture. Moreover, the notion of "tribes" itself is complicated because this category is composed of a multiplicity of individual nations, with a variety of priorities and beliefs.

The Burke Museum's NAAB addresses these challenges by bringing together representatives from the region's many tribes as an advisory group. The inclusion of a tribal liaison, serving as a supported, director-level point of connection between the museum and the NAAB, has created the time and space for listening and consensus-building among members, dramatically enhancing the NAAB's ability to lead the Burke into a future defined by authentic consultation and respectful collaboration that benefits all. We hope that by sharing this story of the Burke's NAAB and tribal liaison and the successes we've experienced—and the hard lessons we've learned—we will help other museums in their own attempts to diversify their leadership structures in pursuit of the ultimate goal of creating a "culture of inclusion that radiates through the institution and into the community."[11]

In closing, we should note that by calling the events and outcomes detailed here a story, we want to convey that they are based on the lived experiences of a specific group of people, working at and with the Burke Museum over the past several decades. Their recollections, paired with the authors' perspectives, create one story of the NAAB, the tribal liaison, and the Burke Museum. There remain other stories to tell.

NOTES

1. Burke Museum, "Bill Holm."

2. James Nason, "A Brief History of the Burke Museum's Direct Engagement with Native American and Ethnic Communities," Document in Burke Museum Archives, 2021.

3. Burke Museum of Natural History and Culture, "Repatriation."

4. Burke Museum of Natural History and Culture, "Floors, Walls and a Shed-Style Roof."

5. During the COVID-19 pandemic, virtual NAAB meetings led to increased participation, as all members—with some technical education and support—had equal access to the gatherings.

6. The NAAB mission is as follows: The Native American Advisory Board (NAAB) guides, advises, and gives direction to the Burke Museum in the areas of

exhibits, collections, community outreach, repatriation, education, research, and collaborative relations with tribal and museum programs. The NAAB's key goal is to build authentic relationships with Washington State and Federally Recognized tribes, including First Nations Canada, Alaska villages, and Indigenous communities to respectfully collaborate and learn together, share knowledge, and create decolonizing practices that support the Burke's mission.

7. OSPI, "Since Time Immemorial: Tribal Sovereignty in Washington State."

8. Burke Museum of Natural History and Culture, "The Ancient One."

9. Polly Olsen (Yakama), Burke Museum tribal liaison, in discussion with the authors, April 2021.

10. American Alliance of Museums, "Facing Change: Insights from the American Alliance of Museums' Diversity, Equity, Accessibility, and Inclusion Working Group."

11. American Alliance of Museums, "Facing Change," 11.

Chapter Sixteen

Integrating Volunteers into Every Stage of a DEAI Initiative

Andrew Palamara and Caitlin Tracey-Miller

The docent could not figure out what was happening. At first he was patient, but he quickly grew confused. He looked around at everyone else in the group, and they seemed to be following along without any trouble. After a few minutes, he finally said under his breath, "I can't understand a word she's saying." He could not grasp why one of his fellow docents suddenly started talking in German. After about ten minutes, the docent who was speaking in German finally stopped speaking and said, "Andrew, is that enough?"

This feeling of confusion was one of the intended results from a workshop that a group of staff and docents organized at the Cincinnati Art Museum (CAM), which focused on increasing awareness of language barriers between English speakers and English-language learners. We do not usually lead training sessions that intentionally confuse the participants, but we took a unique approach for a series of workshops in the spring and summer of 2019. This series never would have happened without involvement from the museum's volunteers.

Volunteers at the CAM play an integral role in engaging with visitors and, therefore, have a wealth of knowledge about visitors' needs. However, prior to 2018, volunteers were rarely involved in the early stages of planning trainings and developing institutional resources. All too often, they were the recipients of the training sessions required for staff, sometimes weeks or months after staff have participated in them. Because employees are on site at the museum more often than volunteers, they have more frequent opportunities to engage in equity work; however, volunteers generally have more of a public presence than many staff. We found this inevitably created a divide between staff and volunteers, particularly when engaging with equity and antiracism work. Wanting to be responsive and recognize this tension, we decided to integrate our volunteers into the training process during the planning stages and invite them to play a more active role in shaping their own development as representatives of the museum.

In 2017, Andrew Palamara, CAM's associate director of docent learning, and Amy Burke, CAM's director of visitor experience, decided that diversity training with overly broad content was not meeting the needs of the museum's largest volunteer groups. At the CAM, those groups are the docent corps, the visitor service aides, and the gift shop associates. From observations, conversations with volunteers, and survey data, we found that past training sessions conveyed information without adequate consideration of volunteers' experiences and perspectives. It was becoming increasingly difficult to invite volunteers to training sessions designed for staff or to adapt trainings to reflect the scope of the volunteers' responsibilities. Also, the staff sessions sometimes lacked specific conversations about how CAM staff and volunteers, in their respective capacities, can work together to examine systemic inequities and create a more inclusive museum. This led to volunteers feeling defensive, as though the sessions were ostensibly accusing them of being racist, or left them feeling confused about how to put what they learned into practice. We needed a new approach.

FORMATION OF THE ADVISORY GROUP

CAM staff reflected on diversity, equity, accessibility, and inclusion (DEAI) in museums and needed to be honest about what we are and are not able to contribute to our own equity work. As a white, cisgender, able-bodied man, Andrew works to help others learn more about themselves and the world around them through art. He seeks to leverage his unearned privilege to foster inclusive dialogues around art that integrate historic and contemporary injustices while admitting this work requires him to practice humility and be mindful of making space for others and collaborating with them.

From the start, we acknowledged a few key principles for laying a new groundwork for DEAI training with our volunteers. First, staff volunteer managers had to play a more prominent role in determining the direction of future DEAI training sessions. We understood the mandates of the museum's strategic plan, specifically to be a public hub for discourse around contemporary issues, while also understanding more about volunteers' needs than other staff. We also needed to make our plan as specific to the scope of our volunteers' work as possible. Theoretical frameworks for DEAI were still useful, but we were compelled to make these training sessions more participatory between staff and the volunteers. In years past, volunteers asked for more practical applications, and we needed to be responsive to their feedback. Finally, we decided to involve a small group of our volunteers in the beginning stages of the planning process. Volunteers are experienced and observant, and they often have more institutional knowledge than the staff due to longer tenures at the museum. More importantly, volunteers are more likely to buy in to a training session or a resource guide if they have an active role in shaping the content.

In early 2018, we formed a volunteer advisory group to have a more collaborative approach to DEAI training with our volunteers. Our expectations were straightforward, so much so that we never gave the group an official name. We envisioned this as an avenue for a dedicated group of staff and volunteers to talk about DEAI work within our volunteer groups. Staff chose representatives from the docent corps, the visitor service aides, and the gift shop associates based on their availability, an interest in DEAI work, and an aptitude for collaborative work. The group consisted of two volunteer managers and three members each from the visitor service aides and the docent corps. We sought to create a diverse group, which included a male volunteer and a Latinx volunteer, but the group was predominantly made up of white women. We saw the value in our white volunteers taking on the labor of the project but knew that it demonstrated the shortcomings in the racial makeup of our volunteers. We also looked for volunteers who were not often asked to be a part of special projects or committees in the past.

We worked to make the process as democratic as possible by maintaining a consistently open dialogue with volunteer members and ensuring that everyone could weigh in before making final decisions. As a group, we came to a collective agreement on the length and frequency of our meetings and the scope of our plans to organize training sessions and develop resources in the coming year that would put DEAI at the center of our volunteers' work.

INCLUDING VOLUNTEERS IN RESEARCH AND EVALUATION

The CAM supports a visitor research department of 1.5 positions and incorporates research into projects across the museum's public-facing operations, including in the development and evaluation of exhibitions, programs, galleries, events, and overall experience. Research is woven throughout the project development process and the team uses a wide variety of methods, including front-end studies, observations, visitor experience intercepts (short surveys collected in-person at the conclusion of a visit), focus groups, and summative evaluations.

The museum frames all research initiatives under an institution-wide umbrella called *CAM Listens*. We provide various ways for people to share their thoughts with the museum, which includes conducting research at community events through iPad surveys, participatory feedback stations, or drawing activities. The team collects feedback from both nonvisitors and visitors through short surveys, social media requests, and in-depth listening sessions or focus groups. Visitor research is regularly incorporated into training for the visitor service aides (VSAides), and the research team and VSAides exist under the same institutional umbrella. Training for VSAides includes a focus on providing personalized facilitated experiences to visitors—listening to each visitor individually to discern their needs and feeling empowered to take extra steps. The research team regularly reports data to volunteers, including net promoter scores,[1] overall experience ratings, and comment trends. The museum acknowledges the core role and impact volunteers have in the experience a visitor has onsite. The volunteer advisory group and the staff representatives decided to incorporate research and evaluation into the formation of a robust action plan for the committee.

Learning more about volunteer comfort level and experiences at the outset was critical to recognizing volunteers' understanding of best practices around DEAI work and identifying opportunities for additional learning and support. It was essential that the voices of each of the three volunteer groups were heard, and we believed that we could reach all groups efficiently through an anonymous survey.

The goal of the survey tool was to learn where volunteers felt there were gaps in their training or experiences that could have been better. In the survey, we asked volunteers about their interactions with visitors and how they felt the museum might break down barriers to visitation or ensure a welcoming and fulfilling museum experience for all. Of the total cohort of 130 volunteers, 70 percent (91 volunteers) responded to the initial survey, including seventy-one docents.

The survey opened with the question: "Can you describe a visitor interaction at the Cincinnati Art Museum during which you wished you had more training or felt you might have said something that made a visitor uncomfortable?" Volunteers responded with a wide range of experiences, including times they did not have backgrounds in a particular artist or exhibition, were not able to answer visitor questions, were not aware of accommodations for a visitor with a disability, or made an incorrect assumption about a visitor's needs or wishes. Some mentioned feeling less comfortable with tour groups representing a range of ages because they felt it somewhat challenging to engage both the adults and children in the group in a way that left everyone satisfied. Others mentioned feeling ill-equipped when presented with language barriers or cultural differences. One volunteer stated, "I worried that some people felt excluded." The survey ended with space for volunteers to share any story they wished with the committee, and many used this space to describe positive experiences with visitors and why they choose to volunteer their time talking to strangers about art.

Volunteers thought broadly about demographics and life experiences when thinking about the diversity of museum visitors and the desire to promote a welcoming environment. Volunteers mentioned serving different generations, races, or cultural experiences outside of their own identity, as well as visitors with disabilities, language barriers, varied levels of comfort with art, varying religious perspectives, genders, and more.

CAM volunteers are acutely aware of the key role they play in visitor experience and see their role as valuable and important. They want to provide the best possible experiences for visitors and want the museum to be a welcoming place. Most were confident in their ability to do this but also wanted to improve.

What Did the Data Tell Us?

The survey results provided a range of valuable takeaways, including increased awareness that volunteers cared about the work of inclusion, even if they differed in levels of comfort or thoughts on implementation. Three quarters of our volunteers felt the museum was already welcoming to everyone, but there was room for growth. Several felt it was essential to continuously grow new audiences to keep a love for the arts and the museum alive for future generations. The results provided an opportunity for the advisory group to think critically about how to best support volunteers' learning and growth. Most volunteers felt confident in their ability to anticipate visitor needs with sensitivity.

Some survey respondents indicated another barrier to fulfilling and engaging in inclusion trainings: staff skepticism about their ability to welcome anyone to the museum. As a result, the staff considered how to mitigate volunteers' frustration and apprehension when developing training sessions moving forward. Some volunteers mentioned opportunities for growth; some admitted to gaps. All want to be the best volunteers they can be. Discomfort is hard but often essential for change. Staff felt that one of their roles was to find ways to reach volunteers effectively in delicate situations.

Overall, volunteers expressed a strong desire for learning tools and training, which is something the committee focused on in the subsequent months and has continued to be an important part of ongoing volunteer engagement. We identified two training topics based on findings from the survey: mitigating language barriers and providing better access for visitors with disabilities.

DEVELOPING TRAINING AND RESOURCES

Once we narrowed our focus to language barriers and accessibility, we split the advisory group into two working teams, each including representatives from visitor experience staff, learning and interpretation staff, docents, and VSAides. Our goal was to provide a mix of ongoing training sessions and resources to demonstrate that DEAI work is a continuous learning process. We gave ourselves a year to develop and schedule regular training sessions and create and disseminate resources like reading lists and feedback forms.

Language Barriers

In *Multiculturalism in Art Museums Today*, museum educators Sofia Gutierrez and Briley Rasmussen articulated their approach with English-language learners (ELL). They suggest that programs do not need to be designed specifically for ELLs; instead, educators could implement teaching strategies that would make programming more inclusive, such as using everyday English instead of academic English.[2] Inspired by these ideas, we put them at the center of our plans for the next series of workshops, which revolved around how our use of language can sometimes be inclusive, as well as how it can exclude people.

We had a few main learning objectives for the workshops. First, we focused on creating an awareness of and empathy for the experiences that ELLs can have at English-dominant museums. In keeping with the work of Gutierrez and Rasmussen, we also sought to promote the practice of empowering visitors to respond to volunteers in their own words and reinforce the idea that ELLs more readily acquire conversational English in settings like museums. We decided to invite docents who speak languages other than English to collaborate with the working groups on developing the training plans.

Our docent corps includes several members who have immigrated to the United States from other countries. All of them had different experiences learning English, whether it was before or after they immigrated to the United States, but they had a shared experience of visiting US art museums as a way of integrating into public life while not needing to speak English fluently to enjoy themselves.

This group of docents gave us something to consider: What if we turn the tables on our English-speaking volunteers and slowly immerse them in an experience that is not in English? We met with them to outline our plans and gauge their interest in assisting with the training. At first, we thought they might be hesitant to commit to something that was intentionally designed to confuse their peers, but they all bought into the idea. We decided to schedule five one-hour workshops over a six-month period to cover several languages: Spanish, German, French, and Russian.

In each workshop, volunteers gathered around an artwork for a short talk from a docent. The docent would introduce the artwork in English and ask the volunteers for their observations. From there, the docent would sporadically use words from their native language, gradually adding more until fully speaking in their own language without asking if the group could understand them. Each docent took a slightly different approach, with some providing visual aids and others who were completely verbal. No matter how they prepared, each one managed to momentarily create an environment in which everyone felt completely lost. After five minutes, we would stop and discuss what the experience was like for everyone in the group. This led to open and effective conversations about what it means to feel welcomed in a public space. Then the docent would pick up the tour again with a different artwork, speaking completely in English.

The group debriefed, comparing the two experiences and reflecting on what they comprehended in each conversation. Some volunteers in the audience followed the docent's gestures or tone of voice. Others relied on words in other languages that sounded like their English counterparts, like how color is spelled the same in English and Spanish but pronounced differently.

Roughly eleven volunteers attended one of five workshops, which is close to half of the museum's volunteers. Our group discussions yielded ideas ranging from greater advocacy for multilingual signage around the museum to buttons worn by volunteers indicating that they are fluent in multiple languages. Advisory group members took notes during each session, and we shared the most common recommendations with CAM's senior staff. One suggestion made by the volunteers was multilingual audio tours, which resulted in docents making short videos about a single artwork in other languages, including Farsi[3] and German,[4] for the museum's YouTube channel.

Accessibility

While half of the advisory group developed and implemented trainings on language barriers, the other half focused on increasing volunteers' awareness of the museum's accessibility policies. Because our accessibility policies had changed dramatically in the previous years, we decided to organize two training sessions with larger groups to brief all volunteers at the same time. CAM staff provided an overview of the museum's accessibility handbook and on-site resources like fidget toys and sensory headphones. We also emphasized the need for person-first terminology when speaking with and about visitors with disabilities (i.e., "person with a disability" instead of "a disabled person"). This was a good opportunity to introduce new resources like social narratives[5] and visual rules lists[6] that we made available on the museum's website but not widely shared with our volunteers. At the end of the session, we showed a preview of upcoming construction projects at the museum that would make the front entrance more accessible, such as new ramps and automatic doors.

After these training sessions, the advisory group created an accessibility feedback form specifically intended for volunteers to use. The form is available on the volunteer groups' websites and in hard copy at the museum. While working at the museum, volunteers can document an accessibility-related issue they witnessed or share an idea that could improve the museum's accessibility policies. The responses are passed along to the cross-departmental staff accessibility committee. To date, many of the volunteers' submissions have expressed needs for more visible wayfinding signage indoors and outdoors and additional places to sit in the galleries. Both are consistently addressed by CAM staff, but input from volunteers gave staff a greater sense of urgency to act.

In 2019, the museum was awarded a grant from the Institute of Museum and Library Services to audit and overhaul accessibility policies, including a series of trainings with community partners starting in the fall of 2019. Prior to securing the grant, CAM staff did not regularly participate in accessibility training. Volunteers, who had received accessibility training developed by the volunteer advisory group in the spring of 2019, were more well-versed than staff in current accessibility policies and resources. Due to the grant, staff members were able to expand on the accessibility work from the volunteer advisory group and integrate trainings across the institution more effectively than we could have done on our own. Volunteers participated in the grant-funded training sessions that took place in the winter and spring of 2020.

Limitations to Our Approach

Without question, there were some limitations to our approach. No matter how hard we tried to engage every volunteer and convey the importance of the trainings and resources we offered, we could not make them mandatory for all volunteers. We chose to engage with those who attended and build from there. Also, in hindsight, staff could have been more transparent in the process of choosing volunteers for the advisory group. Although the people in the advisory group were a great fit, we should have made an open call first.

Finally, we readily recognize that our volunteer groups are predominantly made up of white women, which can limit the diversity of perspectives in the training curriculum and fail to create an equitable grounding for the work. We also acknowledge that the CAM employees that manage volunteers are predominantly white. We still have work to do toward making our staff and volunteer groups better reflect our communities.

NEW PRACTICES

On May 16, 2019, a group of students from the Helen Y. Davis Leadership Academy visited the Museum of Fine Arts Boston, and school administrators subsequently reported accounts of prejudicial remarks and actions from museum staff and visitors toward the students.[7] All of the students in this group were youth of color. As a result, senior leadership at the CAM felt compelled to be proactive and prioritize a series of training sessions on topics like racism and gender identity for staff, which were led by external facilitators. The volunteer managers quickly integrated the work of their advisory group into the broader institutional plan, becoming part of the internal team that organized the four seminars for staff. The data and experiences from the language barrier workshops and accessibility overview were valuable resources to pass along to the outside facilitators when they adapted their sessions for the volunteers in January 2020.

The COVID-19 pandemic forced the CAM to close its doors to the public on March 13, 2020, and sent staff and volunteers home for an indefinite period of time. This effectively put any current work with the advisory group on hold. However, we established a precedent for involving our volunteers in staff-led initiatives that continued through the lockdown. We surveyed all volunteers to gauge their perspectives on the effects of the pandemic and returning to work in the future, and the results have informed staff in meaningful ways.

Docents participated in antiracism roundtable discussions with Andrew in the fall of 2020, in a similar participatory format of the language barrier workshops in 2018. We organized these discussions among cohorts of docents that typically work together on tours. Because these cohorts tend to work more closely and often with each other than any other group of docents, the focus was less on personal development and more on how ideas about equity and justice are connected to museum education. These docents already had a rapport with each other, and in many cases they had established trust that enabled them to discuss antiracism in gallery teaching. Each discussion started with the same question: If you do not talk about racism often on your tours, what holds you back? This opened up a conversation about how we define what is appropriate and relevant in a museum context. For example, several docents said that they only bring up racism when an artwork makes overt reference to racism. However, according to the docents, that tends to happen when the artist is a person of color and rarely ever with the work of a white artist. This insight opened the door for docents to reflect on how they determine when to talk about racism and when to omit it from a conversation. We used artworks from the CAM collection to reflect on our experiences when talking about an artist's racial identity on a tour and how we have responded to racialized assumptions and harmful remarks made by visitors. From the start, we collectively set an intention to resist tidy conclusions after a single discussion. Although there were certainly parts of the debate that ended in disagreement, the docents appreciated the fact that we engaged them in dialogue instead of unilaterally giving them a mandate to follow.

CONCLUSION

Our museum's strategic plan tasked staff with maximizing the impact of the volunteer corps, but we had the freedom to determine how we approached that goal. When we first thought about creating a volunteer advisory group for equity work, it was rooted in the relationships we had already established with our volunteers. However, in our early stages of planning trainings that aimed to foster inclusion, we were not inclusive in our planning process and we knew that had to change. If we intended to rely on our volunteers to be prominent public faces of the museum, we needed to see them as allies and include them in every stage of our equity work.

In hindsight, our volunteer advisory group was an impetus for reconsidering how we listen to our volunteers. We had intended for the advisory group to be a fixture of our volunteer corps, but it has since dissolved. However, through surveys and other forms of data collection, we now have a precedent for hearing thoughts from volunteers before we make important decisions that impact them. In our concentrated focus on language barriers and accessibility, we saw the significance in planning training sessions with docents and creating tangible ways for them to continually engage with ideas of equity and justice well after a training ends.

Although our approach is not perfect, we have seen a marked change in how our volunteers participate in equity work, and much of it started with our volunteer advisory group. The ethos of the advisory group's meetings translated to how we developed training sessions and resources for all volunteers, leading to a more consistent practice of inviting their ideas and input.

This whole process changed our perspective on working with volunteers, and we are seeing it ripple across other departments: there is now a greater emphasis on accessible exhibition design and gathering input from volunteers on renovations of permanent collection galleries. There are still facets of our operations that leave volunteers on the outside looking in, but this short-lived volunteer advisory group showed us how valuable our volunteers can be in the early stages of an initiative, and we are now more equipped to share the benefits of this involvement with other colleagues. We have applied lessons learned from our volunteer advisory group into institution-wide trainings and resources and have demonstrated to all stakeholders that when volunteers are at the table early and often, we are able to build buy-in, meaningfully incorporate volunteer expertise and skills, and more effectively foster inclusive spaces internally and externally. As a result, we are on the path toward being a more inclusive organization.

NOTES

1. The Net Promoter Score is a metric based on the question "How likely are you to recommend ___ to a friend?" on a 1- to 10-scale. Those who choose 9–10 are promoters and below 6 are detractors. The score is a percentage of detractors subtracted from promoters. See "Collaboration for Ongoing Visitor Experience Studies," 11.
2. Gutierrez and Rasmussen, "Code-Switching in the Art Museum: Increasing Access for English Learners," 147–48.
3. Cincinnati Art Museum, "CAM Look in Farsi," 2021, https://www.youtube.com/watch?v=cByWByUslrc&list=PLlxX-wrpnykA4IBUHJpOxqjPLuKURVDsU&index=119.
4. Cincinnati Art Museum, "CAM Look in German," 2021, https://www.youtube.com/watch?v=0GuxsCEflTE&list=PLlxX-wrpnykA4IBUHJpOxqjPLuKURVDsU&index=39.
5. Cincinnati Art Museum, "Entering the Cincinnati Art Museum Social Narrative," 2020, 20200805_20_0115_cam_access_social_narrative_entering_d01_v01_reduced.pdf (cincinnatiartmuseum.org).
6. Cincinnati Art Museum, "Cincinnati Art Museum Visual Rules," 2020, 20_0150_cam_museum_rules_sheet_a01_v02-2456.pdf (cincinnatiartmuseum.org).
7. Guerra, "Students of Color Say They Were Profiled, Harassed at the MFA. Museum Apologizes."

Chapter Seventeen

Old Systems, New Voices

Building Pathways for Change at Seattle Art Museum

Priya Frank, Tina Lee, Regan Pro, and David Rue

The story of equity work is often the story of people and relationships. In this chapter current and former staff members of the Seattle Art Museum (SAM) share individual and collective histories of equity work they have helped initiate and support at the museum. Focusing on community advisory groups, the emerging arts leader internship program, and the equity task force, we describe projects that are founded in authentic relationship building, power-sharing, and reciprocally beneficial partnerships. These values are integral in bringing everyone along in a process of collective movement. The stories in this chapter build on SAM's history of equity work, including board and staff initiatives like the education community engagement committee (ECEC). We, the authors, expand on that work and begin this chapter in 2016, when we were bridged together on key initiatives to further equity work at SAM.

EQUITY WORK AT SAM: COLLABORATING FOR CHANGE

When David Rue, a dancer and aspiring museum professional, interviewed with Tina Lee, exhibitions and publications manager, she was immediately impressed with David's passion for the arts. Although he wasn't the strongest fit for the open position, which required specific technical skills, Tina did not want to lose him to another organization. She connected with Regan Pro, then Kayla Skinner Deputy Director of Education and Public Programs, who was developing a paid internship program designed for individuals from backgrounds historically underrepresented in the field. Regan met with David and was struck by his insights, energy, and experience and fast-tracked the process to hire him. David became SAM's first emerging arts leader (EAL) intern. David's first day also happened to be the first day for Priya Frank, who was hired as SAM's associate director for community programs in the education and public engagement department led by Regan. This new position focused on community partnerships, exhibition programming, and building the equity team,[1] an internal staff advisory group designed to center racial equity at SAM. David, Regan, and Tina were founding members of this group, which was tasked with developing SAM's racial equity plan, following feedback from racial equity trainings for the staff, board, and volunteers. That plan became part of the museum's strategic plan, so those goals impacted the entire institution, and departments were required to develop equity action plans.

In 2020, following the murder of George Floyd, which intensified the Black Lives Matter movement nationally, SAM affirmed its ongoing long-term commitments to equity and inclusion by establishing the position of director of equity, diversity, and inclusion, a senior-level position now held by Priya, and by forming the equity task force with board members and staff. Additionally, Regan and Tina committed to a practice of incorporating feedback from community advisory groups in every special exhibition at the museum.

CENTERING COMMUNITY VOICE THROUGH ADVISORY GROUPS

Tina Lee and Regan Pro

SAM has an established history of convening advisory groups for exhibitions[2] and has long embraced models of community authorship in curatorial engagement, public programs, and education initiatives. Led by the ECEC (a group of trustees and members of the public) SAM sought to share the museum's spaces, platforms, and resources with community partners to decenter the museum and prioritize perspectives that have historically been excluded from the museum.

SAM's early engagement with advisory groups was built off strong local models, most notably the work of the Wing Luke Museum of the Asian Pacific American Experience, which has a twenty-year commitment to a community-developed, community-based planning process for all exhibitions.[3] As Swarupa Anila (former director of interpretive engagement at

Detroit Institute of the Arts) describes, many museums are examining how, "the same collections and interpretive modes of display and meaning-making that serve as sites of learning and aesthetic enjoyment for some audiences can cause trauma and alienation for other audiences."[4] Education and curatorial staff continued to question how our exhibition planning processes might be alienating the audiences we hoped to invite. What or whose values and perspectives were we reflecting or excluding? What were we assuming about our own expertise or canon? How could we move from a didactic, top-down model to one that follows MASS Action's call to move "in the direction of being dialogic (conversational), de-centered (all people given equal consideration), and open source (sharing authority with audiences, particularly those directly affected by the legacies of our spaces)?"[5]

Proposal and Implementation

Believing every exhibition has intersectional themes that would benefit from community expertise, Regan and Chiyo Ishikawa (then the Susan Brotman Deputy Director for Art and Curator of European Painting and Sculpture) wrote a proposal for a yearlong pilot program in which every major special exhibition would have an advisory group. For this practice of community advisory groups to be successful, we sought institutional buy-in across all areas of the museum—particularly from the museum director and board of trustees. There were three key components to our strategy: First, we demonstrated equal curatorial and education commitment in our proposal. Second, after enthusiastically supporting the idea, Kim Rorschach (then the Illsley Ball Nordstrom Director and CEO) presented the proposal idea to senior staff and trustees to establish support from the beginning. Finally, the budget for the advisory groups was embedded into the exhibition budget.

In 2018, SAM launched the pilot year of paid community advisory groups for each of its three major special exhibitions. Advisors would provide feedback that resulted in critical modifications to exhibition checklists and marketing campaigns, and established connections with local organizations and people that enhanced our programming.

There were many lessons learned along the way. But we were careful to publicly and internally celebrate the successes of the initiative, highlighting the ways the process had strengthened our work. At the end of the year, we hosted an evaluation feedback session and invited everyone to share thoughts about how to improve the process. By the end of year two, having community advisors began to feel like an accepted institutional practice rather than an experiment seeking advocates.

Structuring Community Advisory Groups

Our community advisory groups comprise eight people: typically an art historian or educator who has knowledge on the subject of the exhibition, artists whose practice aligns with the art, cultural leaders interested in the exhibition themes, and youth representatives or people who work closely with youth. We aim for age diversity to ensure that the group could speak to the concerns of multiple generations and perspectives. (See box 17.1 for recommendations on selecting advisors.)

BOX 17.1. RECOMMENDATIONS ON ADVISORS

- Consider people who may not already have opportunities to easily share their thoughts with the museum. For example, board members or trustees may have valuable insights to contribute; however, they already have many channels to share their thoughts with museum leadership.
- If the goal of having advisors is to broaden and deepen the expertise informing exhibitions, make sure to honor the varieties of expertise represented and not just reaffirm traditional models of knowledge.
- Avoid having both an academic advisory group (made of academic experts in subject areas) and a community advisory group (made of community members, artists, educators and non-academic experts). This model can often undermine the expertise offered by the community advisory group. All experts should serve on the same group so they can be in dialogue.

A core internal team rotates in and out of the community advisory groups. This core team selects advisors, organizes and facilitates meetings, reports back to each respective department, and advocates for advisors' perspectives as staff work on the exhibition, programming, and marketing plans. It is important to note that staff incorporate working on advisory groups into our existing work.

Meeting Structure and Budget

Funding needed to be built into the exhibition budget, which requires us to have our exhibition schedule confirmed at least two years into the future, and budgeted a year in advance. Expenses include a $500 honorarium for each advisor to attend three to four meetings per year, parking fees, food and beverage, and meeting supplies. (See box 17.2 for recommendations on planning meetings.)

BOX 17.2. RECOMMENDATIONS ON MEETINGS

- Maintain a lower staff to advisor ratio to foster open discussion, especially around sensitive topics. With eight to ten advisors, having more than four to five staff can make a meeting feel like a focus group with too many observers.
- Plan agendas carefully in advance. Advisors need to feel that their time is honored and that staff are using the meetings as effectively as possible.
- Don't ask advisors questions you can't genuinely use their feedback on. For example, if you are discussing an exhibition that comes with a set title, don't ask advisors to weigh in on what the show should be called. Instead, ask them to give marketing or outreach suggestions that could provide context to the title.
- Ask staff to join meetings that will cover topics related to their work. For example, if you are discussing the layout of the galleries, make sure to invite staff members working on exhibition design. It's much more impactful for staff to hear directly from advisors (particularly when their advice counters staff preferences) than to hear feedback secondhand.

Advisory group meetings are structured as follows:

- Meeting One: We outline the roles and responsibilities of the advisory group and request honest feedback on a range of topics. We explain that their roles involve making recommendations, but ultimately the museum makes the final decisions. This clarification is helpful to underscore so the advisors do not feel offended if their ideas are not realized. Our core team then prompts discussion about an exhibition presented by a curator with questions such as: What themes stood out to you? What did you assume about the exhibition going into this meeting? Did your opinions change? What excites/challenges you about this show?
- Meeting Two: This meeting focuses on interpretation. Gallery label samples—especially traumatic, triggering, or controversial images and narratives—are flagged for review and sent to advisors in advance of the

meeting. The exhibition designer presents the exhibition layout plan, which provides a behind-the-scenes opportunity that keeps the advisors engaged. Often feedback from these conversations inform the images selected for the exhibition marketing campaign. Lastly, we invite partnership ideas: Which artists or cultural organizations might be a good fit to partner with on this exhibition? What related events are already planned outside of SAM that we could help support or amplify through this exhibition?
- Meeting Three: We present our proposed exhibition marketing campaign and invite feedback on mockups of title treatments. This is not a critique on design; instead we ask: If you saw this ad in a magazine, would you be inspired to see the show? We also ask for recommendations about media outlets.

During these meetings, there may be times when advisors disagree on issues. It's important to remember that these conflicting viewpoints are valuable to surface during the exhibition planning process so we can accommodate any related changes to the exhibition. Disagreements can also help illuminate the intersecting identities our audience members and visitors bring to the museum and remind us not to treat cultures as a monolith.

By the final meeting we have grown better acquainted with the advisors, and we are often disappointed our time together has ended. We invite advisors to celebrate our work at the exhibition opening event, attend exhibition programs to continue engaging with the museum, and share the news of the exhibition and programs with their networks.

BUILDING PATHWAYS FOR THE ARTS LEADERS OF TOMORROW

David Rue

Just as the authentic and proactive inclusion of community voice is valued in exhibition development, so too are the educational, cultural, and lived experiences of interns valued in the operations and programs at SAM. Stemming from our emphasis on relationship-building and inclusion, SAM launched the EAL internship program in 2016. This paid ten-week position provides emerging arts leaders from diverse backgrounds, especially from historically underrepresented groups in the museum field, with an in-depth understanding of SAM's operations, programming, and audiences. The program is also designed to offer interns a holistic experience combining their expertise, background, and agency within a professional development program. I was asked to be the museum's inaugural EAL intern, an integral step toward my full-time employment at the museum.

Prior to interning at SAM, I was a professional dancer performing with TU Dance in St. Paul, Minnesota, and I had no experience in the world of art administration. I had moved to Seattle the year before and was deeply interested in learning about the business and administrative side of the arts sector while deepening my understanding of how arts organizations operate. I was drawn to the EAL program for its emphasis on helping interns from nontraditional museum backgrounds achieve their career goals while strengthening integral skills for arts careers. Interns work across departments, gain an understanding of museum careers, and develop a community engagement project or program based on their interests and perspectives.

During my internship, I worked with the museum's education and curatorial departments and had formative meetings with museum leadership. I researched the museum's collection and learned about the visual arts in a way I'd never imagined and felt genuinely supported by my colleagues. For example, I developed an in-gallery performance during the *Kehinde Wiley: A New Republic* exhibition, in which classical ballet dancers performed to contemporary hip-hop music, and a hip-hop dancer performed with a live cellist. This performance spoke to themes of genre mashup and Wiley's practice of bringing elements of Black culture into the world of classic European portraiture. This internship encouraged me to use my dance expertise to bring a different approach to in-gallery programming, and this cross collaborative model of artistic hybridity is something that continually influences my career. Following the internship, I became SAM's public engagement associate, joining a team that produces about 250 public programs throughout the year, serving approximately thirty thousand adults.

I now work closely with new cohorts of EAL interns, meeting weekly to discuss their goals and providing tools to help them achieve them. I encourage the interns to express themselves while connecting to SAM's collection and object-based research. We also discuss what internal work culture looks like at SAM and how they can most successfully navigate museum spaces to advocate for themselves. As someone who didn't have a traditional art historical career path, I'm passionate about sharing my experiences with the interns to set themselves up for success.

Through professional development, administrative inquiry, and career building, the EAL internship prepared me to produce large-scale public programs in a way that was both educational and empowering. My experience at SAM has also led to a successful career in Seattle as an arts professional outside of the museum. I have produced multidisciplinary large-scale public programs (art festivals, dance performances, and workshops) on my own using the skills I strengthened through this internship.

In 2015 the Andrew Mellon Foundation released survey results from 278 art museums mostly residing in the United States.[6] This data revealed that 72 percent of museum staff are white and 28 percent represent historically underrepresented minorities. When breaking down the racial diversity by job type, the demographics are more problematic. The Mellon study found that non-Hispanic white staff continue to dominate the job categories most closely associated with the intellectual and educational mission of museums, including those of curators, conservators, educators, and leadership. The demographics of these positions are: 84 percent white, 6 percent Asian, 4 percent Black, and 3 percent two or more races. With the exception of the percentage of Asian staff, these percentages are nowhere near representative of the diversity of the US population. The EAL internship is one model that institutions can follow to turn their commitment to racial equity into a concrete action to shift the historical narrative of what museums look like both internally and externally. My story exemplifies taking a chance on someone who might not be the "traditional" fit. I am honored to witness the growth of this program and be a part of it.

BOARD MEMBERS, COMMUNITY LEADERS, AND STAFF BUILD AN EQUITY TASK FORCE

Priya Frank

At SAM we believe that in order for equity work to be truly effective we must focus on both our internal communities, such as the EAL program and our external communities, including community advisory groups. When I began my new role of director of equity, diversity, and inclusion in July 2020, one of my responsibilities was to center racial equity across all internal constituencies. Museum leadership recognized the need to make sure that everyone is engaged and committed in this work—not just staff but also the board and volunteers—so they launched the equity task force. This advisory body was tasked with developing recommendations for how SAM could further equity work both now and in the future.

The task force idea grew out of conversations between then board president Carla Lewis and Amada Cruz, SAM's Illsley Ball Nordstrom Director and CEO. Both felt it was essential that the CEO/director of the museum and the board president colead this effort together, sending a strong message of commitment to this work. They then asked Dr. Cherry McGee Banks, another SAM board member, to join as the third co-chair. Cherry has extensive experience in multicultural education and a deep investment in SAM's equity work. She developed the framework and structured syllabus for the group, which articulated expectations, timelines, and guidance for the content of each meeting.

Carla, Cherry, and Amada created SAM's equity task force to pool expertise, foster internal connections, and continue building on the museum's commitment to diversity, equity, and inclusion. The twenty-six-person task force consisted of about one-third each of the following stakeholders: board members, staff, and members of one of our board committees called the ECEC, which includes both board members and community leaders. Although each group focused on equity related efforts within their own constituency (e.g., the board of trustees had contributed to an intentional commitment to equity in the strategic plan, which they approved in June 2018), this was their first time working as a cross-collaborative internal group. Amada felt it was important for this task force to represent the entire museum. To make long-standing structural change in any institution, everyone should be part of the process—board members, staff, and community members.

Individuals selected to join the equity task force by the chairs were already dedicated investors to SAM in some capacity. They were asked to contribute their professional expertise, lived experiences, and community networks to this new effort. This would greatly enhance and enrich discussions and provide unique insights to inform the recommendations. Board member Brandon Vaughn, who participated on the task force, stated: "So many organizations . . . both public and private, want to research and implement diversity initiatives for their employees and customers, but more often than not, the people directly involved in the decision making have limited interactions with those who are affected the most. For the Equity Task Force, it was important to SAM's board leadership to include a truly inclusive group that represents the entirety of the SAM community."[7]

Framework and Lens

Virtual task force meetings were held monthly from August 2020 to January 2021 to brainstorm, research, discuss ideas, and learn more about the inner workings of SAM. The group ultimately developed recommendations for how to strengthen and expand our commitment to racial equity and antiracism in four critical departments: human resources, curatorial, development, and communications and marketing. Amada prioritized these four areas because she felt SAM could make significant and measurable progress within each of these departments.

The Research Process

Equity work was already happening in some facet across the institution, so each working group had at least one staff member who could share internal information and a baseline from which the recommendations could then be developed. The co-chairs provided direction for each working group, as follows:

- Human resources working group: Examined recruiting and retention practices; promotions, mentorship opportunities; and staff diversity.
- Curatorial working group: Reviewed past and current curatorial practices with a focus on increasing representation of artists identifying as BIPOC in the collection, exhibitions, and interpretation.
- Development working group: Identified how equity is framed and employed in development in comparable museums, made recommendations for becoming a more welcoming space for all donors, reviewed member demographics, and examined current membership models for inclusivity/exclusivity.
- Communications and marketing working group: Examined current practices and plans to improve outreach to BIPOC communities, reviewed audience data and outreach methods, gauged partnerships, and benchmarked SAM in relation to comparable museums.

There were many different directions that the research could have taken, so the chairs also provided three guiding questions:

1. *What do we need to know* to better understand the current status of the issues identified by our working group?
2. *Where can we go to collect the data* that can help us answer the first question?
3. *What can/should we recommend* in the short term, midterm, and long term to help address equity issues at SAM?

To answer these questions, equity task force members conducted research on SAM and in the field as a whole. Members discussed and learned about traditional models related to these four areas of work and how these origins contribute to current structures in museums.

The equity task force developed a set of recommendations for each of the four areas of focus, building on the good work that was already happening at SAM. Each group provided recommendations that reflected what was needed to take each area of work to the next level, provided a vision statement for how they wanted to center equity, and created a short- and long-term plan.

Each group also identified: (1) overarching goals, (2) subcomponents of the goals, (3) description and measurement, (4) time frame, (5) expected impact, and (6) department intersections. A summary of the recommendations follows:

- The human resources working group created recommendations to foster an inclusive work environment for BIPOC individuals across all departments. Their goals included increasing BIPOC representation through building out career pathways, establishing paid internships, and developing resources for hiring, promoting, and retaining staff. They also recommended gathering key information from staff about their professional and departmental needs to inform future goals and metrics, establishing more focused career development opportunities, and supporting management with tools to foster continued learning about how to lead with an equity lens.
- The curatorial working group recommendations included acquiring works by BIPOC artists and establishing funds to make these acquisitions possible, collaborating more closely with community partners on exhibitions and programming, and expanding the scope of programming to leverage collections and activate both physical and digital channels.
- The development working group focused on centering equitable practices within the department, while also raising funds to support equity related initiatives. Their vision statement described wanting to "build out thoughtful and inclusive SAM fundraising and membership practices that center trust and authenticity, with the end result of a more diversified, engaged, and sustainable support base." Their recommendations included continuing to build authentic relationships in the community and strengthening membership communications strategies to better engage diverse audiences.
- The communications and marketing working group developed strategies for furthering equity work in their department while helping other departments with their communications-related efforts. Their vision statement recognized how communications "guides and shapes the stories the museum tells, connecting art to the lives of the many communities we serve. In our relationships, strategies, and processes, we center those communities, transforming their experience and perception of the museum as an institution that leads according to its values and as a place where everyone belongs." The recommendations included gaining a strong understanding of SAM's current audiences, performing comparative analysis between the museum's audience and local demographics, further connecting with local BIPOC communities, and amplifying equity goals through internal and external communications channels.

All recommendations reflected the importance of feasibility, particularly as staff were challenged by pandemic-related reductions in staff time and reduced budgets. Enacting this plan ultimately fell to the staff, so how do we ensure that this plan is central to the equity work, without overburdening them? The last few meetings of the equity task force were spent translating the recommendations into logistical plans.

Reporting Out Internally and Gathering Feedback

In January 2021, board members on the task force presented the recommendations to the entire board, staff, and the ECEC in three separate meetings. These presentations allowed stakeholders the opportunity to learn more about the work and recommendations, and how their involvement is key to moving this work forward. It also provided an opportunity to gather feedback from each group on the details and feasibility of the plan.

All three constituencies felt that the recommendations were thorough and impressive. They also expressed concerns about staff workload and wanted to be mindful of what was feasible. All three groups also had questions around evaluating "success" and what that looks like across recommendations.

Reflecting on the Process

Taking time to reflect throughout the process was imperative, particularly because working collaboratively across internal communities was a new model for SAM. After every meeting the chairs would debrief and discuss what was needed at the next meeting to help each group further their work. These reflections were particularly important for the chairs in connecting research-related discussions to later meetings about tangible recommendations, a process that took some finessing and guidance.

The chairs held two debrief sessions: one with the entire task force and one with staff who were members of the task force. From staff we learned that it would have been helpful to establish staff member roles before the initial meeting. This cross-collaborative effort was new for some who may not have engaged with board members and ECEC members before. Recognizing the power dynamics and creating more definitive roles could have helped alleviate some staff uncertainty. In hindsight, we learned that taking time to build community agreements would have been helpful in setting the tone for collaborative work across constituencies. In some cases, staff were working outside of their home departments. This was also intentional; we aimed to encourage professional growth and convene a diversity of perspectives. However, many staff described having a learning curve when it came to discussions with board and community members.

What's Next

The equity task force was initially conceived to be a six-month advisory committee, concluding in January 2021. However members of the task force expressed interest in continuing to monitor and assess progress, so we decided to set quarterly check-in meetings.

Senior leadership plays a critical role in taking the recommendations and enacting them with respect to goals, timelines, feasibility, staff, and departmental intersections and overlap. In order to stay on track, these leaders are meeting regularly to assess progress, share needs, and support one another.

We have already had wins related to recommendation areas, such as increased funding for equity work, including grants to redo our American Art Galleries and grow our EAL program. We featured the equity task force work in a front-page article in our spring/summer 2021 newsletter that is mailed to more than thirty-thousand-member households. A section of SAM's website now features our equity work. The board has committed to featuring a topic related to equity at every board meeting. Sharing our work in this book is also another channel for communication.

Final Musings

As a South Asian woman who is a first-generation college graduate, the first person in my family born in the United States and first to be working in the arts, I'm in a field that probably wasn't designed for me. In my role I get to break down those barriers and redefine culture every day. I've always believed that small wins lead to big changes, and in institutions that have operated under traditional structures, it is essential to recognize that advancing racial equity and centering antiracism is everyone's responsibility. This work never ends, but we can each play a role in creating a more equitable museum for our staff, our board, and the wider community.

CONCLUSION

Each of us can do something to advance equity. But it takes all of us to ensure that this work goes beyond buzz words. Bringing everyone along in the movement for institutional change can permanently transform our museums and workplaces into spaces of inclusive connections, healthy communities, and a new way of interacting. We aim to visit a museum and see our cultural experiences and those of our colleagues, families, and friends reflected back at us. To make this happen, equity and inclusion work must be infused into the goals, priorities, regular work plan, and natural rhythm of every element across the institution, for all stakeholders, particularly those in decision-making positions.

The community advisory groups, EAL internship program, and the equity task force are all examples of taking risks, trying new models, power-sharing, and recognizing that having a perfect process was not the point but having the courage to do this together was. None of us inherited a road map for how to do this work; we are the ones building the roadmap. For Regan, Tina, David, and Priya, our aligned values have given us the courage to proceed, even without a roadmap. We knew we had each other to lean on, share ideas, sit in discomfort together, and also see what's possible when we center our work in the authentic relationships that we've built with one another. Recognizing the impact that this work is already having continues to renew our joy, creativity, and hope that change is possible, is coming, and is already here.

NOTES

1. The equity team acts as an advisory group, coleading efforts to improve processes and consult with leadership on issues ranging from messaging, security procedures, and the creation of label texts, to consulting on trainings. Over the years the group has grown to more than thirty-five members from departments all across SAM and has become a catalyst for a culture shift at SAM.

2. As a cultural institution on Indigenous land, we honor our ongoing connection to our Native communities past, present, and future. In 1991, with a grant from the National Endowment for the Humanities, former curator of Northwest Coast Native Art Steve Brown worked with local Native people on the installation of a new gallery space dedicated to displaying Native American art permanently. In 2002, SAM's curator of African and Oceanic Art, Pamela McClusky cocurated the exhibition *Art from Africa: Long Steps Never Broke a Back* with a dozen African and American advisors, who also contributed their knowledge, voices, and music to contextualize works in the exhibition through audio and video presentations (Barbara Brotherton and Pamela McClusky, interview by Tina Lee, Seattle, April 6, 2021).

3. SAM also learned from the Northwest African American Museum and Burke Museum of Natural History and Culture as institutions that also have strong traditions of developing exhibition content in partnership and consultation with experts outside the museum staff. These local models echo excellent work happening nationally at institutions such as the Detroit Institute of the Arts (DIA) or the Oakland Museum of California, which look to dismantle hegemonic practices of representation.

4. Anila, "Inclusion Requires Fracturing," 109.

5. Anderson, Potter, Cook, Gardner, Murawski, Anila, and Machida, "Interpretation: Liberating the Narrative."

6. The Andrew W. Mellon Foundation. "Mellon Foundation Releases the First Comprehensive Survey of Diversity in American Art Museums." July 29, 2015. https://mellon.org/news-blog/articles/Diversity-American-Art-Museums/.

7. Brandon Vaughn, e-mail message to authors, August 26, 2021.

Bibliography

18th Street Arts Center."Core Values." Accessed July 31, 2021. https://18thstreet.org/corevalues/.

———. "Culture Mapping 90404." Accessed July 31, 2021. http://culturemapping90404.org.

Aaron, Carroll. "Doctors and Racial Bias: Still a Long Way to Go." *New York Times*. https://www.nytimes.com/2019/02/25/upshot/doctors-and-racial-bias-still-a-long-way-to-go.html.

Ahmed, Sarah. *On Being Included: Racism and Diversity in Institutional Life*. Durham, NC: Duke University Press, 2012.

American Alliance of Museums. 2018. "Facing Change: Insights from the American Alliance of Museums' Diversity, Equity, Accessibility, and Inclusion Working Group." https://www.aam-us.org/wp-content/uploads/2018/04/AAM-DEAI-Working-Group-Full-Report-2018.pdf.

———. "Museum Assessment Program: About MAP." https://www.aam-us.org/programs/accreditation-excellence-programs/museum-assessment-program-map/.

Anderson, Annie, Emily Potter, Elon Cook, Karleen Gardner, Mike Murawski, Swarupa Anila, and Alyssa Machida. "Interpretation: Liberating the Narrative." MASS Action Toolkit, ed. Elisabeth Callihan, 89–103. Minneapolis, MN: Minneapolis Institute of Art, 2017.

Anderson, Bill, Ashley Narum, and Jennifer Lynn Wolf. "Expanding the Understanding of the Categories of Dysconscious Racism." *The Educational Forum* 83, no. 1 (2019): 4–12. https://doi.org/10.1080/00131725.2018.1505015.

Anderson, Gail. 2019. *Mission Matters*. Washington, DC: American Alliance of Museums.

The Andrew W. Mellon Foundation. "Mellon Foundation Releases the First Comprehensive Survey of Diversity in American Art Museums." July 29, 2015. https://mellon.org/news-blog/articles/Diversity-American-Art-Museums/.

Anila, Swarupa. "Inclusion Requires Fracturing." *Journal of Museum Education* 42, no. 2 (2017): 108–19.

Antar, Anniessa, Elisabeth Callihan, and Adrianne Russell. "A Watershed Moment: Lessons from #MuseumsRespondtoFerguson and MASS Action." *Museum Magazine*, Jan/Feb 2021. https://www.aam-us.org/2021/01/01/a-watershed-moment-lessons-from-museumsrespondtoferguson-and-mass-action/.

Artforum News. "'We Can Do Better,' Claim US Museums Criticized for Hollow Signs of BLM Solidarity." June 3, 2020. https://www.artforum.com/news/we-can-do-better-claim-us-museums-criticized-for-hollow-signs-of-blm-solidarity-83173.

Bailey-Bryant, Joy. "We're Not that Hard to Find." *Museum*, January/February 2017. https://unitedarts.cc/wp-content/uploads/2017/05/were-not-that-hard-to-find.pdf.

Banaji, Mahzarin R., and Anthony G. Greenwald. *Blindspot: Hidden Biases of Good People*. New York: Delacorte Press, 2013.

Benedict, Lily, Matt Berry, MJ Robinson, and Kajette Solomon. "Confronting Ourselves Together: All-Staff Dialogues at the RISD Museum." https://risdmuseum.org/art-design/projects-publications/articles/confronting-ourselves-together.

Bishara, Hakim, and Ilana Novick. "Decolonize This Place Launches 'Nine Weeks of Art and Action' with Protest at Whitney Museum." *Hyperallergic*, March 23, 2019. https://hyperallergic.com/491418/decolonize-this-place-nine-weeks-launch/.

The Broad. "Diversity Apprenticeship Toolbox." https://www.thebroad.org/dap/toolbox.

Brookfield, Stephen D. "Repressive Tolerance and the 'Management' of Diversity." In *Critical Theory and Transformative Learning*, edited by Viktor X. Wang, 1–13. Hershey, PA: IGI Global, 2018.

brown, adrienne maree. *Emergent Strategy: Shaping Change, Changing Worlds*. Chico, CA: AK Press, 2017.

Brownlee, Dana. "The Dangers of Mistaking Diversity for Inclusion in the Workplace." *Forbes*, Sept 15, 2019. https://www.forbes.com/sites/danabrownlee/2019/09/15/the-dangers-of-mistaking-diversity-for-inclusion-in-the-workplace.

Bruin X. UCLA Office of Equity, Diversity and Inclusion. "Lesson 6: Countermeasures." *Implicit Bias* series. https://www.youtube.com/watch?v=RIOGenWu_iA&t=211.

Bryant, Janeen, Barbara Cohen-Stratyner, Stacey Mann, and Levon Williams. "The White Supremacy Elephant in the Room." *American Alliance of Museums*. https://www.aam-us.org/2021/01/01/the-white-supremacy-elephant-in-the-room/.

Bunch III, Lonnie G. "Flies in the Buttermilk: Museums, Diversity, and the Will to Change." https://www.aam-us.org/2019/05/29/flies-in-the-buttermilk-museums-diversity-and-the-will-to-change/.

Burke Museum of Natural History and Culture. "The Ancient One, Kennewick Man | Burke Museum." https://www.burkemuseum.org/news/ancient-one-kennewick-man.

———. "Bill Holm | Burke Museum." https://www.burkemuseum.org/collections-and-research/culture/bill-holm-center/bill-holm.

———. "Floors, Walls and a Shed-Style Roof | Burke Museum." https://www.burkemuseum.org/news/floors-walls-and-shed-style-roof.

———. "Repatriation | Burke Museum." https://www.burkemuseum.org/about/our-work/repatriation.

Burnside, Tina. "African Americans in Minnesota." *Mnopedia*, Minnesota Historical Society. https://www.mnopedia.org/african-americans-minnesota.

Butler, Octavia. *Parable of the Sower.* New York: Four Walls Eight Windows, 1993.

Cain Miller, Claire. "Is Blind Hiring the Best Hiring?" *The New York Times Magazine*, February 25, 2016. https://www.nytimes.com/2016/02/28/magazine/is-blind-hiring-the-best-hiring.html?_r=0.

Callihan, Elisabeth. "From Statements of Solidarity to Transformative Action and Accountability." *MASS Action* (blog). August 31, 2020. https://www.museumaction.org/massaction-blog/2020/8/31/from-statements-of-solidarity-to-transformative-action-amp-accountability.

Castillo, Enrico G., Hallie Scott, and Theresa Sotto. "Building Community and Structural Competency through Art: An Art Museum and Psychiatry Partnership." In *Educating for the Future: Museum Education in the 21st Century*, edited by Jason Porter and Mary Kay Cunningham, chapter 1. Lanham, MD: Rowman & Littlefield, 2022.

Centers for Disease Control and Prevention. "Disability Impacts All of Us." https://www.cdc.gov/ncbddd/disabilityandhealth/infographic-disability-impacts-all.html.

Cohen, LaPlaca. "Culture Track 2017." http://s28475.pcdn.co/wp-content/uploads/2019/06/CT2017-Top-Line-Report.pdf.

Cohen, LaPlaca and Slover Linett. "Culture + Community in a Time of Crisis." http://s28475.pcdn.co/wp-content/uploads/2020/09/CCTC-Key-Findings-from-Wave-1_9.29.pdf.

Cohen, Ronnie. "Young People with Disabilities More Likely to be Arrested." https://www.reuters.com/article/us-health-disabilities-law-enforcement/young-people-with-disabilities-more-likely-to-be-arrested-idUSKBN1DA2SZ.

Collaboration for Ongoing Visitor Experience Studies. "Understanding Our Visitors: Multi-Institutional Science Center Study." (July 2017–June 2018). http://www.understandingvisitors.org/wp-content/uploads/2018/10/COVES-FY18-Aggregate-Report_spreads.pdf.

Crenshaw, Kimberlé W. "Race, Reform, and Retrenchment: Transformation and Legitimation in Antidiscrimination Law." *Harvard Law Review* 101, no. 7 (1988): 1331–87. https://doi.org/10.2307/1341398.

Cultural Competence Learning Institute. "Building and Nurturing DEAI Committees: Theory and Practice in Museums" Public webinar, Association of Science and Technology Centers Programs and Events, August 20, 2020. https://community.astc.org/ccli/get-started/public-webinars.

———. "Would You Rather? September 10, 2021, https://community.astc.org/ccli/resources-for-action/group-activities/would-you-rather.

Dafoe, Taylor. "Arts Workers of Color in Los Angeles Earn 35 Percent Less in Wages than Their White Colleagues, a New Study Finds." *Art News*, May 18, 2021. https://news.artnet.com/art-world/bipoc-arts-workers-1970177.

Dattner, Ben. "A Scorecard for Making Better Hiring Decisions." *Harvard Business Review*, February 4, 2016. https://hbr.org/2016/02/a-scorecard-for-making-better-hiring-decisions.

Dimento, Maria. "Crowdsourced List of Museum Salaries Goes Viral, Exposing Pay Inequities." *The Chronicle of Philanthropy*, August 13, 2019. https://www.philanthropy.com/article/crowdsourced-list-of-museum-salaries-goes-viral-exposing-pay-inequities/.

Discovery Museum Speaker Series. *Talking to Kids about Race and Racism: A Conversation with Dr. Beverly Daniel Tatum Moderated by WBUR's Tiziana Dearing*. Recorded January 27, 2021. Video, 1 hr., 24 min. https://www.youtube.com/watch?v=-sqRicGbxug.

DiTomaso, Nancy. *The American Non-Dilemma: Racial Inequality without Racism*. New York: Russell Sage Foundation, 2013.

Durón, Maximilíano, and Alex Greenberger. "In Open Letters, Art Workers Demand that Institutions Do More to Fight Racism." *ARTnews*, June 19, 2020. https://www.artnews.com/art-news/news/art-workers-systemic-racism-open-letters-1202691764.

Ehrenhalt, Jey. "Beyond the Privilege Walk." *Learning for Justice*. https://www.learningforjustice.org/magazine/beyond-the-privilege-walk.

Ernst & Young LLP, and Royal Bank of Canada. *Outsmarting Our Brains: Overcoming Hidden Biases to Harness Diversity's True Potential*. 2013. https://www.rbc.com/diversity-inclusion/_assets-custom/includes/pdf/Outsmarting_our_brains_Overcoming_hidden_biases.pdf.

Ferdman, Bernardo M. "The Practice of Inclusion in Diverse Organizations: Toward a Systemic and Inclusive Framework." In *Diversity at Work: The Practice of Inclusion*, edited by Bernardo M. Ferdman and Barbara R. Deane, 3–54. San Francisco: Jossey Bass, 2014.

Finkel, Jori. "Meet the Experts Who Root out Racism and Exclusion in the Arts." *The Art Newspaper*, January 11, 2021. https://www.theartnewspaper.com/news/meet-the-experts-who-root-out-racism-and-exclusion-in-the-arts.

Garfein, Steve, Nick Horney, and Marvin Nelson. "Managing Change in Organizations." Paper presented at PMI Global Congress 2013—North America, New Orleans, LA. Newtown Square, PA: Project Management Institute, 2013. https://www.pmi.org/learning/library/managing-change-organizations-5872.

Garibay, Cecilia, and Laura Huerta-Migus. *Becoming a Learning Organization Brief*. Cultural Competence Learning Institute, 2020. https://rb.gy/jblrun.

———. *Organizational Change Brief*. Cultural Competence Learning Institute. 2020. https://rb.gy/c8gzzs.

Garibay, Cecilia, and Jeanne Marie Olson. *CCLI National Landscape Study: The State of DEAI Practices in Museums*. Cultural Competence Learning Institute. 2020. https://rb.gy/kha7bk.

Garton, Eric, and Michael Mankins. "The Pandemic Is Widening a Corporate Productivity Gap." *Harvard Business Review*, June 19, 2021. https://hbr.org/2020/12/the-pandemic-is-widening-a-corporate-productivity-gap.

Geiger, H. Jack. "Racial and Ethnic Disparities in Diagnosis and Treatment: A Review of the Evidence and a Consideration of Causes." https://www.ncbi.nlm.nih.gov/books/NBK220337/.

Glaveski, Steve. "Stop Sabotaging Your Workforce." *Harvard Business Review*, May 27, 2021. https://hbr.org/2021/05/stop-sabotaging-your-workforce.

Goff, Phillip Atiba, Rashad Robinson, Bernice King, and Anthony D. Romero. "The Path to Ending Systemic Racism in the US." Filmed June 3, 2020. Video, 1:06:22. https://www.ted.com/playlists/250/talks_to_help_you_understand_r.

Gotkin, Kevin, Ansel Lurio, Nefertiti Matos, and Madison Zalopany. "Mindful Communication: Language and Disability Discussion and Best Practices." Museum, Arts and Culture Access Consortium, February 7, 2019. https://macaccess.org/rescources/mindful-communication-language-and-disability-discussion-and-best-practices-program-documentation/.

Grady, Constance. "If Museums Want to Diversify, They'll Have to Change. A Lot." *Vox*, November 18, 2020. https://www.vox.com/the-highlight/21542041/museums diversity-guston-national-gallery-hiring.

Greenberg, Alyssa, Anniessa Antar, Elisabeth Callihan. "Change-Making through Pedagogy." in MASS Action Toolkit, ed. Elisabeth Callihan, 156–59. Minneapolis, MN: Minneapolis Institute of Art, 2017.

Greenberger, Alex. "Guggenheim Museum Workers Push to Unionize Amid Wave of Organizing across U.S. Museums." *Art News*, August 2, 2021. https://www.artnews.com/art-news/news/guggenheim-museum-union-drive-uaw-1234600541/.

———. "'The Painting Must Go': Hannah Black Pens Open Letter to the Whitney about Controversial Biennial Work." *ARTnews*, March 21, 2017. https://www.artnews.com/artnews/news/the-painting-must-go-hannah-black-pens-open-letter-to-the-whitney-about-controversial-biennial-work-7992.

Greenberger, Alex, and Tessa Solomon. "Read Statements from Major U.S. Museums about the George Floyd Protests." *ARTnews*, June 2, 2020. https://www.artnews.com/art-news/news/museums-statements-george-floyd-protests-1202689578/.

Guerra, Cristela. "Students of Color Say They Were Profiled, Harassed at the MFA. Museum Apologizes." *WBUR*, May 23, 2019. https://www.wbur.org/news/2019/05/23/students-of-color-profiled-mfa-apologizes.

Guffey, Elizabeth. "Beyond Compliance." *VoCA Journal*, December 7, 2020. https://journal.voca.network/beyond-compliance/.

Gutierrez, Sofia, and Briley Rasmussen. "Code-Switching in the Art Museum: Increasing Access for English Learners." In *Multiculturalism in Art Museums Today*, edited by Joni Boyd Acuff and Laura Evans, chapter 10. Lanham, MD: Rowman & Littlefield, 2014.

Harvard University, Project Implicit. "Preliminary Information." https://implicit.harvard.edu/implicit/takeatest.html.

Hendrick, Keonna, and Melissa Crum, "Multicultural Critical Reflective Practice and Contemporary Art." In *Multiculturalism in Art Museums Today*, edited by Joni Boyd Acuff and Laura Evans, 271–98. Lanham, MD: Rowman & Littlefield, 2014.

Hsieh, Kathy. "Continuum on Becoming a Fully Inclusive Arts and Cultural Organization." Crossroads Ministry. https://www.seattle.gov/Documents/Departments/Arts/Downloads/Grants/Civic%20Partners/Continuum%20on%20Becoming%20a%20Fully%20Inclusive%20Arts%20and%20Cultural%20Organization.pdf.

Hultman, Ken. "Resistance to Change, Managing." In *Encyclopedia of Information Systems*, Volume 3, edited by Hossein Bidgoli, 693–705. San Diego, CA: Academic Press, 2003.

Jackson, Bailey W. "Theory and Practice Of Multicultural Organization Development." In *The NTL Handbook of Organization Development and Change: Principles, Practices, and Perspectives*, edited by Brenda B. Jones and Michael Brazzel, 175–92. Hoboken, NJ: Wiley, 2014.

James, Osamudia R. "White Like Me: The Negative Impact of the Diversity Rationale on White Identity Formation." *New York University Law Review* 89, no. 2 (2014): 425–512.

Jones, Kenneth, and Tema Okun, "White Supremacy Culture." In *Dismantling Racism: A Workbook for Social Change Group*, 28–35. ChangeWork, 2001. https://resourcegeneration.org/wp-content/uploads/2018/01/2016-dRworks-workbook.pdf.

Junebug Productions. "Story Circle." July 19, 2021. https://www.junebugproductions.org/story-circle.

Knight, Rebecca. "7 Practical Ways to Reduce Bias in Your Hiring Process." *Harvard Business Review*, June 12, 2017. https://hbr.org/2017/06/7-practical-ways-to-reduce-bias-in-your-hiring-process.

Li, Shirley. "American Museums Are Going Through an Identity Crisis." *The Atlantic*, November 28, 2020. https://www.theatlantic.com/culture/archive/2020/11/american-museums-are-going-through-identity-crisis/617221/.

Linton, Simi. *Claiming Disability: Knowledge and Identity*. New York: New York University Press, 1998.

MASS Action. "MASS Action Toolkit," edited by Elisabeth Callihan. Minneapolis, MN: Minneapolis Institute of Art, 2017. https://www.museumaction.org/s/TOOLKIT_10_2017.pdf.

Mayorga-Gallo, Sarah. "The White-Centering Logic of Diversity Ideology." *American Behavioral Scientist* 63, no. 13 (2019): 1789–809.

McNellis, Patrick. *The Compression Planning Advantage: A Blueprint for Resolving Complex Issues*. CreateSpace Independent Publishing Platform, 2009.

Merriam-Webster. "Trust," September 10, 2021. https://www.merriam-webster.com/dictionary/trust.

Minneapolis Institute of Art. "Inclusion, Diversity, Equity and Accessibility Policy." 2016. https://new.artsmia.org/about/diversity-and-inclusion-policy.

Minneapolis Park and Recreation Board. "Resolution 2020-350." December 9, 2020. http://minneapolisparksmn.iqm2.com/Citizens/Detail_LegiFile.aspx?MeetingID=2175&ID=5252.

Minnesota Historical Society. "Minnesota Historical Society Wins Two Prestigious Media and Technology Awards." May 1. 2012. https://www.mnhs.org/media/news/5205.

———. "Minnesota Historical Society: Mission, Vision, Values and Strategic Priorities." https://www.mnhs.org/about/mission.

———. "Minnesota Treaties. The US-Dakota War of 1862." https://www.usdakotawar.org/history/treaties/minnesota-treaties.

Miranda, Carolina. "Column: Are Art Museums Still Racist? The COVID Reset." *Los Angeles Times.* October 22, 2020. https://www.latimes.com/entertainment-arts/story/2020-10-22/art-museums-racism-covid-reset.

Moore, Porchia. "Reflexive Cartography: Or, a Ritual for the Dying Museum Landscape—the Socio-political Impact of Change in Museums." *The Incluseum* (blog). August 6, 2020. https://incluseum.com/2020/08/06/reflexive-cartography-or-a-ritual-for-the-dying-museum-landscape-the-socio-political-impact-of-change-in-museums.

Morey Group. *The Broad 2019 Annual Visitor Survey Report.*

Moving Healthcare Upstream. "When a Picture Tells the Story: The Pair of ACEs Tree." March 20, 2017. https://www.movinghealthcareupstream.org/when-a-picture-tells-the-story-the-pair-of-aces-tree/.

MTV. "MTV's Look Different Campaign." https://www.mtvact.com/features/Look-Different.

Mullainathan, Sendhil. "Racial Bias, Even When We Have Good Intentions." *New York Times*, January 3, 2015. https://www.nytimes.com/2015/01/04/upshot/the-measuring-sticks-of-racial-bias-.html.

Nason, James. "A Brief History of the Burke Museum's Direct Engagement with Native American and Ethnic Communities." Burke Museum Archives, 2021.

National Disability Institute. "Race, Ethnicity and Disability: The Financial Impact of Systemic Inequality and Intersectionality." https://www.nationaldisabilityinstitute.org/wp-content/uploads/2020/08/race-ethnicity-and-disability-financial-impact.pdf.

National Museum of African American History and Culture. "Whiteness." *Talking about Race*, June 19, 2021. https://nmaahc.si.edu/learn/talking-about-race/topics/whiteness.

Newton, Paul, and Helen Bristoll. *Spatial Ability Practice Test 1.* www.psychometric-success.com.

O'Neil, Sean. "A Crisis of Whiteness in Canada's Art Museums." *Canadian Art*, June 23, 2020. https://canadianart.ca/features/a-crisis-of-whiteness/.

OSPI. "Since Time Immemorial: Tribal Sovereignty in Washington State | OSPI." https://www.k12.wa.us/student-success/resources-subject-area/time-immemorial-tribal-sovereignty-washington-state.

Page, Kira. "The 'Problem' Woman of Colour in the Workplace." *COCo-net* (blog). March 8, 2018. https://coco-net.org/problem-woman-colour-nonprofit-organizations.

Palmer, Parker. *The Courage to Teach.* San Francisco: Jossey-Bass, 1998.

Papalia, Carmen. "A New Model for Access in the Museum." *Disability Studies Quarterly* 33, no. 3 (2013).

Paquet Kinsley, Rose, and Aletheia Wittman. "Bringing Self-Examination to the Center of Social Justice Work in Museums." *Museum Magazine* (2016 January/February): 40–45.

Patterson, Adam, Aletheia Wittman, Chieko Phillips, Gamynne Guillotte, Therese Quinn, and Adrianne Russell. "Getting Started: What We Need to Change and Why." In MASS Action Toolkit, ed. Elisabeth Callihan, 11–16. Minneapolis, MN: Minneapolis Institute of Art, 2017.

Perszyk, Danielle R., Ryan F. Lei, Galen V. Bodenhausen, Jennifer A. Richeson, and Sandra R. Waxman. "Bias at the Intersection of Race and Gender: Evidence from Preschool-Aged Children." *Developmental Science*, 22e12788 (2019): 1–2.

Power, Angelique. "On the Death of Equity." Recorded June 23, 2020 for the Americans for the Arts Annual Convention. Video, 27:35.

Race and Social Justice Initiative. "Racial Equity Toolkit: To Assess Policies, Initiatives, Services, Programs, and Budget Issues." http://www.seattle.gov/Documents/Departments/RSJI/Racial%20Equity%20Toolkit%20COVID19.pdf.

Race Forward. "Principles for Racially Equitable Policy Platforms." August 6, 2020. https://www.raceforward.org/practice/tools/principles-racially-equitable-policy-platforms.

Raicovich, Laura. *Culture Strike: Art and Museums in an Age of Protest*. London: Verso, 2021.

———. "One Museum's Complicated Attempt to Repatriate a 'Benin Bronze.'" June 24, 2019. https://hyperallergic.com/506634/benin-bronze-head-interview/.

Randle, Aaron. "'We Were Tired of Asking': Why Open Letters Have Become Many Activists' Tool of Choice for Exposing Racism at Museums." *Art News*, July 15, 2020. https://news.artnet.com/art-world/museum-open-letters-activism-1894150.

RISD Museum. "RISD Museum's Anti-Racist Work." https://risdmuseum.org/art-design/projects-publications/articles/risd-museum-anti-racist-work.

Rosenberg, Marshall B. *Nonviolent Communication: A Language of Life*. California: PuddleDancer Press, 2015.

Schein, Edgar H. *Organizational Culture and Leadership*. San Francisco: Jossey Bass, 2010.

Seattle Antiracism. "Actionable Solidarity: Walking the Talk." Filmed July 12, 2021. https://www.youtube.com/watch?v=gLABUYOo2_M.

Senge, P. *The Fifth Discipline*. New York, NY: Doubleday, 1990.

Shoenberger, Elisa. "What Does It Mean to Decolonize a Museum?" *MuseumNext*, December 11, 2019. https://www.museumnext.com/article/what-does-it-mean-to-decolonize-a-museum/.

Solomon, Danyelle, Connor Maxwell, and Abril Castro. "Systematic Inequality and American Democracy." August 7, 2019. https://www.americanprogress.org/issues/race/reports/2019/08/07/473003/systematic-inequality-american-democracy/.

Solomon, Jessica. "Facilitator Tips for Virtual Meetings 1: Turn that Grid into a Circle." Art in Praxis (@artinpraxis) Instagram post, July 14, 2021. https://www.instagram.com/p/CRT85gvlXLK/.

Stevenson, Bryan. "The Truth Starts Here: Museums' Role in Truth, Reconciliation, and Healing." *Keynote*, American Alliance of Museums Annual Meeting. June 7. 2021.

Sue, Derald Wing. *Microaggressions in Everyday Life.* Hoboken, NJ: John Wiley & Sons, Inc., 2010.

Subbaraman, Nidhi. "Grieving and Frustrated: Black Scientists Call Out Racism in the Wake of Police Killings." *Nature*. June 8, 2020. https://www.nature.com/articles/d41586-020-01705-x.

Tatum, Beverly Daniel. *Why Are All the Black Kids Sitting Together in the Cafeteria? And Other Conversations about Race*. New York, NY: Basic Books, 2017.

Thompson, Karl. "What Percentage of Your Life Will You Spend at Work? August 16, 2016. https://revisesociology.com/2016/08/16/percentage-life-work/.

Trauma Informed Oregon. "Guiding Principles of Trauma-Informed Care." https://traumainformedoregon.org/wp-content/uploads/2020/02/Principles-of-Trauma-Informed-Care.pdf.

Tulshyan, Ruchika. "How to Reduce Personal Bias When Hiring." *Harvard Business Review*, June 28, 2019. https://hbr.org/2019/06/how-to-reduce-personal-bias-when-hiring.

US Department of Arts and Culture. "People's State of the Union." June 19, 2021. https://usdac.us/psotu.

Van Der Valk, Adrienne, and Anya Malley. "What's My Complicity? Talking White Fragility with Robin DiAngelo." *Teaching Tolerance Magazine* 62 (Summer 2019). https://www.learningforjustice.org/magazine/summer-2019/whats-my-complicity-talking-white-fragility-with-robin-diangelo.

Vankin, Deborah. "What's Drawing Millennials to Downtown LA's Broad Museum." *Los Angeles Times*, March 20, 2016. https://www.latimes.com/entertainment/arts/la-et-cm-the-broad-young20160320-story.html.

Webb, Maynard. "How to Alter Your Hiring Practices to Increase Diversity." *Forbes Magazine*, October 29, 2017. https://www.forbes.com/sites/maynardwebb/2017/10/29/how-to-alter-your-hiring-practices-to-increase-diversity/?sh=63591cf12029.

Westermann, Mariët, Roger Schonfeld, and Liam Sweeney. "Art Museum Staff Demographic Survey 2018." *The Andrew W. Mellon Foundation*. January 28, 2019. https://mellon.org/news-blog/articles/art-museum-staff-demographic-survey-2018/.

Winters, Mary Frances. "From Diversity to Inclusion: An Inclusion Equation." In *Diversity at Work: The Practice of Inclusion*, edited by Bernardo M. Ferdman and Barbara R. Deane, 205–28. San Francisco: Jossey Bass, 2014.

Wittman, Aletheia. "Creating a Framework for Institutional Genealogy." *The Incluseum* (blog). August 20, 2021. https://incluseum.com/2021/08/20/institutional-genealogy-framework.

W. K. Kellogg Foundation. "Restoring to Wholeness—Racial Healing for Ourselves, Our Relationships, and Our Communities." December 2017. https://www.ala.org/tools/sites/ala.ools/files/content/Restoring%20to%20Wholeness%20WKKF%20Racial%20Healing%20Publication.pdf.

Wong, Jessica. "AGO to Keep Free Entry for 25 and Under, $35 Annual Pass." *CBC News*, November 26, 2019. https://www.cbc.ca/news/entertainment/ago-annual-pass-permanent-1.5373672.

World Health Organization. "Disability." https://www.who.int/health-topics/disability#tab=tab_1.

Yoshino, Kenji. *Covering: The Hidden Assault on Our Civil Rights.* New York: Random House, 2006.

Index

Page numbers in italics indicate a figure or table.

About the Editors

Priya Frank (she/her) has over 25 years of investment in equity and social justice work. Currently, she is the director of equity, diversity, and inclusion at the Seattle Art Museum. Frank was recognized as one of 2018's Most Influential People by *Seattle Magazine*, and was named to *Puget Sound Business Journal*'s top 40 under 40 list in 2019. She holds a BA in communications and American ethnic studies from the University of Washington Seattle and an MA in cultural studies from the University of Washington Bothell.

Theresa Sotto (she/her) has worked at the crossroads of education, equity, and the arts for more than twenty years. She is currently the Ruth R. Marder Director of Learning and Community Engagement at the Walters Art Museum. She previously worked at the Hammer Museum, Getty Museum, University of Arizona Poetry Center, and John F. Kennedy Center for the Performing Arts. She frequently presents on topics related to inclusive teaching, implicit bias, and equity initiatives.

About the Contributors

Anniessa Antar is a nomadic educator, museum transformer, and cultural organizer living on occupied Dakota and Anishinaabe land. Antar worked at the Minneapolis Institute of Art as the activation specialist from 2019 to 2021, where she collaborated with artists and community partners to create engaging events. She is also one of the co-coordinators of Museum As Site for Social (MASS) Action, a collaborative project which seeks to align museums with more racially just and liberatory practices.

Alexander Barrera (he/him) was born and raised in Santa Ana, California, where his passion for producing events developed by volunteering to support large-scale community programs. He currently executes public programs at Hauser & Wirth Los Angeles as their events manager. Alexander previously worked at the Hammer Museum, Center for the Art of Performance at UCLA, and the University of Southern California. He received a BA in visual communications from the University of San Diego.

Sue Bell Yank is executive director of Clockshop and was formerly deputy director of 18th Street Arts Center. Her work in arts, entertainment, and public schools intersects with her interests in affordable cities, socially engaged art, and pedagogy. She is the chair of the City of Glendale Arts and Culture Commission and has consulted on audience development and strategic arts marketing. Yank received a BA from Harvard and an MA in public art studies from the University of Southern California.

Lily Benedict (she/her) is a museum educator and curator from Providence, Rhode Island, whose explorations land in the intersections of art, history, the environment, and social justice. She works with young people as a museum educator for K–12 school and teacher programs at the RISD Museum of Art. She has a BA in anthropology from Cornell University and an MA in public humanities from Brown University.

Christian Blake is currently director of equity, diversity, and inclusion at MLSE Foundation and MLSE LaunchPad, and previously worked at the Royal Ontario Museum where he led the museum's community engagement, inclusion, and well-being portfolios. He is also adjunct faculty at the University of Toronto and continues his practice as an occupational therapist through Level Up Gaming, an organization that he cofounded.

Rex Buck Jr. (1955–2022) was leader of the Wanapum of Priest Rapids. He was an original member of the Burke's Native American Advisory Board and worked extensively on the repatriation of The Ancient One. He served as the chair of the NAAB's executive committee from 2019 to 2022.

Tara Burns is the specialist, family and K–12 audiences at the Hammer Museum where she organizes K–12 initiatives and family programs for the Academic Programs Department. Burns has also worked at the Skirball Cultural Center and the Los Angeles County Museum of Art. She earned her BA in history from Barnard College and her MA in educational studies from Loyola Marymount University.

Elisabeth Callihan is a museum practitioner working at the intersection of education, equity, and engagement, cocreating programs that catalyze meaningful connections through art. She most recently served as the head of multigenerational learning at the Minneapolis Institute of Art and, prior to that, was the manager of public programs at the Brooklyn Museum. She is the cofounder of Museum As Site for Social (MASS) Action.

Ashanti Davis (she/her) is exhibition manager at the Fleet Science Center in San Diego, California, and an arts and culture change agent. She received her MA in museum studies from Johns Hopkins University in 2021. She looks forward to continuing her work as a leader in the arts and culture sector and catalyzing meaningful change through lenses of social justice, curiosity, and creativity for all organizational staff and communities.

Marit Dewhurst (she/her) is director of art education and associate professor of art and museum education at the City College of New York. Her research and teaching focuses on art and social justice, community building, and culturally sustaining pedagogy. In addition to several articles and book chapters, she has written two books, *Social Justice Art: A Framework for Activist Art Pedagogy* (2014) and *Teachers Bridging Difference: Exploring Identity with Art* (2018).

Regina N. Ford is the senior vice president of operations of the Pacific Science Center in Seattle, Washington. Regina has more than twenty years of human resources and organizational effectiveness experience and more than ten years of experience as a diversity, equity, and inclusion leader at publicly traded Fortune 500 companies. Regina holds a BA cum laude in economics from Harvard University and MBA Beta Gamma Sigma in finance from Pepperdine Graziadio School of Business.

Cecilia Garibay is the CEO of Garibay Group, a nationally recognized audience research and consulting firm working on culturally responsive issues in informal learning environments. Garibay Group is a founding partner of CCLI, the author of the *CCLI National Landscape Study: DEAI Practices in Museums*, and an ongoing faculty member for CCLI, focusing on appreciative inquiry, data collection, and evaluation.

Neil Gordon has been the CEO of the Discovery Museum since 2009. Prior positions include COO, Boston Children's Museum; Boston budget director; and associate director for the Boston office of Jobs and Community Services. Neil was board chair of the Association of Children's Museums, treasurer of New England Museum Association, and founding president of the Friends of Fort Point Channel. Neil holds degrees from the Harvard Kennedy School and Dickinson College.

Mel Harper (she/her) is an interpretive projects manager and current Ailsa Mellon Bruce sabbatical fellow at the National Gallery of Art, where she collaborates with curators, designers, and more to craft interpretation for the museum's temporary exhibitions. Mel received her MA in Black visual culture from Howard University, where she taught African American art history and managed the prints and photographs collection at the Moorland-Spingarn Research Center.

Keonna Hendrick has spent more than a decade championing cultural equity using antiracist frameworks in museums and arts organizations. In 2021 she was appointed as the Brooklyn Museum's first director of diversity, equity, inclusion, and access. She has taught at Pratt Institute; Teacher's College, Columbia University; and School of Visual Arts. Hendrick holds a BA from Wake Forest University, and an MA from the Ohio State University.

Marilee Jennings is executive director of Children's Discovery Museum of San Jose. Jennings's experience as CEO of a local museum institution, former president of a national association (ACM, 2014–2016), and current board service of a national association (ASTC, 2020) provides unique and critical perspectives to CCLI, especially in supporting CEOs in engaging with the important work of equity and organizational change.

Katherine Larson joined the Corning Museum of Glass in 2016 as a curatorial assistant and is now curator of ancient glass. She has a PhD from the University of Michigan and has worked in science, archaeology, and art museums. She identifies professionally as an archaeologist and recovering classicist, struggling to contend with the white supremist, colonial legacy of and in archaeology, history, and museums.

Julia Latané is head of art preparation and installation at the Los Angeles County Museum of Art (LACMA). She was head preparator at The Broad from 2014 to 2018 and at the Autry Museum of the American West from 2008 to 2014. She cofounded the Museum of Contemporary Art, Tucson in 1997, and served as president of the board. Latané serves on the Preparation, Art Handling, Collection Care Information Network (PACCIN) advisory board.

Tina Lee (she/her) is the senior manager of exhibitions and publications at Seattle Art Museum. She received her BFA from the University of Washington, MFA in arts leadership from Seattle University, and a US Fulbright Fellowship. She is a first-generation Korean American born and raised in Seattle.

George Luna-Peña (he/him/his) serves as the program director for the Diversity Apprenticeship Program (DAP) at The Broad in Los Angeles, California. The DAP provides paid, full-time apprenticeships in preparation/art handling to apprentices from underrepresented groups in museums. Before joining The Broad, Luna-Peña was a research manager for the Media and Participatory Politics Group at the University of Southern California and the special projects coordinator at Generation Justice in Albuquerque, New Mexico.

Jenni Martin, director of strategic initiatives at Children's Discovery Museum of San Jose, is also CCLI project director and lead faculty, bringing a depth of experience in equity and inclusion practice over her thirty-two years in the informal education field. In her twenty-three years at Children's Discovery Museum, Martin has led its DEAI committee and stewarded its cultural competency efforts to ensure its growth as a community anchor.

Brindha Muniappan s the senior director of the museum experience at the Discovery Museum in Acton, Massachusetts. Her work continues a focus on building and diversifying audiences through intentional collaborations. Before joining the Discovery Museum, Brindha led the education and public programs team at the MIT Museum and was a current science and technology educator at the Boston Museum of Science. She earned her SB and PhD at MIT.

Polly Olsen (Yakama) is director of DEAI and tribal liaison at the Burke Museum of Natural History and Culture. She has nineteen years of involvement in academia, health care, and museums, enjoying success in collaboration, program development, and planning and implementation. Her professional and life experiences—and her passion to serve communities—have led Olsen to thrive in her career. Olsen earned a BA in liberal arts/cultural anthropology from the University of Washington.

Andrew Palamara (he/him/his) is the gallery coordinator of the Emmanuel Art Gallery and Experience Gallery at University of Colorado Denver. He previously worked at the Cincinnati Art Museum, Dallas Museum of Art, and MASS MoCA. He holds a BFA in graphic design and illustration from Belmont University and an MA in art education from the University of North Texas.

Regan Pro is the deputy director of public programs and social impact at the Lucas Museum of Narrative Art where she collaborates with brilliant, creative partners to build a new museum dedicated to visual storytelling. Previously she was the Kayla Skinner Deputy Director of Education and Public Engagement at the Seattle Art Museum and has held positions at the University of Washington Museology Program, the Addison Gallery of American Art, Path with Art, and Project Zero.

Sumathi Raghavan is the manager of corporate and foundation relations at the Burke Museum of Natural History and Culture. In addition to her grant-writing responsibilities, she serves on the museum's equity and inclusion committee. She has previously worked in publishing, as a librarian, and for a local South Asian arts and social justice nonprofit, Tasveer. She is a graduate of Wellesley College and the University of Chicago.

MJ Robinson is a freelance artist, educator, and community organizer. Robinson fosters creative curiosity and encourages playful group visioning in movements for social justice --with a particular focus on racial and environmental justice, LGBTQIA2S+ joy and well-being, and prison abolition in Providence, Rhode Island, and beyond. They studied studio art and creative writing at Oberlin College and children's book illustration at Rhode Island School of Design.

Francesca Rosenberg is the director of community, access, and school programs at The Museum of Modern Art (MoMA). In her twenty-seven years at MoMA, Francesca and her team have won national and international respect for MoMA's efforts to make the museum accessible to all. Most recently, MoMA received awards from the Alzheimer's Association; AAM; Museums and the Web; Ashoka's Zero Project for social impact and scalability; and the Hearing Loss Association of America.

David Rue is a dance artist and creative professional born in Liberia and raised in Minnesota. Through his work in public engagement at Seattle Art Museum and public programs at Friends of Waterfront Seattle, he conceptualizes and implements arts programming that helps adult audiences more deeply engage with the visual and performing arts using the lens of equity, excellence, and joy.

Lara Schweller is the associate educator of community and access programs at The Museum of Modern Art (MoMA). Schweller works on accessibility across MoMA, collaborating with staff on initiatives to ensure building and exhibition accessibility as well as disability equality training. Schweller's work in education focuses on the museum's award-winning education programming for individuals with disabilities and the museum's creative aging initiative, Prime Time.

Kajette Solomon is RISD Museum's first social equity and inclusion program specialist. Her role endeavors to shape, implement, and manage the museum's efforts to build an equitable, diverse, and inclusive institution for all. Solomon is an American Association of Museum volunteers board member and a participant in the Rhode Island Foundation's Equity Leadership Initiative. She holds a BA in art history from Arcadia University and an MA in modern and contemporary art history, theory, and criticism from Purchase College.

Dr. Julie K. Stein served as executive director of the Burke Museum from 2005 to 2022. She previously served as curator of archaeology (1990–1999), supervising repatriation, including that of The Ancient One/Kennewick Man (reburied in 2017). Stein's leadership exemplified respectful collaboration with tribal communities and set a path to continue this work. An emeritus professor of Anthropology at the University of Washington, Stein received her MA and PhD degrees from the University of Minnesota.

Nick Stephens is an Illinois native living and working in Los Angeles, California. His career in museums has spanned a decade, and he is most passionate about organizing community around progressive ideologies and diversifying the future of museum leadership. He is currently the development director at Craft Contemporary and has previously held positions at the Hammer Museum and the Museum of Contemporary Art Chicago. He received his BA in art history from the University of Illinois Chicago.

Stacey Gevero Swanby was formerly the director of visitor services at The Broad. She led a team known for an innovative and inclusive approach to the visitor experience. She began her museum career at the community-based Wing Luke Museum of the Asian Pacific American Experience in Seattle's Chinatown International District. Swanby seeks to change the stories that are told in museums and to amplify the voices of those that are little heard within the museum field.

Chris Taylor is currently the chief inclusion officer for the state of Minnesota, where he has designed and is implementing a statewide strategy for equity. Prior to joining the state, he was the chief inclusion officer for the Minnesota Historical Society where he created institutional strategy for equity and inclusion to center equity in the work of all departments of the institution. Taylor recently earned an EdD in organization development and change.

Caitlin Tracey-Miller is the assistant director of visitor research and evaluation at the Cincinnati Art Museum, where she is passionate about accessible and welcoming museum spaces that encourage engagement, inspiration, and connection. She loves collecting visitor voices and sharing those voices in a helpful and meaningful way. Tracey-Miller graduated with an MA in museum studies from the University Toronto and with a BA in English from Earlham College.

Lianne Uesato has worked at the Corning Museum of Glass as an assistant conservator since 2017. She completed an MA in art conservation at Buffalo State College and worked in private practices and museums of various sizes across the United States. Raised in Honolulu before becoming a nomadic conservator, she is a curious misfit observing museum culture.

Marissa Volpe is the chief of equity and engagement at History Colorado where she accompanies a statewide community of Colorado stakeholders toward the full participation in preserving and celebrating the history of Colorado. Additionally, her work aims to educate and engage the staff of History Colorado in the application of diversity, equity, and inclusion through best practices in communication, decision-making, and daily practices to promote a culture of belonging.